Johan Preis

DRAKENSBERG  S

120 graded hikes and trails in the 'Berg

DAVID BRISTOW

C. STRUIK PUBLISHERS

Struik Publishers (an operating division
of Struik Holdings (Pty) Ltd)
Struik House
Oswald Pirow Street
Foreshore
Cape Town 8001

Reg. No: 80/02842/07

First published 1988

Text © David Bristow
Photographs © David Bristow, with the exception of the following: Jeanette de Leeuw: page 73 no.5; Natal Parks Board: front cover (lammergeier), page 36, page 71 no. 4, page 79 no. 7, pages 131 and 151; Ralph Taylor: front cover (centre top); Deon Tromp: page 43, page 73 nos. 2 and 4, pages 75 nos. 7 and 10, page 85 no. 2, page 114 and back cover (right below), and Des Watkins: page 72 no. 1, page 73 no. 3, page 75 no. 9, page 90 no. 1 and page 139.

Designed by Sabine Chadwick
Edited by Bev Bernstone
Cover design by Abdul Amien
Illustrated by Felicity Harris
Maps by Philippa Scott and Anne Westoby
Index by Ethleen Lastovica
Photoset and reproduction by ProSet-Flexoplate, Cape Town
Printed and bound by Printpak Books, Cape

All rights reserved. No part of this publication may be reproduced, stored in a system or transmitted, in any form or by any means, electronic, mechanical, photocopying, recording or otherwise, without the written permission of the copyright owners.

ISBN 0 86977 457 3

CAPTIONS FOR COVER (FRONT)

(Left, top) Hikers crossing the Bushman's River en route *to Sehlaba-Thebe. (Left, bottom) Rainbow Gorge in the Cathedral area. (Centre, top) The Cathedral range. (Centre, left) A juvenile lammergeier. (Centre, right) Bushman rock paintings. (Right, top) Mnweni. (Right, bottom) The view from Spare Rib Cave.*

CAPTIONS FOR COVER (BACK)

(Left, top) A Chironid *bloom. (Left, below) The mountain hut below Giant's Castle. (Centre, left) The author stands atop Dragon's Back. (Centre, right)* Themeda-Festuca *montane grasslands. (Right, top) Fern forest. (Right, below) The Sentinel, Royal Natal National Park.*

FOREWORD

The Natal Drakensberg is one of South Africa's most outstanding attractions, which draws hundreds of thousands of visitors annually to its scenic beauty, crisp mountain air, and crystal clear waters.

Some come simply to relax, while others come to pit their skills against the array of craggy peaks. One thing is common to all, though: hiking, whether this be a leisurely promenade across the lawn, a gentle stroll to the nearest stream, or a strenuous hike to the very foot of the rocky buttresses. For nearly all, the desire is to go just a little bit farther, to get away from the sights, smells and sounds of man-made intrusions.

The Drakensberg is, however, not always kind to those who use it. A gentle summer's morning can, by midday, become a nightmare of thunderstorms with their death-dealing lightning and crashing rolls of thunder that echo endlessly down the long valleys. Or it may, within minutes, be turned into dense fog that defies the sight for more than a few metres. A crisp winter's morning, with crackling frost in a fairytale land of crystal icicles, can turn into a blinding snowstorm that can last for two or three days, trapping the unwary and resisting all attempts at reaching safety.

For those who know and understand the moods of the mountains, the Drakensberg is a place of peace and endless delights, of the fulfilment of pleasures, and of the wonders of adventure. For the newcomer it is a place where new experiences abound and where the love of nature is born. All are drawn to return again and again, and it is thus that the desire to explore the furthermost limits of one's growing love for the outdoors is aroused.

One cannot think of the Drakensberg without thinking too of its fragility as one of the few unspoilt ecosystems we have left in South Africa. Not only is it important for the spiritual enrichment that it brings, but it is vital as a source of water. To hike in the Drakensberg is to marry the intangible and the tangible. It creates a sense of being one with nature and a commitment to ensuring the future of such beauty for the benefit of future generations. This is the essence of conservation. More can be learnt about it from contact with the mountains than years of reading and listening.

If David Bristow's sensitive treatment of the innumerable Drakensberg hikes, rambles and strolls encourages its readers to explore them, then it will have contributed immeasurably to the conservation of our environment. Certainly those who have been there and who follow his directions will learn something new from it, and the book will elicit memories and emotions with the turn of every page.

We have precious little left that is pristine, and my appeal to all who use the Drakensberg is to leave it as they find it. Everyone has the right to enjoy it, but nobody has the right to spoil it.

John Vincent

Assistant Director (Interpretation and Public Relations)

Natal Parks Board

PUBLISHER'S NOTE

While every effort has been made by the publisher to ensure the accuracy of both the hike descriptions and the maps, it is the hiker's personal responsibility to use the best maps available, in this case those compiled by Peter Slingsby for the Directorate of Forestry of the Department of Environment Affairs.

Contents

ACKNOWLEDGEMENTS

To all the hikers I met along the way, thank you. I would also like to thank the following in particular:

- For permission to use their excellent photographs: Jeanette de Leeuw, the Natal Parks Board, Ralph Taylor, Deon Tromp and Des Watkins
- the Forestry and Natal Parks Board officials who assisted me in the field, particularly Nico van den Berg, as well as those who helped with the checking of the manuscript, especially Dr John Vincent
- Graham, Yvonne and Chris Godenir for their ever-welcoming kindness
- Ed Salomons of Inkosana Lodge for good company, food and wine
- Don and Shirley, with whom I have shared many mountain adventures, for renewed vitality at Sehlaba-Thebe
- Reg Pearse of Emkhizweni for information offered over tea and the generous donation of personal maps
- Felicity Harris for her carefully executed line drawings, and Philippa Scott and Anne Westoby, who produced high-quality maps from my confused sketches
- Tracey Hawthorne, who helped prepare the manuscript and encouraged me during my 'long march'
- Peter Borchert, Ellis Pender, Sabine Chadwick and Bev Bernstone at Struik for making this publication possible.

Introduction

Half-way up Waaihoek Peak in the Hex River Mountains there is a plaque which warns the weary climber:

The way is long and getting longer.
The road goes uphill all the way, and even further.
I wish you luck. You'll need it.

The way is dark and getting darker.
The hut is high and even higher.
I wish you luck.
There is none.

James Thurber

This expresses my own attitude to hiking in the Drakensberg – every road is ultimately 'uphill all the way, and even further'. Yet it is this that makes mountaineering so rewarding – only those who pay the price of getting there can enjoy that other-worldly environment. No-one who has hiked or climbed among the awesome peaks of the 'Berg can fail to be bonded to them with a personal, even spiritual intensity. The mists that swirl around the massive spires, lightning that cracks into the rock buttresses, the sunshine that bursts through stormclouds to wash the basalt a deep crimson, and the great mountain birds that soar effortlessly across the face of the Escarpment – all leave fresh, exhilarating impressions on our minds and draw us back evermore.

There is a part of these mountains that has been overlooked by most mountaineers, and this is the Little Berg and its valleys, forests and gorges. Admittedly, most of my time in the Drakensberg has been dedicated to getting to the top. During two and a half glorious months of the autumn of 1987, I walked from one end of the 'Berg to the other and it was the Little Berg that fascinated me most. One great attraction of the area is that one can venture there without the attendant dangers of the High 'Berg, and yet it is no less beautiful and remote. There are fewer chances of seeing anyone in the long, fertile gorges of the Ntonjelane rivers, for instance, than on the summit. The secret caves, the waterfalls and pools, the fern-carpeted forests, the birds and animals make up a far richer world than that of the harsh summit.

There is something about the summits of the Drakensberg, however, that is irresistible to the mountaineer, something rarefied and pure. This feeling of being above and apart from the world is akin to the elevating feeling one experiences in the Gothic cathedrals of Europe, and it is no surprise that this architectural style echoes the forms of Europe's famous mountain ranges. From Olympus to Everest, mountains have long been associated with spiritual involvement and just about every major range in the world is associated with a local of deity. Perhaps this is what drives us to sweat and curse our way up long mountain paths.

What is difficult to comprehend is how people still manage – in spite of pleas, notices, warnings and threats – to litter paths, deface cave walls and cause erosion by taking short cuts. There is intense pressure on the Drakensberg for increased recreational facilities, yet there is talk of the need to close off areas, limit access, concrete paths and so on, much of which could be avoided by following simple but essential guidelines of behaviour; those same guidelines that come as pleas, notices, warnings and threats. One hopes that a love of the mountains will guide hikers to treat this delicate ecosystem in the manner befitting such a place.

The Drakensberg is the subcontinent's most important catchment area, and few hikers realize that each step they take has a direct effect on the quality of the water. The steepness of the terrain and the poorly developed soils increase the 'Berg's susceptibility to erosion. By the time you can see the erosion, however, it is already too late to stop it. Once the top soil has been eroded away, the ground loses its ability to absorb and store rainwater and so there is increased runoff, causing higher degrees of erosion and susceptibility to drought. Once the top soil is gone, it is unlikely to be replaced until hikers and farmers leave the area for something like a hundred years or more.

Land Control. The Drakensberg has been largely under the control of the Forestry Directorate's conservation division, with the Natal Parks Board controlling the game and nature reserves. Recently, the Forestry Directorate was been stripped of its conservation role and now the areas previously under its control are entwined in bureaucratic debate. At the time of writing the fate of these areas was uncertain, but there are two alternatives: the first is that the provincial authorities, who now pay the former Forestry conservation officials, will maintain control over the conservation and catchment areas of the Drakensberg and continue to manage them for recreation as Wilderness Areas, as did the Forestry Directorate. The other possibility is that the Natal Parks Board will gain control over much of the Wilderness Areas and State Forests and manage them as they do their parks.

Regardless of this bureaucratic entanglement, firm steps have to be taken to avoid the degradation of the Drakensberg. Many of the popular caves in the mountains have been defaced by hikers who do not deserve to be there – perhaps one should have to earn merit badges or belong to a controlling club to gain access. I think not, but how else can the managers preserve the wonders of the Drakensberg. I believe the answer lies in each person's behaviour, to do as the National Hiking Way motto tells us: to take only photographs and leave only footprints.

Permits. Before embarking on your next 'Berg trip, find out about the conditions regarding access to each area and the authority in charge. At the time of writing, you need to purchase a permit from the local Forest Station to enter any State Forest and another to enter a Wilderness Area. Natal Parks Board has its own access permits and regulations and each holiday period they have to turn away multitudes of would-be hikers who have not booked; as I said, they have much stricter access rules than Forestry areas. But even in Wilderness Areas, if you are planning to hike during a holiday period it is advisable to book your permit well in advance, as there is a limit to the number of people allowed. There isn't enough space for everyone to have their own wilderness to themselves, but the experience should still be one of minimum contact with others. Of course, you could avoid the holiday periods and have the entire range to yourself.

Grading of hikes. I have graded each hike in order to give the hiker some idea of what he or she is tackling. The grading gives a distance in kilometres, then an average time taken to complete the hike, then a strenuousness grading, and finally general notes about the hike, the area and perhaps something interesting about its history or ecology. The duration factor is calculated as follows: it takes an average fit person carrying a moderately heavy pack one hour to cover three kilometres over ground that is not steep. For an uphill section one moves at about two to two and a half kilometres per hour. With a heavy pack this can be decreased to one and a half kilometres per hour. If one is fitter than average, one may reduce the time accordingly. No account has been taken of the stops one would normally take on a hike – I like to stop fairly often for tea or water, to swim or take photographs. The weather and temperature, your physical state, the weight of your pack and the composition of your party will influence the duration of a hike, but three kilometres per hour is a good base measurement to use. All distances and durations given are for a one-way journey, unless specified as a round trip. So be sure to check whether you are going mainly up or down and make the necessary adjustments.

I have not given any kind of preference grading as I feel that each hike has its own merits. The five severity or strenuousness gradings of my system are as follows:

- Easy – a short hike, with no steep sections, from one to five kilometres or a maximum of two hours' duration.
- Fair – this may be short (one to three kilometres) but steep, or longer than five kilometres but never strenuous.
- Moderate – this is usually a day's outing, with no sustained ascents. Generally, a hike of this grade would have a one-way distance of not more than seven kilometres.
- Severe – this is a fairly long and very steep, or very long and fairly steep hike. There will almost certainly be some sustained climbing (but not rock climbing) and possibly frequent up-and-down sections.
- Extreme – this will usually be a trip to the top of the Escarpment, in other words very long and very steep. Not all trips to the summit are equal in severity, but then that is what the general section is there to detail.

Scope. This book covers most walks in the Drakensberg mountains, from strolls around popular camp sites and hotels to the longer ascents of the summit plateau and traverses along the summit and the Contour Path. I cannot pretend to know the mountains better than anyone else, and there are many people who know certain areas of these mountains far better than I ever shall. It is unavoidable in a book of this scope that errors will arise, and it would be appreciated if anyone spotting errors, seeing omissions or knowing of anecdotes that would enrich the copy, would write to the author, care of the publisher, furnishing information which could be used in a possible future edition of this guide.

Maps and the mountain register. A vital part of hiking in the 'Berg is the ability to read maps accurately, as the Drakensberg is no place to fool around in. Never hike alone to the summit, in fact never proceed to the top of the 'Berg without someone who knows the mountains and has been there before. Peter Slingsby, commissioned by the Forestry Directorate, has compiled a set of three, two-sided maps which cover the range from Mont-aux-Sources to Thaba-Ntsu in 1 : 50 000 scale. These maps are the definitive reference to the Drakensberg and an essential item of every hiker's pack. I have used these maps for the base data of all my own maps, with some corrections made according to maps compiled by Reg Pearse, and I refer to Slingsby's maps as 'the map' throughout.

It is important to sign the Mountain Register if you plan to spend one or more nights out in the mountains, as it is used in mountain rescues. If you fail to complete the register, you will be legally liable to cover all expenses of a rescue, including the use of helicopters. Rescue teams from the MCSA and other organizations risk their lives to help others, so do co-operate where possible.

Place names. A confusing part of compiling this guide has been in deciding how to spell the various place names, considering the different forms encountered in different sources. Zulu names were often corrupted and anglicized, so that Thukela became Tugela, and eNjesuthi became Injasuti. These corrupted forms have been in common use for so long that few hikers would recognize the more correct spelling for places they know well. Where an incorrect form of a place name is commonly used it has been retained in that form, but in the cases of others, like Mkhomazi (instead of the colonial Umkomaas), the more correct spelling is used. The naming of peaks is even more problematic, with some peaks having a San, a Zulu, an Afrikaans and an English name. I have tried to follow the same rule as above, but in many cases I have dropped the English or Afrikaans version where previously a Zulu one existed. This is simply according to the laws of taxonomy which are used in the scientific naming of things. Thus, Gatberg becomes Intunja, and Rockeries Tower remains Mponjwane (although this too is incorrect, see page 53).

Abbreviations. Only a few abbreviations are used in this book. They are:
NPB – Natal Parks Board
NHWB/S – National Hiking Ways Board/System
MCSA – Mountain Club of South Africa.

Numbering of hikes and key to maps. For easy reference, a prefix has been added to each hike, thereby indicating the region where the hike commences. In this way, GG1 refers to Golden Gate Hike 1, AM2 to Amphitheatre Hike 2 and MW3 to Mnweni Hike 3 and so on.

The key to the regional maps, which appear in the colour section, is on page 66. The following key is applicable to the trail maps which accompany each hike.

Hiking ethics and helpful hints. I have an ecological bias in these matters, something that will become obvious as you use this guide. I also have strong feelings regarding hiking ethics, instilled by years of mountaineering and association with the MCSA. These ideas are contained in boxes throughout the book, under headings such as How to Best Enjoy Your Hike, Mountain Hygiene and Fires and Fishing. I also include some hints which might prove useful, such as information on snakes, mountain photography and what to wear and carry.

I hope my own enthusiasm for the natural environment will encourage you to pursue each topic that I have raised. The books listed for further reading are authoritative and fascinating. I have most of them in my own library and when the Cape winters set in, I open my 'Berg books and dream; then I listen to the weather reports, check my snow gear and stock up on supplies. . . and so perhaps I will meet you there.

KEY TO THE SKETCH MAPS

– – ►	Hiking route
——	Major road
— — • • •	Possible detour/other hike
=====	Jeep track
• 3 299	Mountain peak
	Cave
	Chain ladder
	Bridge
	Forested area
	Plantation
	Waterfall
	Dam
H	Hotel
NPB	Natal Parks Board
	Camp site
	Caravan park
	Hut
— • — • —	Game fence

A SHORT NATURAL HISTORY OF THE DRAKENSBERG

Historical Geology and Topography

The geological history of the Drakensberg is fairly simple to comprehend – it is the time scale which is often difficult to grasp. The high peaks and escarpment of these mountains are the capping atop many horizontal layers of the Karoo Supergroup of rocks which cover about two thirds of South Africa, much like the icing on a tiered wedding cake. The Karoo period began about 250 million years ago (the earth is about four and a half billion years old), when the present continents of Africa, South America, Australia, Antarctica, as well as parts of the Middle East, India and Madagascar formed one super-continent referred to as Gondwanaland.

At this time present-day southern Africa was covered by a vast sheet of ice. When this vast glacier melted, it left behind a sludge of eroded material which solidified into the Dwyka Group of rocks, the first layer of the Karoo Supergroup. The area encircled by these deposits was like an enormous inland sea and over the many millions of years that followed, the Ecca and Beaufort beds were laid as horizontal layers of shale, sandstone and mudstone in the sea's basin. Conditions varied greatly but were characterized by swampy landscapes where the amphibians, which had emerged from the cold seas, slowly evolved into mammals.

After about 30 million years of watery conditions, the interior of Gondwanaland began to dry up: swamps became lakes and lakes became estuaries, and these in turn became dry plains and then wide, wind-swept deserts. The sandy deposits are referred to as the Stormberg Group of rocks, and it is these rocks that make up the present-day Drakensberg.

The first Stormberg layer is the Molteno Group, consisting of mainly blue-grey sandstones which form the ledges and terraces at the foot of the Little Berg. Next came the Red Beds, with their typical red to purple mudstones and shales, which now form the steep grassy slopes below the Cave Sandstone cliffs. These rocks are seldom exposed in today's landscape, but the increasing aridity, which caused the deposition of these rocks, is thought to have brought about the extinction of the mammal-like dinosaurs of the Karoo period.

The large-grained, yellowish Cave Sandstones seem to have been largely wind deposited (aeolian). They are extremely soft and erosive, which accounts for the cliffs that define the Little Berg and the many caves and overhangs that were home to the Bushmen for perhaps thousands of years. Primitive dassie-size mammals survived this period to represent our link with earliest life. At the end of the Cave Sandstone period the super-continent of Gondwanaland began to heave and buckle and split apart, accompanied by large-scale volcanic activity.

About 190 million years ago, great fissures opened in present-day Lesotho and molten lava spewed from the earth's boiling core, covering the area from the Natal coastline into the interior of the Orange Free State. With the breakup of Gondwanaland the influence of the sea and consecutive periods of continental uplifting (itself due partly to erosion) caused the establishment of an erosion cycle which continues today. What we see as the Drakensberg is really a step which is being continually worn back by water and gravity. There is no 'other side' to the mountains that one sees from Natal, for beyond one's

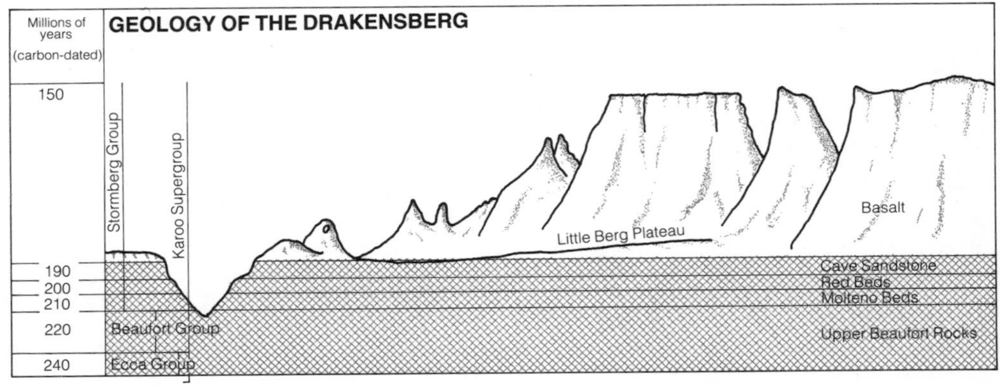

line of vision lies the mountain fortress of Lesotho, a high plateau country surrounded on all sides by high escarpments.

When the last of the basalt covering has been chiselled away – at a rate of about one centimetre every five years – the softer sandstones below will soon be planed by the rivers in the area and then the climate will change and with it the soils, the vegetation and the animals. Then the area will look something like it was before the Stormberg period began.

Climate

Climate is generally considered to be the average weather pattern recorded over a few decades. Weather, on the other hand, is the daily state of the atmosphere and it is this that most concerns us as hikers in the Drakensberg. There are definite seasonal weather conditions in the 'Berg, with summers being generally wet but warm and winters dry and cold. As this is a major mountain range with vast altitudinal differences, the daily weather there is highly variable; in fact, snow storms are known to hit the high peaks at any time of the year.

An important factor determining the weather is synoptic conditions, or the positions of high and low pressure systems around the subcontinent and the winds they produce. During the summer there is usually a low pressure cell over the interior of southern Africa, with high pressure systems over the Indian Ocean. Wind tends to flow from the high to the low pressure area, bringing moist air across Natal from the sea. As this warm, moist air reaches the Drakensberg it is forced upwards; it then cools and heavy summer storm clouds develop over the mountains.

During the winter this pattern is reversed. There is a high pressure cell over the land, and low pressure cells move across the country from the south-west. The high pressure cell causes generally cold, dry conditions during the winter. There is, however, an additional factor at work – the movement of cold fronts. These are moving masses of cold and warm air which are called temperate cyclones. The cold front part of the system arrives first and is heralded by high cirrus clouds (horses tails). These are followed by thick banks of nimbo-stratus rain clouds which may bring rain, hail, sleet or snow.

An anomaly of winter in Natal is the occurrence of high temperatures when strong westerly winds course over the Escarpment; these hot, dry berg winds cross the dry interior, warming up as they descend the mountains to sweep towards the coast.

Autumn and spring are transitional periods between the two seasonal extremes and they are accompanied by very changeable weather, although the days are usually warm and the nights cool. This is the best time for hiking, but even then hikers must be prepared for all extremes. For those who have the right equipment, nothing quite beats hiking on the summit plateau when it is covered by a soft quilt of snow.

Climate and weather are the muscles behind the tools that shape the land. Although water is the main agent of erosion in the Drakensberg, a lightning bolt cracking into the basalt spires can loose a shower of rock, which is more visible than the continuous erosion that goes on undetected. This is all part of the natural processes which shape the land; erosion caused by man, however, is avoidable.

Vegetation

The vegetation of the Drakensberg is effected ona local scale by both altitude (height above sea level) and aspect (direction to the sun). Basically, the greater the altitude the greater the temperature range and the greater the stresses on the things which live there. The north-facing slopes receive more direct sunlight than south-facing ones and are generally hotter and drier. The rate of evaporation on the north-facing slopes is extremely high and the animals and plants living there have to be hardy, but not as hardy as those finding a niche on the top of the mountains.

Silver protea
(*Protea roupelliae*)

There are three major vegetation zones of the Drakensberg, with a number of species and communities of plants being common to more than one zone. The Montane Belt includes the protea savanna and Afro-montane forests of the lower slopes and gorges. The main species, which are found among the grasses on the south-facing slopes, are *Protea caffra* with its silvery leaf hairs and reddish stalks and leaf base and *P. roupelliae*, which is similar but lacks the silvery hairs and reddish colour. Both are medium-sized trees. *P. subvestita* has a yellowish flower and grows as a shrub with dense, vertical branches; *P. dracomontana* is a low shrub found in the higher Sub-Alpine Belt, while *P. nubegina* is represented by a single, remote community in the north.

The major grasses are *Themeda triandra* (red-grass) and *Festuca costata* (tussock grass), although there are many other types of grass to be found, especially in moist areas. Tree ferns (*Alsophila dregei*) and cycads (*Encephalartos ghellinkii*) are commonly found along rivers and in marshy areas.

The forests are characterized by two species of yellowwood, *Podocarpus falcatus* (Outeniqua yellowwood) and *P. latifolius* (the real yellowwood). Other common trees are the mountain hard pear (*Olinia emarginata*), Assegai wood (*Curtesia dentata*), Cape Holly (*Ilex mitis*) with its

Highveld protea
(*Protea caffra*)

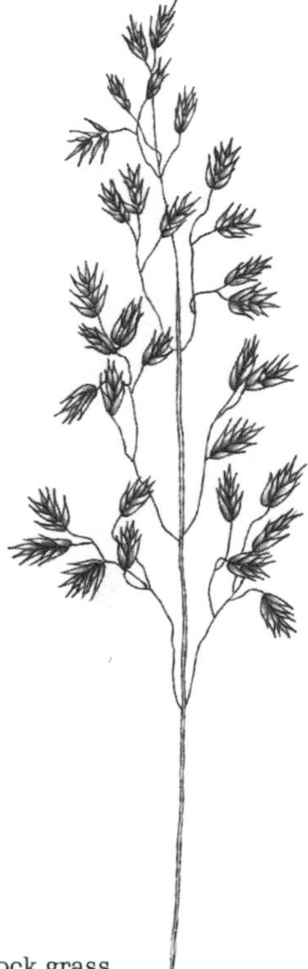

Tussock grass
(*Festuca costata*)

Red grass
(*Themeda trianda*)

whitish bark and white stinkwood (*Celtis africana*). Outside the forests, along rivers and among boulders, the most common trees of the Drakensberg are to be found: ouhout (*Leucosidea sericea*) and sagewood (*Buddleia salviifolia*), which forms communities with mountain taaibos (*Rhus dentata*) and common spike thorn (*Maytenus heterophylla*).

The Sub-Alpine Belt extends from around the tops of the forested gorges to the base of the basalt walls of the Escarpment. This zone takes in most of the Little Berg plateaux and is covered almost exclusively by *Themeda* grasslands. Fynbos is found in the sheltered areas, with *Leucosidea-Buddleia* scrub along the river banks. Many bulbous plants, such as watsonias and irises, burst into flower every spring among the golden grass plains. Higher up the

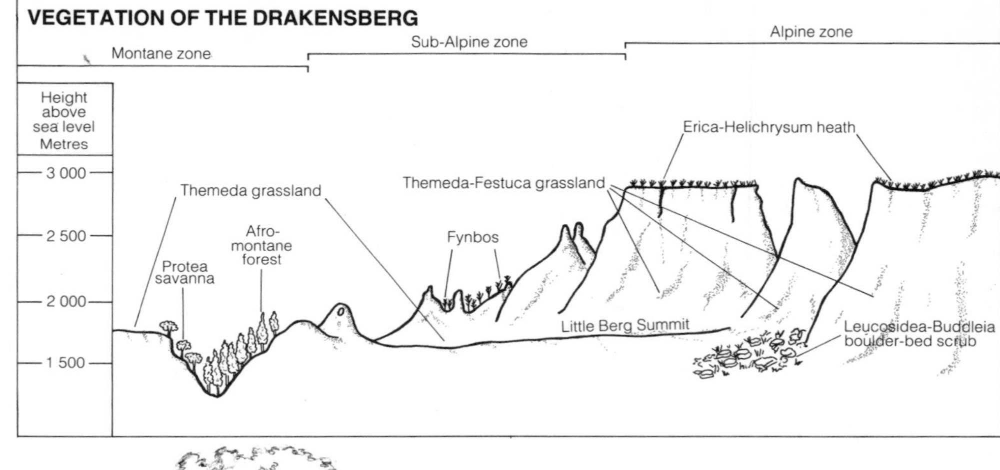

Real yellowwood (*Podocarpus latifolius*)

White stinkwood (*Celtis africana*)

Natal bottlebrush (*Greyia sutherlandii*)

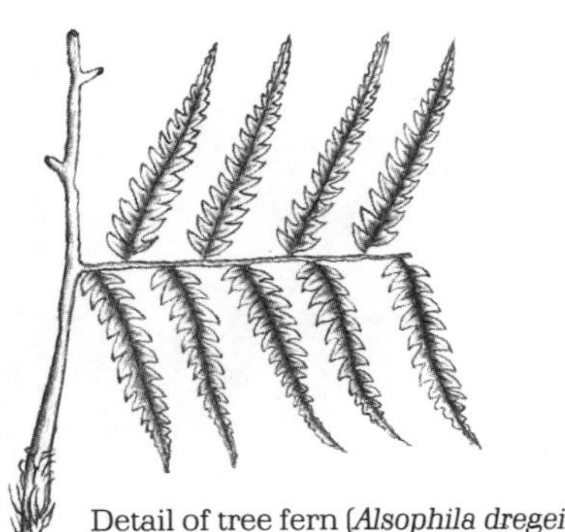
Detail of tree fern (*Alsophila dregei*)

Detail of Nana-berry (*Rhus dentata*)

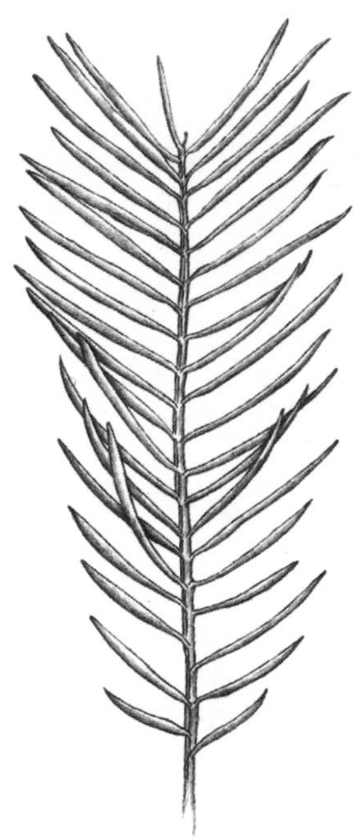
Detail of cycad (*Encephalartos ghellinckii*)

Red-hot poker (*Kniphofia* sp.)

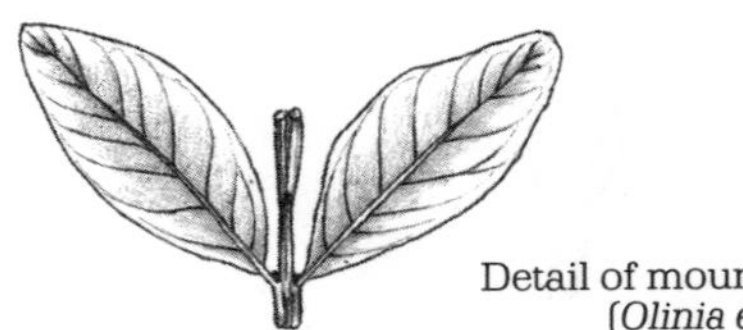
Detail of mountain olinia (*Olinia emarginata*)

mountains, on the steeper slopes below the basalt walls, the composition of the grasslands changes to *Themeda-Festuca* community. These are called sour grasses, because they survive in winter by withdrawing nutrients into their roots, which makes them unpalatable to grazers.

There are neither trees nor anything growing taller than one metre in the Alpine zone. The most common plants are *Ericas*, with tiny rolled-up leaves. The other main component of the heaths are Everlastings (*Helichrysum*) with their papery flowers which play an important role in Zulu and Xhosa sorcery. Small tussock grasses grow here, providing grazing for the cattle, horses and goats of the Basotho herdsmen. The bogs and streams are stroked with splashes of red and yellow when the warmth of spring draws out *Kniphofia, Moraea* flowers, and *Erica* and *Helichrysum* blooms.

The mountain ranges of Africa south of the

Detail of sagewood (*Buddleja salviifolia*)

River lily
(*Schizostylis coccinea*)

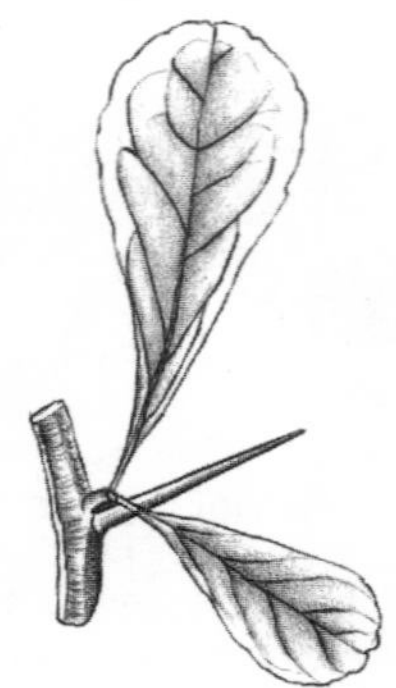

Detail of spike thorn
(*Maytenus heterophylla*)

Erica (Ericaceae family)

Everlasting (*Helichrysum* sp.)

Sahara are like ecological islands connected by common genetic elements which skip along these islands with the climatic tides. Species of the Cape Fynbos have found suitable niches in these mountainous environments and erica heaths, proteas and other typical Fynbos plants are found there. The Cape Fynbos Biome is a highly stressed environment for plants and so the summits of the sub-Saharan mountains are covered by the *Erica-Helichrysum* heaths, which can survive these stressed conditions and which one associates with Fynbos.

The *Podocarpus* (yellowwood) forests found in the Drakensberg are more accurately called Afro-montane forests, for they, too, are found throughout the mountains of Africa. Of course, as one moves south along the continent's eastern mountain spine from Ethiopia to the Cape, the species composition changes and

Moraea (*Moraea* sp.)

Guernsey lily (*Nerine sarniensis*)

decreases, with an overlap of species between adjoining areas.

Macro- and micro-habitats exist in the Drakensberg, where certain factors determine why a particular plant species grows only in one small confined area. In the Oqalweni Valley of Cathedral, for instance, the rare 'Berg cycad flourishes near the river.

Of the factors playing a major role in controlling the flora of the Drakensberg, the first that comes to mind is fire. The vegetation here has adapted to frequent burning and has developed mechanisms to cope with these conditions. Fire is a natural process in ecology; man, however, tends to change everything – he burns the veld too often, fells the trees and allows his cattle to overgraze the grass, leaving extensive erosion in his wake.

Detail of ouhout (*Leucosidea sericea*)

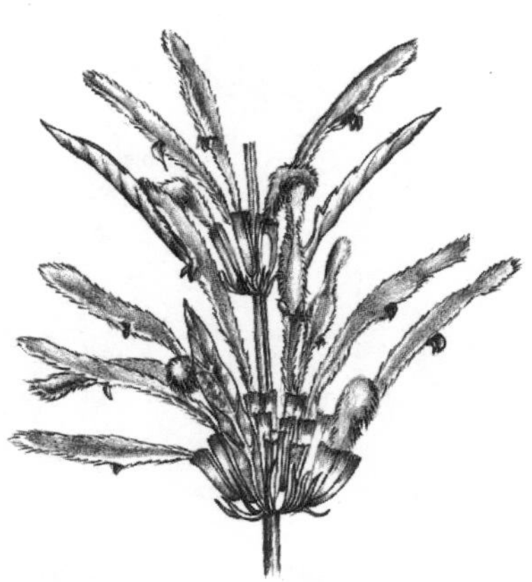

Wild dagga (*Leonotis leonurus* var. *leonurus*)

Detail of African holly (*Ilex mitis*)

Animals

The first animals of the Drakensberg were dinosaurs which lived here about 200 million years ago. Some of these reptiles left their footprints in the soft sand and mudstone, and fossilized remains of these footprints can be seen in the rock in Lesotho near Leribe and in the Giant's Castle Game Reserve. Increasingly dry conditions drove the reptiles away, but there was a small mammal, about the size of a dassie, which survived and continued the genetic evolution, evidence of which has been preserved in multiple layers of the Karoo rocks.

Mountains everywhere are stressed environments where animals have to make special adaptations to cope with extreme conditions; they have to be versatile like baboons, specially endowed with thick fur like dassies, able to hibernate like reptiles or fly like birds. There are, of course, many types of animals which have adapted to life in the 'Berg: there are five species of mongoose and eight conspicuous species of rodent, as well as hares, porcupines and otters more common than their shy natures would imply, cats like leopards, lynxes, servals and wild cats, and jackals. But these are all rarely seen and a good field guide will be most helpful in providing detail. Two species which are most conspicuous are baboons and dassies.

Baboons (*Papio* spp.) are considered by some to be the noisiest, most obnoxious animals in the mountains. They are highly sociable creatures, superb rock climbers and can be found from the top to the bottom of mountains, living in trees, in caves or on rock ledges. They eat just about anything and their only natural enemy is the leopard. Dassies (*Procavia capensis*) are very agile rock dwellers and in spite of being the favourite food of many larger carnivores and raptors, they may be approached within a few metres. There is also a nocturnal tree dassie (*Dendrohyrax arboreus*) which can be seen in the forests.

Birds best characterize the Drakensberg, and none more so than the lammergeier or bearded vulture (*Gypaetus barbatus*). These great mountain birds were once found throughout southern Africa, but their range decreased with the wild herds on which they depended. Today they are found only in the Drakensberg and in Lesotho and are considered to be the most endangered birds on the subcontinent. Only a few years ago a lammergeier sighting was considered by mountaineers to be a rare and marvellous thing.

More recently a number of lammergeier 'restaurants' have been established in the mountains and the birds are now more visible. From below the lammergeier can be recognized by its enormous backswept wings and a diamond-shaped tail. The adult has a golden chest, a black 'beard' and mask and a scarlet eye ring. After the lammergeier, the black eagle (*Aquila verreauxii*) is the crown prince of the mountains and it is easily recognized by its large size, overall black colour, white cross on the back and white 'windows' on the under-wing.

The most conspicuous raptor in the mountains is the jackal buzzard (*Buteo rufofuscus*), which could be mistaken for a small eagle. They are often seen perched on telephone poles along the road and when they take off, the buff-coloured chest and rump are at once diagnostic. From below, a jackal buzzard can be identified by the black trailing edge to the wing, with a white middle section and a pale leading edge. The Cape vulture (*Gyps coprotheres*) is the only true vulture found in the Drakensberg, where a large breeding colony can be found in the

Mountain reedbuck
(*Redunca fulvorufula*)

Bushbuck (*Trageliscus scriptus*)

Oribi (*Ourebia orebi*)

pocked cliffs of Vulture's Retreat, behind the Dragon's Back at the top of Gray's Pass.

The lanner falcon (*Falco biarmicus*) is one of the swiftest fliers among the raptors and is recognized by its black 'flying mask' and narrow, back-swept wings. It is one of the smaller birds of prey, but is slightly bigger than the more common rock kestrel (*Hirundo fuligula*). The kestrel is the supreme hovering craft, with a distinctive black tail bar and reddish body. The smallest raptor of the Drakensberg but the commonest in the country is the black-shouldered kite (*Elanus caeruleus*). There are, of course, many other birds in the Drakensberg – about 250 at the last count – which may be discovered among the forests and peaks of the 'Berg and the pages of suitable field guides.

The eland (*Taurotragus oryx*) is the largest antelope and the largest animal found in the Drakensberg. They were the Bushmen's favourite game and their link with the metaphysical, which is why the eland is so well represented in the rock art here. They are equally at home in the mountains as in the dry savanna of the Kalahari. The most numerous antelope in the mountains are grey rhebuck (*Pelea capreolus*) and they are found mainly above the Cave Sandstone level. The first sign of these alert creatures is usually their sharp bark of alarm. They then bound off up the grass slope, their bushy white tails held erect as they bob along. They are medium-sized antelope with shaggy grey coats, elongated ears and short horns which point slightly forwards.

The grey rhebuck is sometimes confused with what is considered to be the shyest

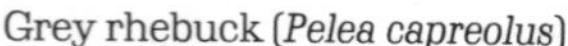

Grey rhebuck (*Pelea capreolus*)

Klipspringer (*Oreotragus oreotragus*)

antelope of all, the oribi (*Ourebia ourebi*), although the chances of seeing an oribi are very slim indeed. They are smaller than the rhebuck and are more fawn coloured. They lie concealed in tall grass and only break when you are almost on top of them.

As ubiquitous as the rhebuck is the mountain reedbuck (*Redunca fulvorufula*), which collects in smaller groups and is even shyer than the former species. They lie up during the day in glades and will always run uphill when approached. They are distinguished from the rhebuck by their reddish upper and white underparts, and by their longer, curved horns. The bushbuck (*Trageliscus scriptus*) is easier to identify but seldom seen, preferring the habitat of forests and riverine bush. They are smallish but robust and fast, with attractive markings consisting of white spots on the reddish flanks and black stripes on the back, as well as a black collar.

The grey duiker (*Sylvicapra grimmia*) keeps largely to the same habitat as the bushbuck, but may also be seen in cultivated fields. Its name reveals its shy nature as it dives for cover when fleeing. It is a uniform grey colour with short, spiky horns. Slightly smaller than the duiker, the klipspringer (*Oreotragus oreotragus*) has padded hoofs, which allow quite remarkable jumping on rocky terrain. Although similar to the grey duiker in size and colour, they have short muzzles and very short tails, while the coat is shaggy and coarse. Only the male has horns, which are short and straight. They seem to be confined to the Fynbos belt in the Drakensberg, above an altitude of 2 400 metres, that is above the Little Berg. Blesbok, red hartebeest and black wildebeest have been reintroduced to their former ranges in the 'Berg and are found mainly in the Golden Gate and Giant's Castle areas.

There are 24 species of snakes found in these

Puffadder (*Bitis arietans*)

Spitting cobra or rinkhals (*Hemachatus haemachatus*)

mountains, only three of which need concern hikers. The most dangerous is the puff adder (*Bitis arietans*) because it is highly venomous and relies on camouflage for protection. It will only strike if it thinks that you are about to step on it; most bites are on or below the ankle, so by wearing hiking boots you will be reducing the danger considerably. Field guides say that these snakes are seldom found above 2 000 metres, but I have seen them at about 2 500 metres. They are fat snakes with broad heads and have vivid chevron markings of brown and yellow for the entire length of their bodies.

The berg adder (*Bitis atropos atropos*) is much smaller than the puff adder, with black and grey diamond patterns on the back, but it also has the typical sluggish look of an adder. While a puff adder bite is potentially fatal, no-one is known to have died from a berg adder bite. The symptoms are, however, something with which every hiker should be familiar, as a few hours after being bitten you will not be able to walk.

The rinkhals (*Hemachatus haemachatus*) is also dangerous, its spray being potentially more serious than its bite. Wearing sunglasses is the best preventative measure against the deadly accurate jet of venom, which can cause intense pain and blindness if not treated immediately. You should see the snake first though, as it will rear cobra-like, with hood extended, before it sprays. Its colour may vary from brown to black with white or yellow banded markings along the throat.

There are three basic types of lizard found in the 'Berg. The small, frail-looking geckos (Gekkonidae family) with sucker-like toes are the only lizards that communicate vocally. Then there are agamas (Algamide family) or koggelmandertjies, with their prehistoric, horny appearance. They may be large and colourful and love to sun themselves on boulders, but run fast with bodies held high. Finally, there are the skinks (Scincidae family), or typical lizards, with short, fat bodies, short legs and smooth skins. They are usually olive green to brown in colour with yellowish stripes down their bodies.

Very little has been recorded about insects in the area, but it is certainly an entomologist's dream. Nowhere have I seen river valleys so dense with the gossamer of spider webs, and such a variety of spinners; the forests seem to vibrate with dazzling butterflies, which flutter like confetti over the grasslands, alighting on flowers where they bloom; the grasslands teem with grasshoppers and vividly coloured locusts, and noisiest of all are the cicadas, those frenetic Christmas beetles whose high-pitched 'singing' can be quite deafening on midsummer afternoons and evenings.

GOLDEN GATE

The Golden Gate Highlands National Park is characterized by a series of imposing sandstone bastions which flank the Little Caledon River and is one of the few game reserves in the country proclaimed for its scenic splendour rather than its ecological importance. Even before its proclamation in 1963, and the opening of the Rhebuck Trail, Golden Gate was a popular camping and hiking getaway. Apart from the two-day hiking trail, there are many short, easy walks and rambles, as well as horse rides.

With the exception of a few isolated basalt peaks, the Park comprises Little Berg plateaux and their incised valleys. The exposed Cave Sandstone layer is creamy-yellow with the softer coppery ferrous Red Beds below; at sunset the colour slowly dissolves through a vivid range of purple, cerise and gold before shadow darkens the cliffs. Although both rock layers are highly erodable, the lower Red Beds are more so and they become undercut, giving the cliffs their characteristically prominent, overhanging structure. Above the sandstone cliff line, which runs in and around the Park at an altitude of about 1 980 metres, there is a 'contour line' of dolerite just above the basalt horizon which also follows the perimeter of the Park at about 2 210 metres.

Hikers exploring this game reserve can expect to see eland, gemsbok, mountain zebra, mountain reedbuck and grey rhebuck, as well as the largest herds of black wildebeest in the country. Smaller animals include wild cat, mongoose, jackal, aardwolf and otter. To make the best of this opportunity, hikers should wear dull-coloured clothing, avoid using 'dayglo' packs and pay heed to basic veld craft such as walking softly and quietly without breaking the skyline, checking spoor on the path and using the wind direction when tracking. The best way to spot animals is to scan unfocussed around you, keeping alert for any unusual shape, colour or movement in the surroundings.

Keeping a pair of binoculars on hand is helpful, especially to identify birds such as sunbirds and woodpeckers, harriers, buzzards and eagles, and the more ellusive passerines such as cisticolas and warblers, swifts and swallows which sometimes fill the sky in reeling, swooping multitudes. The high sandstone cliffs are the natural habitat of black eagles, redwinged starlings, rock martins and rock pigeons. With patience you should be able to capture them on film in their natural setting. The cliffs opposite Glen Reenen have a nest that was until recently used by a pair of breeding lammergeiers, but unfortunately these rarest of southern African birds have not been seen at Golden Gate for some time.

The main Brandwag camp in the Park offers modern, luxury accommodation of which the National Parks Board can be proud. A restaurant, book shop and modern hotel facilities are available and visitors can choose to stay in suites or in self-contained chalets. At the Glen Reenen camp there is a small but lush caravan park and camp site on the banks of the Little Caledon River; if more privacy and comfort is required there are bungalows for hire, as well as a provisions store and petrol station. One- or two-hour horse rides are available from the stables near Brandwag camp.

One criticism of the Park is the huge gap that exists between the grade of the shorter walks and that of the single hiking trail here. The Rhebuck Trail is more strenuous than most two-day hiking trails as the path seldom contours, so it is up, down, up, down for all of 30 kilometres. After this, only the outing to the top of Wodehouse Kop (also on the Rhebuck Trail) is anything of a physical challenge.

The Rhebuck Trail *Hike GG1*

Route: *Round trip from Glen Reenen camp site*
Distance: *30 kilometres*
Duration: *2 days*
Grade: *Severe to Extreme*
General: *This trail circumnavigates most of the Park, taking you over the highest and lowest points with scant regard to sparing the legs by contouring. The official times given to complete the various sections were obviously calculated by a marathon runner without the burden of a pack. But don't let this put you off (as it did the party who joined me on the first day's outing), for the trail does take you through scenic countryside with the chance of excellent game viewing – which is the point of it all, I suppose. Bookings must be made through the National Parks Board booking office. Although the trail is strenuous, any physically competent person can complete it – just start early and don't rush. Also, be careful not to interpret the numbers on the Park's map as kilometre markers, as they mark places of interest.*

▶ **Day 1** (15 km): From Rugged Glen camp site (no. 2 on the Park's map), the path crosses the Little Caledon River footbridge (no. 1) towards Echo Gorge, but the path forks off at a small stream to the left and then up to the large overhanging cliffs below Wodehouse Kop. Stop a while under the cliffs to watch the birdlife, insects, spiders and enjoy the shade, for it's the last you have for a long stretch. Continue along to the end of the cliff line and climb the rock ramp, using the convenient but unnecessary chain ladder. You will now be standing on the lip of the sandstone cliffs with a panoramic view of the Little Caledon River valley and across the eastern Orange Free State. You are now on top of the famous Brandwag (no. 3).

▶ Turn around and look up to the high peak behind you, just slightly lower than Wodehouse Kop (2 438 m), for that is where you are heading. The path is obvious, and after a few hundred metres it follows a fence line to the first basalt band which must be negotiated. On the grassy slopes you are sure to see Victorin's scrub warblers, cloud cisticolas, and that common hawk of the mountains, the black harrier. When you get to the low cliff band the path becomes indistinct: if you like the exposure go straight up the corner, but it is easier to traverse a short way around to the left, and then pick your way diagonally up and around back to the corner on the right. The clearly defined path carries on up the ridge, crosses over, between two high points (both 2 427 m, no. 4), to the left-hand side of the mountain and then goes over to the left and down. There are intermittent path markers along the way, so you can't really get lost.

If you drop your pack and then proceed stealthily, down the right-hand (eastern) slope of the mountain towards Wodehouse Kop (2 438 m), you should come within close range of gemsbok, eland, wildebeest and mountain zebra on the terrace below. This is also where the shyer antelope lie low during the day.

▶ Once back on the path, head down to the plain where a small number of pans attract wildebeest, gemsbok and springbuck. The path heads across a plain, crosses a stream and follows the left-hand bank to some pools and the Bridal Veil Falls, and a short detour from the main path will enable you to gain a grand view of Boskloof (no. 5). When the *Kniphofias* (red-hot pokers) bloom along the river courses they attract a colourful parade of birds and butterflies: sit patiently nearby and you will be able to observe and photograph them at close quarters.

▶ Further along, the path heads into Boskloof and follows the river where it has cut a series of smooth pools, criss-crossing it before reaching the Bushman Cave (no. 6). These are as pleasant surroundings as you will find for a lunch spot and it happens to be half-way. From here, the path climbs for a short way up to the right, curving around Tweeling Kop, and then descends to the Wilgenhof Youth Camp (no. 7) over a slip-

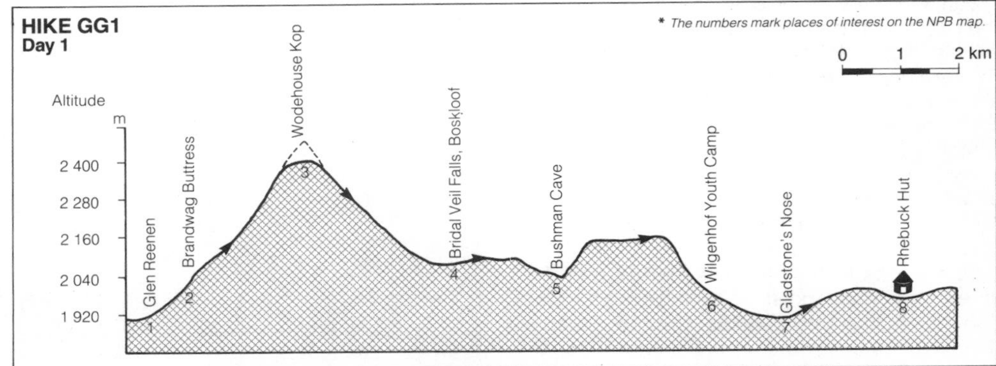

A classic view of the Golden Gate.

pery rocky section where the path becomes indistinct.

▶ From Wilgenhof, the path passes the sandstone bastion called Gladstone's Nose (no. 8) and then follows the Ribbokspruit for about 2,5 km. This section can be quite boring, passing old rubbish dumps and excavations, following a track for most of the way. The Rhebuck Hut is situated 1 km beyond the end of the track, after you have passed through an ouhout (*Leucosidea sericea*) thicket, where the twisted trunks and branches create a haunted atmosphere. Ouhout is the most common bush or small tree of the Drakensberg, growing mainly along forest margins and river banks. The camp can accommodate 18 people in three rooms. There is also a braai boma and a room with gas cookers and a gas light. Cathedral Cave is tucked away in the cliff line on the opposite side of the river from the huts; it is more of a cleft than a cave, though.

▶ **Day 2** (15 km): The second section is simple: you go up to the top of Generaals Kop (2 732 m) and then down again. Keep plasters and water handy. From the hut the path follows the Ribbokspruit to its source, passing The Crevasse gorge (no. 10), a waterfall and pool formed by a dolerite shelf (no. 11) and thick grass slopes and finally a boggy area where the river begins. Just above here you come to the Park boundary (no. 12) where a fence prevents you from suddenly tumbling over the edge into Lesotho. From here there are spectacular views of the dominating Ribbokkop (2 837 m), of the villages and fields far below in the Caledon River valley and of the Maluti Mountains beyond.

One thinks of lizards as favouring hot, dry areas but this moist, often freezing zone abounds in agamas and skinks which scamper across the rocks, bodies raised high, and hurtle into cracks at the vibration of approaching boots. The sharp whistle of rhebuck is often heard, but they are hard to see – as you hear the sound stop and look, for it is usually issued as the animal breaks its cover to bound off uphill. Always keep a look out for snakes in the grass – I had a close encounter with a brilliant yellow and black rinkhals, but it got a bigger fright than I did and quickly slithered away. I always hike with a staff, to prod suspicious things in the grass or trees, to help me cross rivers and break cobwebs, and as a handy tripod for close-up photography.

▶ The path follows the fence to a corner and then you are faced with a decision: you can either follow the fence up a very steep grassy bank and then scramble through a basalt band to the top of the peak, or you can deviate to the left and follow a terrace around the Generaals Kop (no. 13 and definitely unlucky for some). The marked trail goes up the very steep bank but if you are already despondent I doubt the wisdom of choosing this alternative; another path can be followed along the outer edge of the terrace and this should be considered – unless, like me, you have the mountaineer's curse.

▶ If you do climb to the top of the peak, retrace your steps to the bottom of the basalt band and then turn right and curve around to the right, down to the level grassy terrace and then right, down to a gully at the far-eastern end of it, across a stony plateau. The path descends through a boggy area where *Moraea* blooms can be seen from spring to late summer, and then follows the prominent spur away from the peak where baboons and springbuck are commonly seen. The path then follows the spine of the spur all the way to the Langtoon Dam (no. 14), around the dam wall and then along the right-hand bank of the Buffelspruit to an artificial rock pool (no. 15) and to, by now, a compulsory swim only a few hundred metres short of Glen Reenen camp.

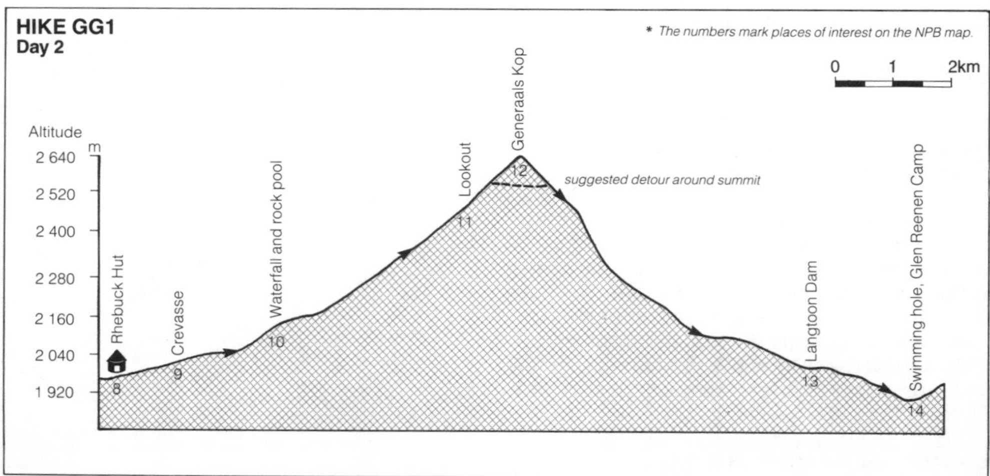

Echo Ravine *Hike GG2*

Route: *Glen Reenen camp site to Echo Ravine*
Distance: *1 kilometre*
Duration: *20 minutes*
Grade: *Easy*
General: *This and the following three hikes begin at the same point. They are all short and easy, so you can combine them for a few hours' outing. A map of the hikes is displayed on a board in the camp site, next to the footbridge; when I saw it, it was faded but it gives an idea of the general layout of the paths.*

▶ From Glen Reenen cross the river via the footbridge and continue straight up into the ravine, through dense ouhout bush. Sunbirds and white eyes are common here, but if you are observant and quiet you could also see olive woodpeckers in the bush. Although the walk terminates at the base of the cliffs, you might be tempted to explore higher up the various ravines, as far as you think is safe. Just remember that the gorge is a natural water trap and can become dangerous when wet.

Mushroom Rocks *Hike GG3*

Route: *Round trip from Glen Reenen camp site via Mushroom Rocks*
Distance: *1,2 kilometres*
Duration: *30 minutes*
Grade: *Easy*
General: *This hike begins at and returns to Glen Reenen camp along the main tarred road.*

▶ From Glen Reenen camp site cross the Little Caledon River footbridge and head up the path to Echo Ravine. At the first junction turn right towards the impressive overhanging rocks which, for obvious reasons, are called Mushroom Rocks. You are likely to see brilliant malachite sunbirds with their characteristic curved beaks and long tails, darting across the tops of trees. At sunset the last light plays on the natural vegetable stains, oxides and lichens, turning them into a technicolour fantasy of transient shades. Return along the same route or continue around the bulge and then recross the river to meet up with the road, following it back to camp.

One of the many species of Helichrysum *or Everlastings.*

Boskloof *Hike GG4*

Route: *Glen Reenen camp site to Boskloof*
Distance: *1,6 kilometres*
Duration: *35 minutes*
Grade: *Easy*
General: *For bird-watching this is the best short walk in the Park, and the longer round trip could lead to hours of bird-watching in the kloof. This Boskloof must not be confused with the larger Boskloof on the northern boundary of the Park.*

▸ About 320 m along the Echo Ravine path (Hike GG2) turn left and continue for about another 300 m parallel to the main cliff line to a fork in the path. Take the right-hand branch and follow it deep into a gorge. (After rain this gorge becomes very wet and potentially dangerous.) Return either by the outbound route or turn right at the next fork and you will emerge near the Brandwag Buttress.

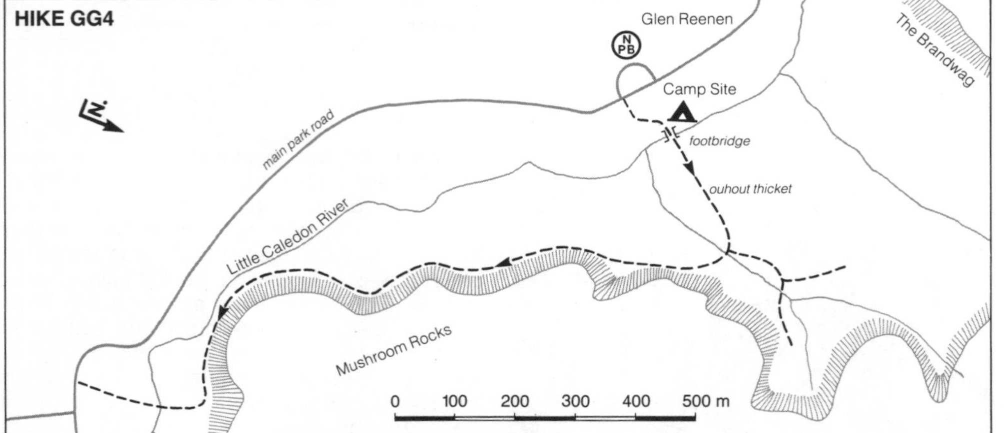

The Brandwag *Hike GG5*

Route: *Glen Reenen camp site to Brandwag Buttress*
Distance: *1 kilometre*
Duration: *20 minutes*
Grade: *Easy*
General: *Although there is a steep section on this hike, there are no real obstacles and its short distance does not qualify it for a more difficult grading. This hike constitutes the first section of the Rhebuck Trail (Hike GG1). The name of the buttress means 'sentinel', for it stands guard over the valley, fiery in the twilight.*

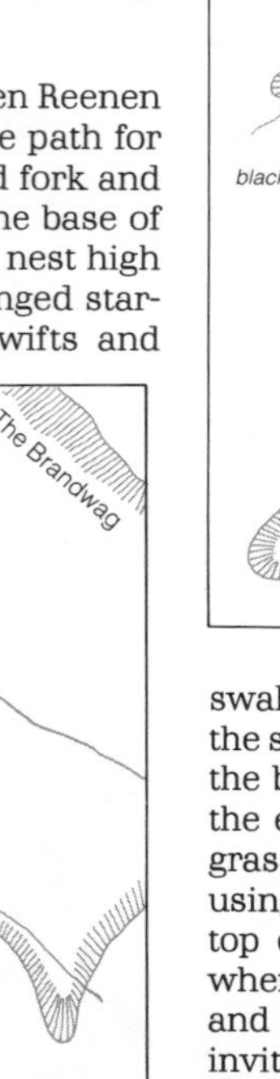

▸ Cross over the foot-bridge from Glen Reenen camp site and follow the Echo Ravine path for 320 m to the fork; take the right-hand fork and then cross the stream and head to the base of the buttress. Look for a black eagle's nest high up on a ledge. The ubiquitous redwinged starlings, rock pigeons and martins, swifts and

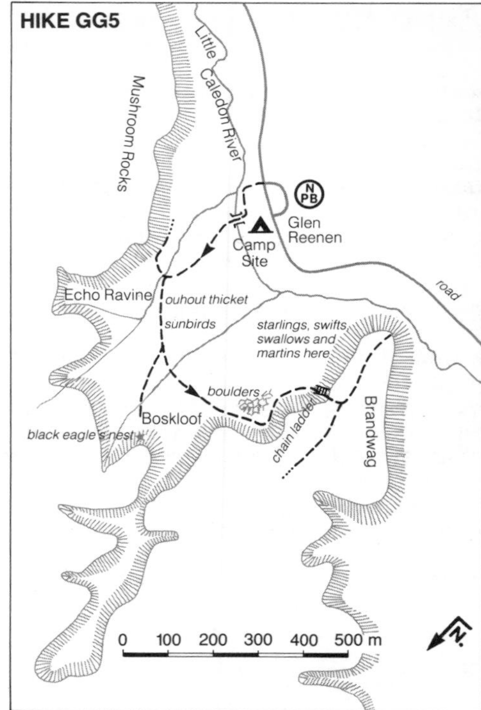

swallows swirl around the cliffs, dive-attacking the swarms of insects that gather in midair near the birds' nests. Continue over the boulders to the end of the cliffs and then climb the steep, grassy slope and rocks to the top of the cliffs, using the chain up the last 20 m if necessary. On top of the cliffs there is a level terrace from where one can survey this section of the Park and the river valley below. Behind you is the inviting Wodehouse Kop and from there the views are even better.

Wodehouse Kop *Hike GG6*

Route: *Glen Reenen camp site to Wodehouse Kop*
Distance: *4 kilometres*
Duration: *1 to 2 hours*
Grade: *Fair to Moderate*
General: *This short, steep hike is a relatively easy way to the top of Wodehouse Kop. At 2 438 m, this peak is still well short of the average Escarpment height of around 3 000 m, but the views are great.*

▶ Proceed to the top of the Brandwag (see Hike GG5) and then take a breather, as the going gets progressively steeper from this point. Follow the path marked by yellow Rhebuck Trail markers, first along the plateau and then along the fence up the steep grassy slope to a clearly visible band of dolerite. Black harriers can be seen gliding low over the slopes, while warblers, cisticolas and neddickies sing from grass stalks or on fence wires. Carry the latest edition of *Roberts Birds*, which has an easy-to-follow key on the cisticolas, to help you avoid frustration in trying to identify them. Buck are not commonly found on this slope but they often lie on the terraces to the left and below, sunning themselves through the day.

▶ At the rock band proceed straight up, or if you don't like the exposure, proceed around to the left for about 15 m and then go diagonally up the rock band, working your way back to the corner. From here it is a clearly defined but steep path to the top of the nearest peak. The Park brochure says that this climb should take you an hour, with hiking pack. Anyone who can accomplish this feat is ready for much higher things, in which case follow the trail markers for two days. Wodehouse Kop is now off to the right, so traverse around on a faint footpath to the highest point.

Looking up Ribbokspruit Valley towards Generaals Kop on the Rhebuck Trail (Hike GG1).

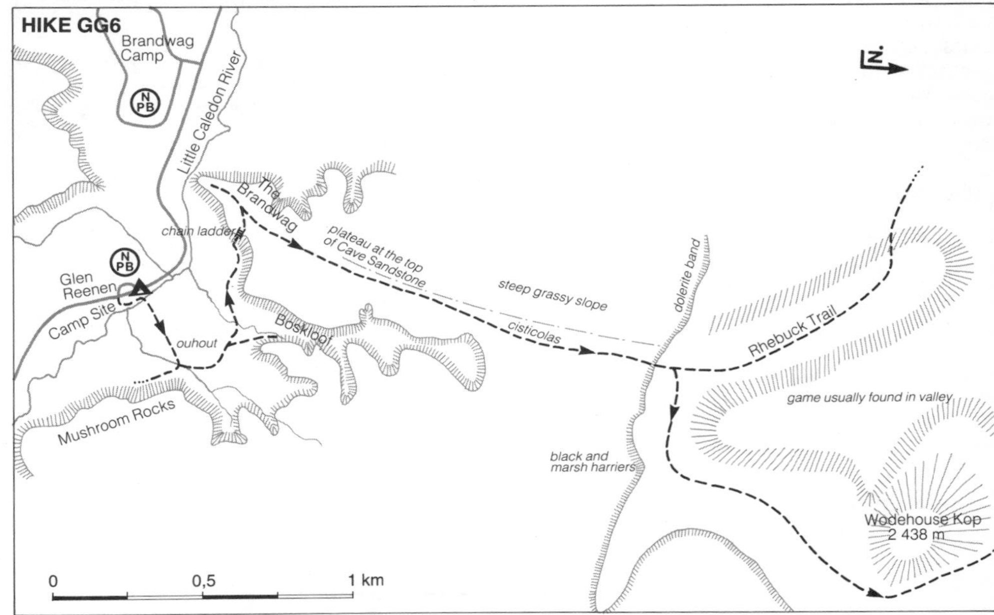

Holkrans *Hike GG7*

Route: *Brandwag camp site to Holkrans cave*
Distance: *1,5 kilometres*
Duration: *30 minutes*
Grade: *Easy*
General: *A photograph of the Holkrans cave can be seen in Anthony Bannister's definitive photographic book,* The National Parks of South Africa. *This is the only hike in the Park beginning at the Brandwag camp, but I found it to be the most interesting short hike in the area.*

▶ From the car park behind the main building entrance, follow the sign to the beginning of the path which climbs up to the base of the towering cliffs behind the camp. Follow the cliff line around to the right and the path leads to the cave. Wooden steps lead up into the cave, the top half of which has been fenced off. Interesting erosional formations are evident on the walls of the cave, and the cave entrance frames the splendid view across the valley and distant hills.

▶ From the cave you can return via the same route, or you can continue to the apex of the valley into which the cave faces, and then follow a path along the base of the valley back to the Brandwag car park.

FIRES

While fires greatly enhance camp-side atmosphere, they are highly dangerous and are banned from Wilderness Areas (fires are allowed at official camp sites only). The ecology of the Drakensberg is extremely sensitive to fire and an untimely fire could spell extinction for some species.

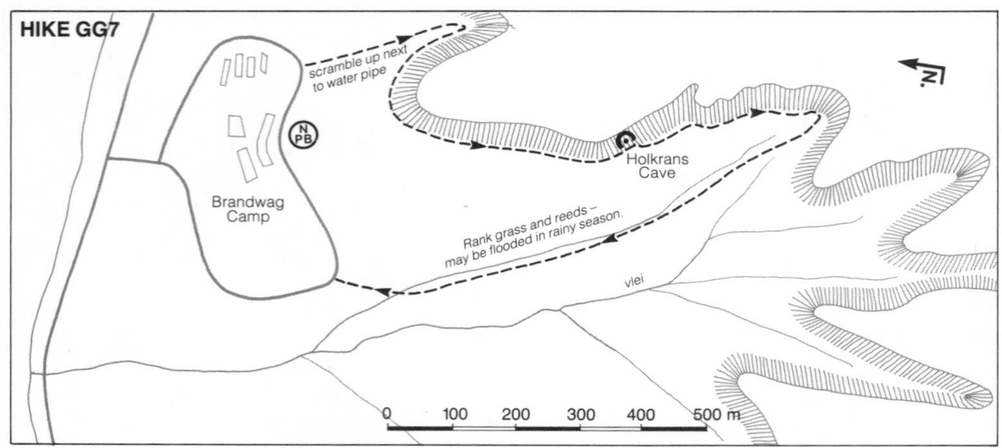

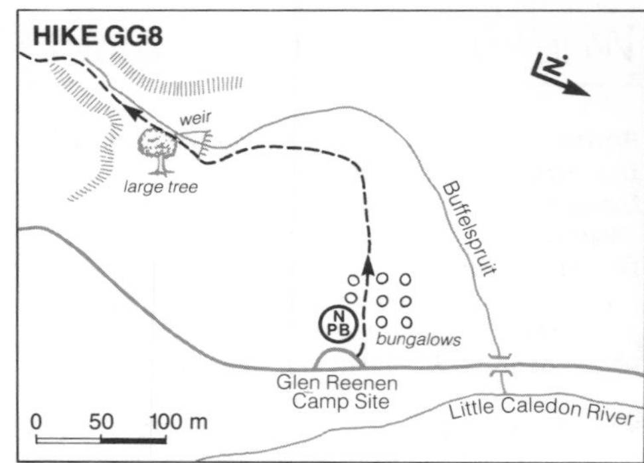

Rock Pool and Langtoon Dam *Hike GG8*

Route: *Glen Reenen camp site to Langtoon Dam*
Distance: *1,2 kilometres*
Duration: *35 minutes*
Grade: *Easy*
General: *This short hike is perfect on a hot day: it follows the course of a stream to a swimming hole and then wanders further on to a pretty dam where waterfowl and other birds can be seen. At dawn and dusk this is a good spot to watch for game.*

▶ From Glen Reenen follow the stream behind the bungalows to the swimming reservoir, five minutes' walk from the camp site. After a plunge in the rock pool and a snooze in the shade of the overhanging willow tree, put on your takkies and follow the path up to the left-hand bank of the stream. After a while the path crosses over to the opposite bank and passes through rank grass and bush.

▶ The walk is scenic with periodic shade along the way. The path recrosses the Buffelsspruit River and follows a narrow ledge along low cliffs until you reach the wall of the Langtoon Dam. Here you can climb up the rock corner on your left to get to the top of the wall and then around to the dam itself. The high peak beyond the dam is Generaals Kop (see Day 2, the Rhebuck Trail, Hike GG1).

Little Caledon River Dam *Hike GG9*

Route: *Glen Reenen or Brandwag camp site to Little Caledon River Dam*
Distance: *3 kilometres*
Duration: *1 hour*
Grade: *Easy*
General: *This is not really a hike, as it follows the main tarred road in the Park, in a westerly direction along the Little Caledon River to the dam. Birdlife is the attraction here.*

▶ From either Glen Reenen or Brandwag camps, follow the road along the Little Caledon River to the small dam near Gladstone's Nose buttress, which forms one of the 'gates' after which the Park is named. These formations have been a gateway to numerous travellers over the years, including various Voortrekker parties and the armies and refugees of the Difaqane wars during the 1820s.

A shady car park and graveyard stand on the raised bank above the dam. The reservoir should be explored, but you must be prepared to get your shoes wet and muddied if you want to do it properly. Redknobbed coots, yellowbilled ducks, cormorants and sometimes darters can be seen on the water or sunning themselves on the thickly reeded banks. In the wooded area you should see pigeons and doves, giant woodpeckers, hadedas and hamerkops. . . the list will increase the longer you watch.

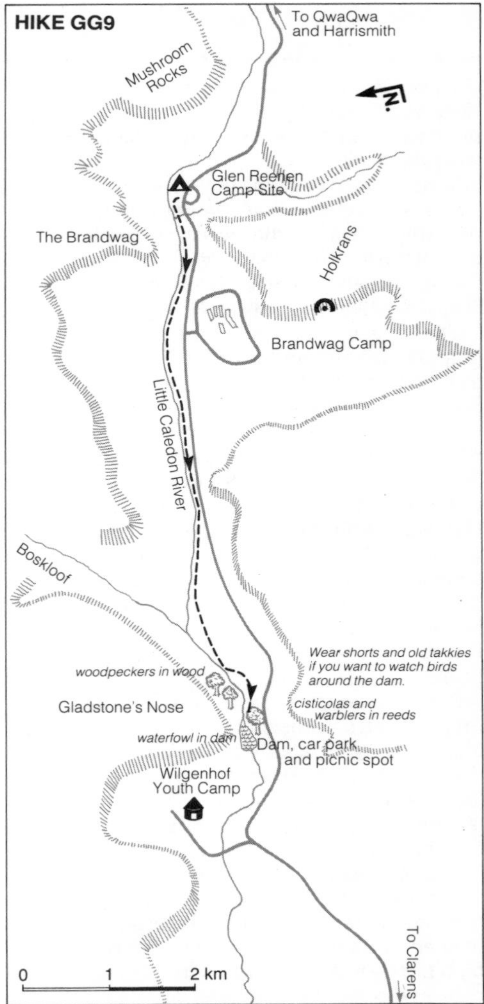

Aeons of erosion have sculpted the sandstone cliffs, forming strange shapes like that of the Mushroom Rocks.

THE AMPHITHEATRE

Everyone who knows the 'Berg has their favourite spot there. The Royal Natal National Park was the first place in the 'Berg that I visited as a child and it remains my favourite. The scenery is among the most dramatic in the world: the Amphitheatre, the main geographical feature of the area, is an awesome rock wall, about five kilometres in length, over which the Tugela (Thukela) River plunges in three gigantic leaps.

The Tugela, together with the Namahadi (Elands), Bilanjil and Khubedu rivers, rises on the slopes of the aptly named Mont-aux-Sources. At 3 282 metres, this peak was once thought to be the highest point of the subcontinent. (In fact it is only the ninth highest peak in South Africa.) Mont-aux-Sources was named by the French missionaries Arbousset and Daumas, who believed the Khubedu River, which also rises from this point, to be the source of the Orange River. It has since been established that the Senqu, rising above Mnweni some 15 kilometres to the south, is in fact the longest and strongest contender to the title.

Over 500 metres from top to bottom, the Amphitheatre presents the greatest single altitude drop in southern Africa and was the venue of the earliest chapter in the climbing history of the Drakensberg. Climbing parties bivouacked at the legendary Rydal Mount hotel and they trekked from there up to the foot of the Namahadi Pass by wagon.

Gone are the days of whiskered, maverick mountaineers in their knickerbockers and women climbers in tweed skirts and lace-up, high heel boots. Gone, too, is the Rydal Mount – now just a lonely ruin on a high steppe near Witsieshoek. Nevertheless mountaineers can still stay in luxury, in the land of mists at the Witsieshoek Mountain Resort, which was originally a two-hut stopover for travellers.

The Natal National Park was proclaimed in 1916 but only acquired its 'royal' prefix after a visit there by the British Royal Family in 1947. In 1949 the first attempt was made to reintroduce blesbok to the Park, but they died while being transported by horse cart from the Orange Free State. Later, a similar attempt was made with black wildebeest, but these 'clown princes of the veld' proved to have an irresistible urge to leap over the precipices of the Little Berg; the last wildebeest leapt to its death in 1982. Grey rhebuck, mountain reedbuck, bushbuck, smaller antelope such as the klipspringer, and a variety of birdlife can still be seen in the Park, which was proclaimed largely for its magnificent scenery.

But a sadder chapter of history concerns the hunting of Bushmen in this region. Late last century, the government of Natal employed bounty hunters to track Bushman raiding parties and then drive them into the high 'Berg passes, where they were ambushed and killed.

Situated below Witsieshoek, the Royal Natal National Park has a fine caravan park and camp site, as well as the exclusive Royal Natal National Park Hotel and the Tendele hutted camp. All are set in the most magnificent landscape on the subcontinent. The Park thus offers a complete cross section of accommodation, making it the most sought-after resort in the Drakensberg. Access is strictly controlled by the Natal Parks Board on a first-come-first-served basis, preferably by booking.

The Cavern hotel lies in the beautiful Putterill Valley, over Surprise Ridge from Rugged Glen. Offering cosy, friendly accommodation, it is one of the few remaining family hotels that still provide traditional mountain hospitality and

The Tugela River and its gorge (Hike AM3) offer some of the most awe-inspiring scenery in the area.

solitude. The hotel is run by Peter and Rhona Carte, who preside over a special and historic part of the mountains and actively promote the interests of mountaineers. Residents have access to the adjacent Park and to a number of other interesting hikes starting from The Cavern, such as that to Cannibal Cave (Hike AM9). Non-residents are allowed to hike and camp on hotel property by arrangement only.

Little Switzerland resort and conference centre lies higher up on the Oliviershoek Pass and hikers can venture out from there, but the Amphitheatre area is beyond a day's range from this hotel. The Hlalanathi chalet, caravan and camping resort is situated on a bank of the Tugela River, downstream from the Park, and offers one of the finest views of the Escarpment, from the Amphitheatre to Stimela Ridge. The gardens of this resort attract many birds, such as black, collared and malachite sunbirds and groundscraper thrushes.

Mont-aux-Sources via Basotho Gate and the Chain Ladder *Hike AM1*

Route: *Mahai camp site to the Chain Ladder*
Distance: *20 kilometres*
Duration: *9 hours (in other words, a long day)*
Grade: *Extreme*
General: *I consider the view from the top of the Amphitheatre to be the most spectacular in South Africa. Although the hike takes one day, three full days should be allotted to the round trip to take full advantage of the area. Traditionally, the route begins in the Mahai camp site, but nowadays most hikers drive the extra 100 or so kilometres through Witsieshoek to the Sentinel car park and so reduce the hike by six or seven hours. This means Mont-aux-Sources is within reach of just about anyone willing to climb the Chain Ladder, although there is a limit of 100 people allowed up the Chain Ladder each day. Inevitably, this accessibility has also led to the degradation of the caves, paths, upper Tugela basin and the general atmosphere of the area. Such is progress. But beware, for easy access to this inhospitable place has also increased the dangers to hikers. Never venture up the Chain Ladder without sufficient food and clothing and a tent to sit out the most violent of storms. Take heed of the graves of those who have flaunted the fury of the dragon.*

▸ Starting at the Mahai camp site, proceed past Lookout Rock where you turn right, cross the Mahai River and then turn left below Plowman's Kop and Gudu Bush. The path then loops back to the river: here you can choose to follow the easier left-hand bank, or the right-hand path past Mahai Cave set in a forest patch. The two paths meet again at a four-way crossing on a ridge on the left-hand bank above the Mahai River, about 5 km from the camp site. Continue parallel to the river, crossing above the Mahai Falls, and on up Gudu Pass to Basotho Gate. Do not follow the Dooley Water path from the four-way crossing (that is, away from the river around a spur) as this path is closed near the top of the Little Berg.

During the Difaqane wars of the 1820s, Basotho Gate was used as an escape route by people fleeing Zulu impis over the mountains and into the sanctuary of Maluti, 'the high place' or present-day Lesotho. Where once only jagged ridges and human skeletons greeted weary travellers, there now stands one of the Drakensberg's favourite ports of call. If you have scheduled your departure wisely you should be in time for breakfast, tea or lunch at the Witsieshoek Mountain Resort, 7 km from Mahai. If you make it in time for Sunday breakfast you might be lucky enough to see vultures, lammergeiers and other raptors taking their fill at the resort's bird 'restaurant'.

▸ Follow the gravel road from Witsieshoek for 10 km, past Breakfast Rock (a favourite halt before the road and hotel existed) to the Sentinel car park. Due to vandalism to hikers' cars, a guard post and security fence have been erected; toilets and limited sleeping facilities have also been provided. You must sign the QwaQwa mountain register here if you wish to proceed up the Chain Ladder; also carry a passport if you intend exploring over the watershed into Lesotho or in case you get lost – a common occurrence.

▸ Continue up one wide and then a series of tighter zigzags to the base of the north face of the Sentinel: this face was first climbed in 1959 by Angus and Pam Leppan. The peak itself was first climbed in 1910 from the west by W. Wybergh and N. McLeod, but what was then a mountaineering odyssey is now an easy, and spectacular, D-grade slog. Recently some high-grade rock routes have been forged up the Sentinel's various faces. Views of Sentinel Peak, the Witches on your left and the Maluti Mountains to the right are magnificent, the peaks often being snow-covered in winter and mist-shrouded in summer.

▸ Do not take short cuts up the zigzags as overuse has seriously degraded the mountain, in spite of the conservation authorities' efforts in recent years to control soil erosion. Apart from minimizing erosion, zigzag paths are easier on a hiker's legs, and in the final analysis it is quicker to take the lesser gradient.

▶ From the top of the zigzags the path skirts the base of the Sentinel and then passes the Sentinel Gully to skirt the Western Buttress. This section of the path is more or less level but involves a short scramble. Be careful in wet weather, as this section can be slippery. In autumn you should pass cascades of pink *Nerine* flowers, while in spring and summer orchids, irises and *Moraea* blooms are evident. The path passes the two Sentinel caves – one apparently used now as a toilet and as a garbage dump – and proceeds easily to the Chain Ladder (the litter along here is abominable, so pick up a few papers and it will soon all be gone). From the car park it is 3 km to the bottom of the Chain Ladder. Many people seem to fear the 30-metre ascent of the ladder; if so, they should not venture into the mountains and should rather remain at the car park and take photographs.

▶ From the top of the Chain Ladder there is a good view of Kloof Gully and its waterfall. From the cairn here one path follows the high ground – a low ridge going up to the right – to Crow's Nest Cave, set in a rock band, and thence on to the summit of Mont-aux-Sources, easily recognizable in clear weather as the highest point in the area. Another path heads off to the left along flatter ground, crosses the Tugela River after about 500 m and continues straight on to the old MCSA hut, which is now restored and used as a guard hut by KwaZulu conservation rangers. It is likely that in the future the KwaZulu authorities will open an official camp site in front of the guard hut, but with limited access – an unfortunate but necessary step considering the damage caused there by hikers (near the lip of the Tugela Falls I filled two black garbage bags with litter in less than 30 minutes).

Weather permitting, a worthwhile detour could be made up the slope of the Western Buttress to follow the entire length of the Amphitheatre lip as far as the Inner Tower of the Eastern Buttress. The views of the Escarpment and down into the Tugela River valley are without equal in the Drakensberg. Between the two towers of the Eastern Buttress is a sliver of rock of nearly the same height – this is Devil's Tooth.

It is possible to hike all the way along the Escarpment plateau from the top of the Chain Ladder to Sani Pass. This would take about two weeks of continual walking but has recently been run in three days by a trio of fellrunning enthusiasts – for this type of trip you should be familiar enough with the area so as not to need a guide. An exploration around the top of the Amphitheatre will take the best part of a day. Alternatively, you can spend a few days exploring the surrounding plateau and perhaps follow the main footpath from the hut over the rise into the Khubedu Valley.

By following the most easterly tributary of this river upstream, southwards parallel to the Escarpment, you can proceed to the Ifidi area for a day's outing or longer. Keep in mind, however, that the Ifidi Cave is nothing more than a meagre overhang and a descent of the Ifidi Pass involves some serious abseiling. From the hut it is about 7 km to the Ifidi Cave, from where you have views of Mount Oompie, the Ifidi Pinnacles and the Singati Valley.

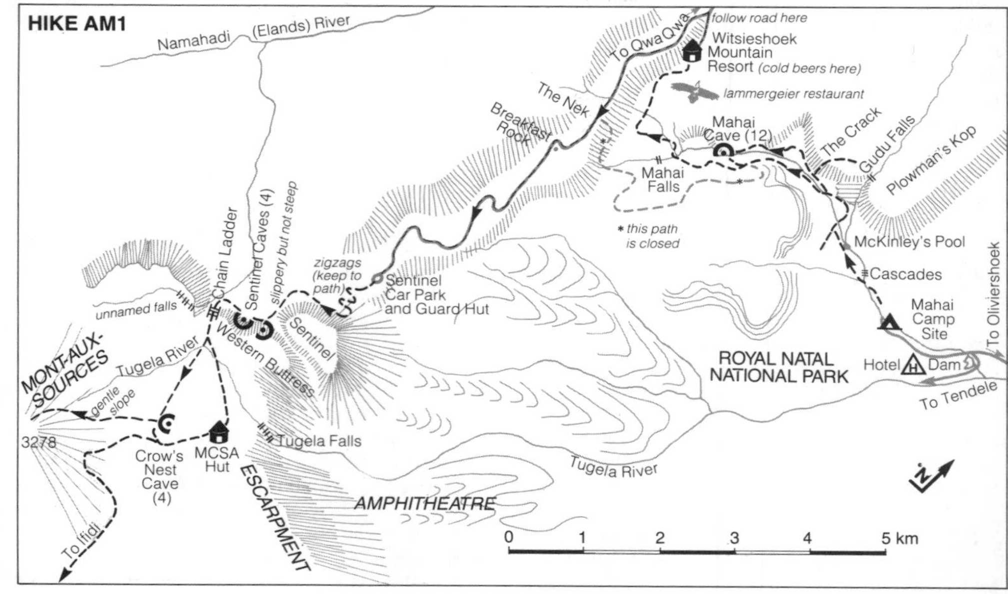

Escarpment traverse – Amphitheatre to Cathedral Hike AM2

Route: *Sentinel car park to Cathedral Peak*
Distance: *62 kilometres*
Duration: *4 to 5 days*
Grade: *Severe*
General: *This section of the Escarpment traverse is, in my opinion, the finest of all. It is not so long as to become an endurance test, and about the maximum distance for carrying a comfortable self-sufficient load. The route passes the most dramatic parts of the Drakensberg, including the Amphitheatre, Mbundini, Mnweni and the Rockeries, the Saddle and the Cathedral range itself – if you come back from this trip without stunning memories and photographs, you will have been unlucky or just not looking. Access to both ends of the traverse is good and this makes the logistics easy. The distances for each day's hike are flexible, but have been designed to terminate at a well-known cave: just remember*

HIKE AM2
Day 1
To Mont-aux-Sources
chain ladder
Sentinel Caves
Namahadi (Elands) River
climb through rock bands
MCSA Hut
Western Buttress
Sentinel
Do not take short cut
vlei
Tugela Falls
Remember your passport!
zigzags
AMPHITHEATRE
Car Park
Tugela River
gentle valley
small overhang 100 m above pass
uphill
Ifidi Cave
pass with two pinnacles
Devil's Tooth
Eastern Buttress
To Witsieshoek
0
1
2
3 km

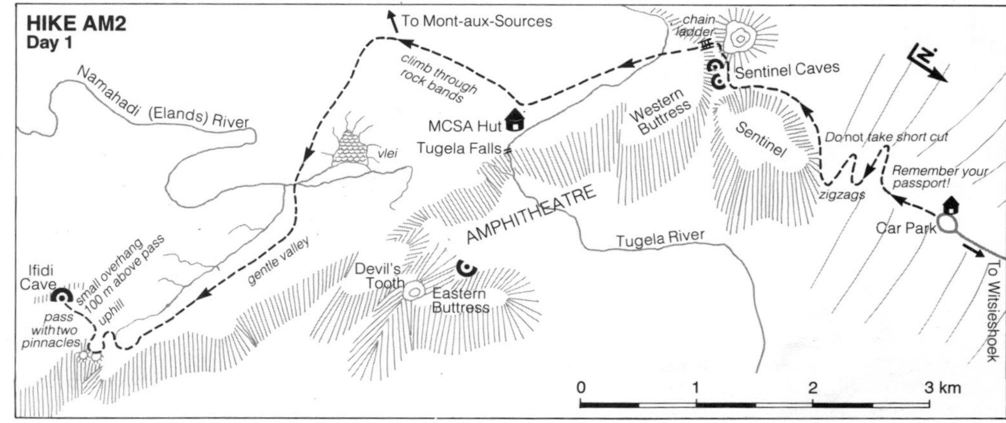

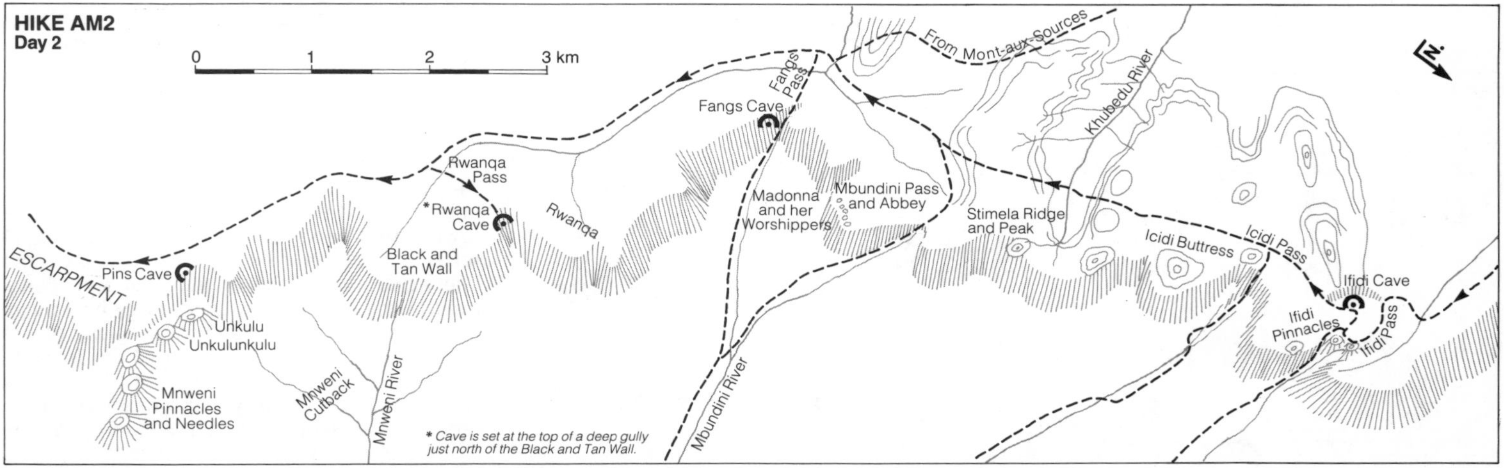

HIKE AM2
Day 2
0
1
2
3 km
From Mont-aux-Sources
Fangs Pass
Fangs Cave
Khubedu River
Rwanqa Pass
*Rwanqa Cave
Rwanqa
Madonna and her Worshippers
Mbundini Pass and Abbey
Stimela Ridge and Peak
Icidi Buttress
Icidi Pass
Ifidi Cave
Ifidi Pinnacles
Ifidi Pass
Black and Tan Wall
ESCARPMENT
Pins Cave
Unkulu
Unkulunkulu
Mnweni Pinnacles and Needles
Mnweni Cutback
Mnweni River
Mbundini River
* Cave is set at the top of a deep gully just north of the Black and Tan Wall.

that the caves may be occupied or difficult to find, so it is essential to carry a good, lightweight tent. Also, distances are approximate as each party will find its own route.

▶ **Day 1** (12 km): Begin at the Sentinel car park and follow the zigzag path up to the base of the Sentinel, passing the Witches and excellent views of the Eastern Buttress and Devil's Tooth (Hike AM1). Traverse around the Sentinel and the Western Buttress, past the caves and on to the Chain Ladder. Ascend the ladder and cross the Tugela River, following the path to the old MCSA hut and then southwards over the ridge and into the Khubedu Valley. Follow the most easterly tributary southwards, as close to the Escarpment as possible, to reach Ifidi Cave (a small overhang). Alternatively, if the weather is suitable, just hug the Escarpment until you reach Ifidi Cave.

▶ **Day 2** (11 km): You can take an inland route to bypass the Ifidi and Icidi buttresses, or follow the more uneven Escarpment route, but either way it is worth keeping close to Stimela Ridge to get good views of the Gothic-like Mbundini area. For the best views of this area, take a detour to the Mbundini Abbey, with views over to the Fangs. Follow the Escarpment to Fangs Pass where Fangs Cave can be found a little way down the pass on the right-hand side, just where the rock steepens. Should you want to cover more distance on this day, continue southwards for another 2,5 km to Rwanqa Cave. The cave is found in the pass of the same name, in a deep gully before the Black and Tan Wall. As with Fangs Cave, Rwanqa Cave is situated a little way down the pass and off to the right.

▶ **Day 3** (15 km): Continue past the Black and Tan Wall above the remote and magnificent Mnweni area, 'the place of fingers'. A fairly distinctive path can be found next to the deep gully on the southern side of the Black and Tan Wall. The path does a wide detour inland, around the Mnweni Cutback, Hanging Valleys and Ukikicane, and then turns back to the Escarpment to meet the head of the Mnweni Pass. Let your camera cool down here for a while, for the best is yet to come. The path crosses the Senqu River, the source of the Orange River, and leads out onto a headland

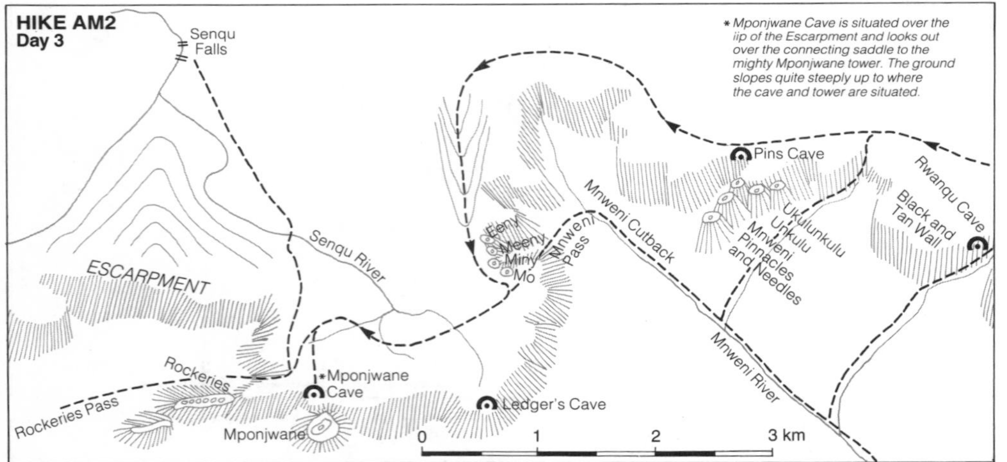

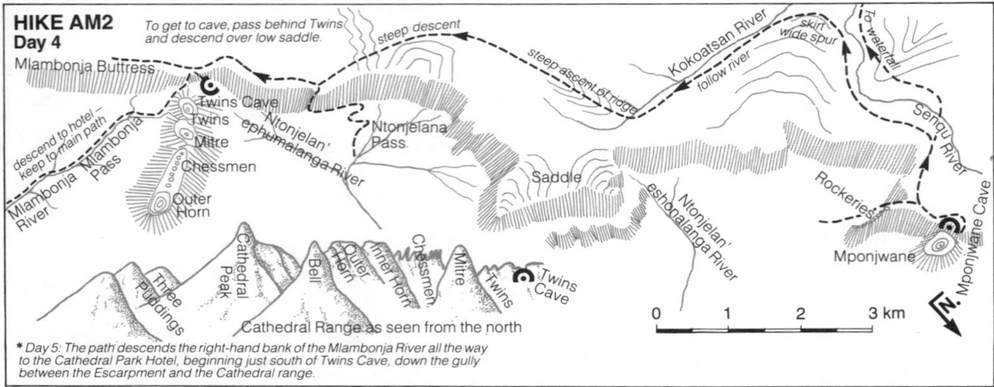

* Day 5: The path descends the right-hand bank of the Mlambonja River all the way to the Cathedral Park Hotel, beginning just south of Twins Cave, down the gully between the Escarpment and the Cathedral range.

The Tugela Gorge cuts its way through mountains of the Royal Natal National Park.

above the Mnweni Needles, the Rockeries and the great Mponjwane or Rockeries Tower. Mponjwane Cave is situated directly west of Mponjwane Peak, facing the dividing gap below the Escarpment lip.

(A short cartographical note: The Zulu word 'mponjwane' refers to the little horns on a heifer's head; anyone having seen the mighty Mponjwane will realize that this is an inappropriate name. In fact, reference to early maps of the Drakensberg shows that it was the original name for the peak next to the Horns, named Cathedral in the range of the same name, while Mponjwane was named Cathedral Peak – the present-day names are the result of historical mapping error. People looking at Cathedral Peak must wonder how it got its name, for it is in no way reminiscent of such a lofty structure.)

▶ **Day 4** (15 km): You would have to be a late sleeper or enveloped in cloud not to be greeted by a stunning sunrise from your night's eyrie. A kilometre inland from Mponjwane Cave is the head of Rockeries Pass, from where you can see the eight pinnacles of the Rockeries ridge. From there a path leads inland for 4 km to a waterfall on the Senqu River that, when frozen in winter, offers an unusual sight, complete with winter sports on the frozen river. Thereafter, follow a tributary to the south-east, back to the Escarpment near Nguza Pass (which, I am told, means 'backside'). Pass the Saddle, which juts out from the Escarpment and resembles a saddle from below, and then inland again around a wide, rounded valley and on to the head of Ntonjelana Pass.

▶ From this pass a definite path follows the lip of the Escarpment to a point behind the Cathedral Range from where you can see the Twins (which as you will realize should have been called the Triplets) and the Mitre. There is a junction behind a high point, where Mlambonja Pass goes down over a concealed lip; because it does not head out in a gully, the pass is easy to miss in foul weather. To find Twins Cave, go down the pass for a short way until you can work your way around to the left and find the cave up on the right, below the Twins. This is one of the most popular caves in the Drakensberg for a number of obvious reasons.

▶ **Day 5** (11 km): The last day's hike takes you all the way down the bone-jarring Mlambonja Pass, following the course of the river to the Cathedral Peak Hotel. Mlambonja means 'hungry dog' (as opposed to eNjasuthi – 'the well-fed dog') and refers to the scarcity of game that early Nguni hunters experienced here. Enter the pass to the south of Twins Cave and follow the main gully down past the Chessmen and the Horns. Do not take the Contour Path to the left after 3 km, but keep on going steeply down the right-hand bank of the river for 11 km. (For more information on this area refer to the chapter on Cathedral Peak).

Tugela Gorge *Hike AM3*

Route: *Tugela River car park to Tugela Gorge*
Distance: *7 kilometres*
Duration: *+ 2 hours*
Grade: *Moderate*
General: *This is undoubtedly the most popular medium-distance hike in the area, and with good reason. The route goes through alternative stretches of protea veld and forest, and the scenery beyond the gorge is rivalled only by the view from the top of the Tugela Falls.*

▶ The path begins at the car park below Tendele camp, on the banks of the Tugela River. Directions are unnecessary as the path is well defined and simply follows the river. From the car park the path veers away from the river for 1 km. At the first junction (marked by a concrete direction cairn), turn sharp left to cross the Devil's Hoek River and continue up to the left to enter the main Tugela Valley.

If you look down to the river, you will notice an interesting geomorphological formation called braiding, where the dissipation of high energy (from the river dropping over the falls) causes the deposition of material in this characteristically plaited manner. The river's energy is further reduced by its eroding of the spectacular gorge at the foot of the falls.

▶ The first section of the path contours well above the river, passing through protea savanna, where it can become oppressively hot in summer (a good cue to carry some water or juice). This vegetation is typical of the warmer and drier north-facing slopes, which receive year-round sunshine, as opposed to the cool, forested south-facing slopes and moist gorges. The protea trees here are either of the species *roupelliae* (usually identified by the silvery leaf

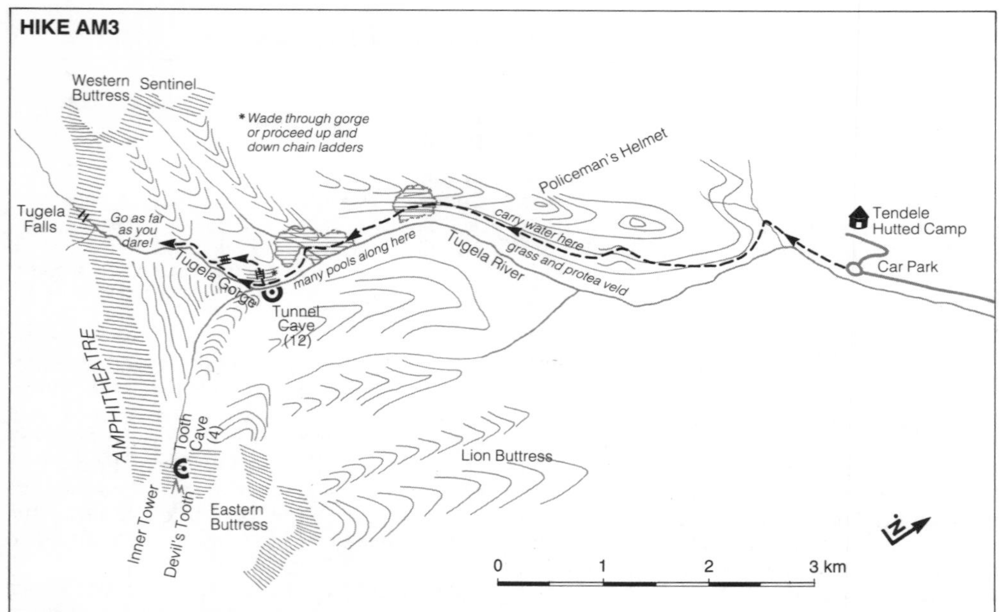

hairs) or *caffra* (sometimes erroneously called *multibracteata*). The latter species is found in the Eastern Cape, Natal and Transvaal and is similar in appearance to the waboom (*P.nitida*) found in the Fynbos region.

The grass cover consists mainly of *Themeda* sp. and *Festuca* sp. types and is referred to as Highveld *'suurveld'*, for during the cold winter months these grasses withdraw their nutrients into their roots and become unpalatable to grazers. In the days before farms and fences, animals would feed high up in the mountains during the summer and then descend to the sweet Thornveld pastures for the winter. This poses an unresolved problem for nature reserves in the Drakensberg, where efforts are made to recreate natural conditions.

▶ Below Policeman's Helmet you will enter the first small patch of forest along the hike. These forests are commonly called yellowwood forests after their once-dominant species, *Podocarpus latifolius* and *falcatus*. Yellowwoods, mountain hard pear, African holly, Cape beech and ash, cabbage trees, stinkwood, wild peach and wild olive (ironwood) are the large trees of these Afro-montane forests, while monkeys' rope climbers (*Secamone*) and old man's beard lichen (*Usnea*) cling to their trunks and branches.

A variety of ferns and herbs grow among the forest litter and along stream banks, where orchids and other flowers also thrive. On the forest fringes you may find the widespread ouhout and wild sage trees, as well as various *Rhus* sp. (characterized by their tri-foliate branch ends), the common spike thorn (*Maytenus heterophylla*) and various climbers.

▶ The main gorge is reached, usually after a crossing or two, at the confluence of the Tugela River and Eastern Buttress gully; there is no need to mention the location of pools along this stretch as they are so numerous. From this point you will gain excellent views of the Inner and Outer Towers, and the more dramatic Devil's Tooth and its Toothpick. The Tooth was thought by early climbers to be an unconquerable proposition, until 1950 when E. Scholes, D. Bell and P. Campbell completed the then most daring and technical climb in the 'Berg to stand on top of this looming spire. The Tooth is still considered to be one of the finest and most difficult rock climbs of the Drakensberg.

▶ Before the entrance to the gorge itself, a short chain ladder on the left allows you to circumvent the wading necessary to get through the gorge. Most people stop for lunch at this point and then head back, missing the finest part of the gorge and the startling close-up views of the Amphitheatre wall and Tugela Falls gained beyond the gorge. Only experienced climbers should, however, proceed up the two gullies of the Sentinel and Western Buttress.

▶ With the chain ladder behind you, take the path directly in front of you leading up the steep left-hand bank of the Devil's Tooth Gully to the Tunnel Cave. This cave affords another good vantage point of the area. In the narrower parts of the gorge hikers should be alert for sudden thunderstorms, which can bring down a frightening deluge of water and boulders within minutes.

Otto's Walk and Bushman Paintings *Hike AM4*

Route: *NPB visitors' centre to Sigubudu Valley*
Distance: *2 kilometres*
Duration: *45 minutes*
Grade: *Easy*
General: *A pleasant, self-guided forest walk along the Tugela River with classic views of the long sweep of the Amphitheatre and of the lofty peak of the Sentinel (3 165 km). A small donation to do this walk should be made at the visitors' centre nearby, where a trail booklet is obtainable.*

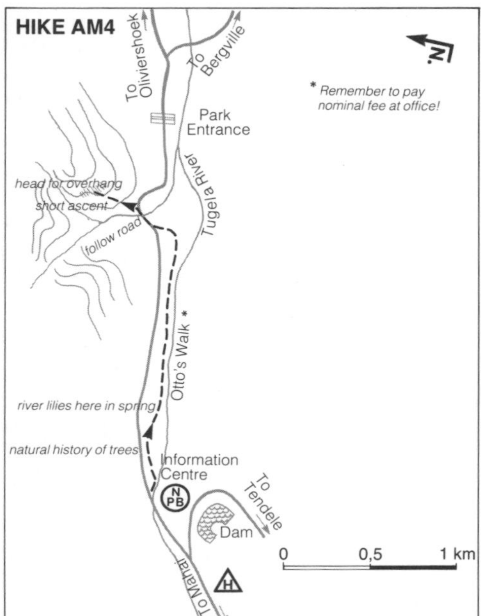

▶ Begin at the north-eastern corner of the visitors' centre car park where a sign marks the start of the trail. Some trees are signposted with short natural histories. A feature of the river bank in autumn is the profusion of a pink variety of the normally scarlet river lily, *Schizostylis coccinea*.

▶ At the point where Otto's Walk reaches the road continue towards the Park gate for a few hundred metres. The Sigubudu Valley will be on your left (it is signposted). From the outward curve of the road a path proceeds up the valley to some of the rare Bushman paintings in the Park. The artwork can be found on a short, west-facing slab of rock.

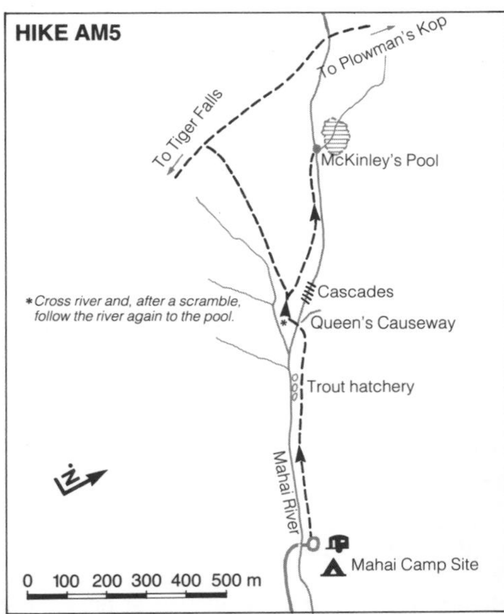

These rare Bushman paintings of antelope can be found in a remote 'Berg cave which is out of bounds to hikers.

McKinley's Pool *Hike AM5*

Route: *Mahai camp site to McKinley's Pool*
Distance: *1,5 kilometres*
Duration: *30 minutes*
Grade: *Easy*
General: *Probably the easiest, most popular short walk in the Park along a pretty section of the Mahai River, where the British Royal Family once walked.*

▶ From the Mahai camp site, walk up the road to the trout hatchery and cross the Queen's Causeway; from here the Cascades can be seen upriver. At the Cascades take the right-hand path along the river bank to McKinley's Pool. (Malcolm Pearse shows how one can use photography to capture the essence of flowing water in his pictures of the Cascades in *A Camera in Quathlamba*.) From the pool you can boulder-hop a good distance upstream, the banks abounding with blooms at all seasons. Keep a lookout for the multitudes of spiders, which spin many-shaped webs across the river, and watch how they achieve this extraordinary feat.

Gudu Bush and Falls

Hike AM6

Route: *Mahai camp site to Gudu Falls*
Distance: *2,3 kilometres*
Duration: *1 hour*
Grade: *Easy to Fair*
General: *A walk through diverse habitats and scenery with a cold but invigorating swim at the end.*

▶ From the camp site follow the Mahai River path past the trout hatchery and the Cascades, and turn right at the junction 1,5 km from the start of the hike. This takes you across the river and onto a ridge. At a second junction on the ridge turn right and head towards Gudu Bush. You will pass through diverse vegetation; the variety includes bracken and thick grass, tree ferns and cycads, various veld flowers in different seasons and the occasional yellowwood tree sheltered by rocks.

▶ A path (not shown on Slingsby's map)

The feet of the dassie are kept moist by glandular secretions, thereby enabling it to climb sheer rockfaces.

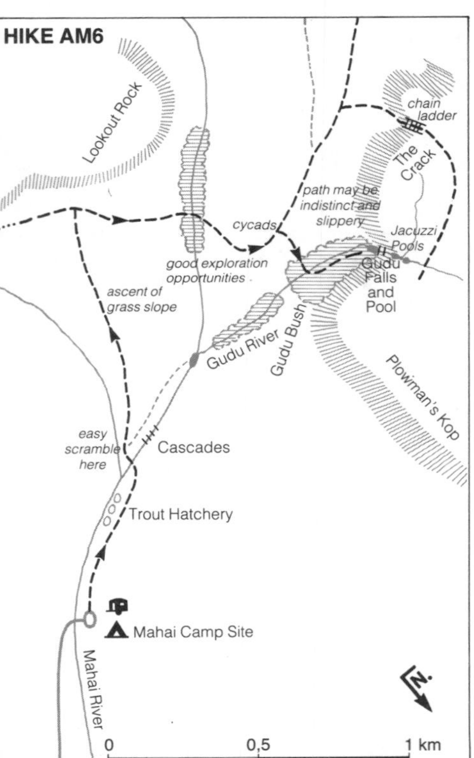

enters the forest and then turns left up the right-hand bank of the river. The path ends on a bank above a large pool, into which the Gudu Falls plunge. Due to a chemical quirk, falling water cools, so the temperature of the pool is like Cape Town's Atlantic coast in summer – shocking, but then that's a 'Berg pool for you at the best of times. Keep a lookout in the forest for interesting flowers in spring.

Plowman's Kop Hike AM7

Route: *Round trip from Mahai camp site via Plowman's Kop*
Distance: *7 kilometres*
Duration: *2 to 3 hours*
Grade: *Moderate*
General: *If you enjoy the wonders of nature a whole day can be allocated for this hike, even though it takes only a few hours. The hike takes in most or all of the previous hike (Gudu Falls, Hike AM6) and then proceeds to pools above the falls on top of Plowman's Kop. Adequate opportunity exists for variation, exploration and relaxation.*

▶ Follow the Gudu Bush path (Hike AM6) to the edge of the forest, turn left and continue up the right-hand bank of the Mahai River for another 700 m. If you are amenable, a short detour into

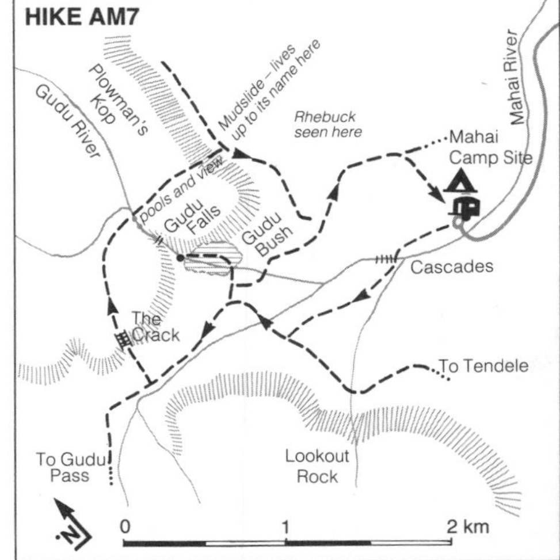

Gudu Bush and to the falls is certainly worth the effort and aesthetically completes the route.

▶ The path up Plowman's Kop via The Crack is clearly defined and interesting. A short chain ladder up The Crack helps you over the only tricky section of rock. Once at the top of the hill, head for the high ground to the right and then make for the top of the Gudu Falls. A series of natural jacuzzi pools, connected by short 'bum' slides, lead around a corner to the lip of the falls. The sides of the channel picturesquely frame the Sentinel, Amphitheatre and Mahai Valley below.

▶ Continue along Plowman's Kop and then down the very steep Mudslide, which lives up to its name in wet conditions. At the bottom of the slide turn right for about 800 m, then left for another 800 m. Mountain reedbuck and even bushbuck can sometimes be seen in this bush area. You should now meet a well-constructed path with erosion gabions leading down to the camp site or, 200 m further on, to a path leading off to the hotel on your right.

Fairy Glen and The Grotto

Hike AM8

Route: *Mahai camp site to The Grotto*
Distance: *5,5 kilometres*
Duration: *+ 2 hours*
Grade: *Moderate*
General: *This is a river and forest walk with good exploration opportunities. The names above should be enough to entice you.*

▶ From the Mahai camp site, the hotel and visitors' centre paths lead uphill, for 1,6 and 2 km respectively, to Fairy Glen on the Golide Stream,

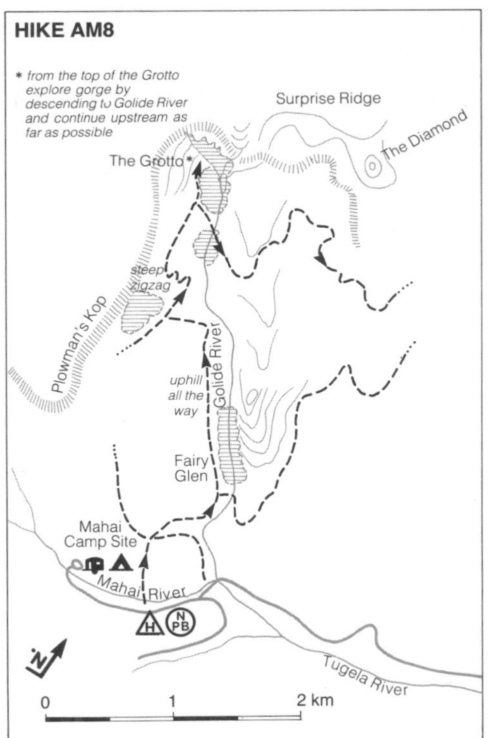

with a delightful picnic spot in the Glen wood. Continue up the left-hand bank of the stream, above the forest, for 2 km. The path veers away from the stream to a T-junction. Turn right here for 200 m and then zigzag up a steep slope on the eastern side of Plowman's Kop. The path then levels off and heads towards and along the river, again above a forest patch.

▶ Between the second and a nearby third forest patch a path leads off to the right, to cross the stream; but to get to The Grotto keep left to follow the path above the river to an impressive gorge cut into the sandstone. The Grotto actually consists of two connecting gorges, both worthy of exploration. While the main path to the left keeps above the river, you can go down to the river (turn right at the previous junction) and then make your own way up into the gorges.

Otto's Walk (Hike AM4) follows the Tugela River, taking in classic views of the Amphitheatre.

Surprise Ridge and Cannibal Cave *Hike AM9*

Route: *Mahai camp site to Cannibal Cave*
Distance: *7 kilometres*
Duration: *3 hours*
Grade: *Moderate*
General: *This hike can be lengthened into a round trip, returning via The Diamond, Castle Rocks and The Grotto rather than via the approach route. Cannibal Cave is on land owned by The Cavern hotel, but access is by right of way. This huge cave is of historical interest and affords good views of the surrounding countryside.*

▶ Proceed to Fairy Glen (Hike AM8), but cross the Golide Stream at the junction on the left-hand bank below the forest. Skirt around and up a spur and then contour into another valley, crossing a stream 1 km above a forest. A path leads into the forest above the Sunday Falls, which are worth the 1-km detour downstream. The path then climbs a steep bank, turns sharply to the right and climbs again around a spur and up to Surprise Ridge, crossing several streams on the way. The views from here are what give the ridge its name, so before proceeding to Cannibal Cave, amble along the ridge, taking in the splendid sights. At 1 889 m, Camel's Hump is the highest point of the ridge.

▶ At the four-way junction proceed over the ridge and around the northern side of The Diamond to the cave 1,2 km ahead. This is the largest Drakensberg cave I have seen and a very wide angle lens is needed to do it photographic justice. During the mid-nineteenth century the cave was used as a lair by one of the cannibal bands which roamed around the area of present-day Lesotho. Chief Sidinane and his marauders attacked lone stragglers or small groups travelling through the area after the Difaqane wars, then strung their victims up in the cave to keep them fresh for eating. If travellers and wanderers were in short supply, the cannibals bartered and ate their own wives and children. Popular images of missionaries in Africa stewing in large pots and of cannibals chanting gruesome songs around the fire were derived largely from tales brought back to Europe by evangelical visitors to these regions.

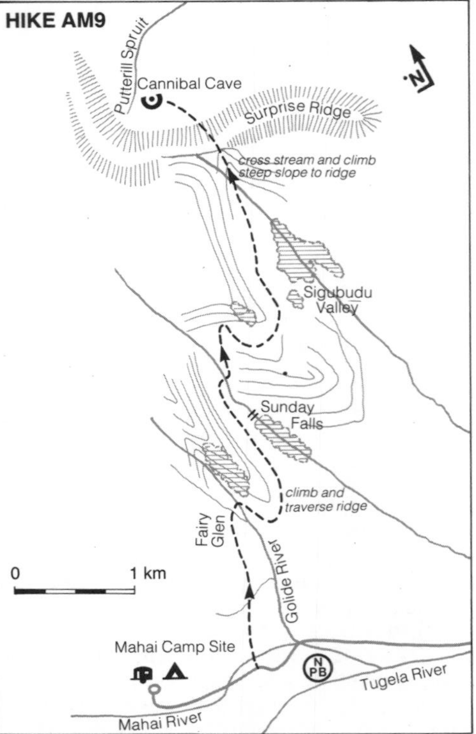

Faint remains of Bushman art can just be detected on a slab near the middle of the cave. The only successful, published photograph of the cave that I know of can be seen in Malcolm Pearse's black and white masterpiece, *A Camera in Quathlamba*.

Sigubudu Ridge and Valley *Hike AM10*

Route: *Round trip from Mahai camp site via Sigubudu Valley*
Distance: *12 kilometres*
Duration: *4 to 5 hours*
Grade: *Moderate*
General: *Start early if you want close-up views of game such as mountain reedbuck and grey rhebuck; remember that you, too, are a large predator so move stealthily. Not all of the paths on this hike are distinct and a general sense of orienteering is necessary.*

▶ Proceed towards the site of the Sigubudu Bushman paintings near the Park entrance (Hike AM4). Before you reach the cliffs flanking the Sigubudu Valley, a path leads to the right, up a hill and onto a plateau above the paintings. Once on the plateau, turn left and find your way up the high ground between the Sigubudu and Forgotten valleys, proceeding northwards.

▶ A path through the protea veld continues steeply up the left-hand side of a spur, just above a forest, and then to the top of the Sigubudu Valley on its right-hand bank. Bear left around the Sigubudu Valley to meet the Sunday Falls path. The path crosses an unnamed river (on which lies the Sunday Falls) and then heads

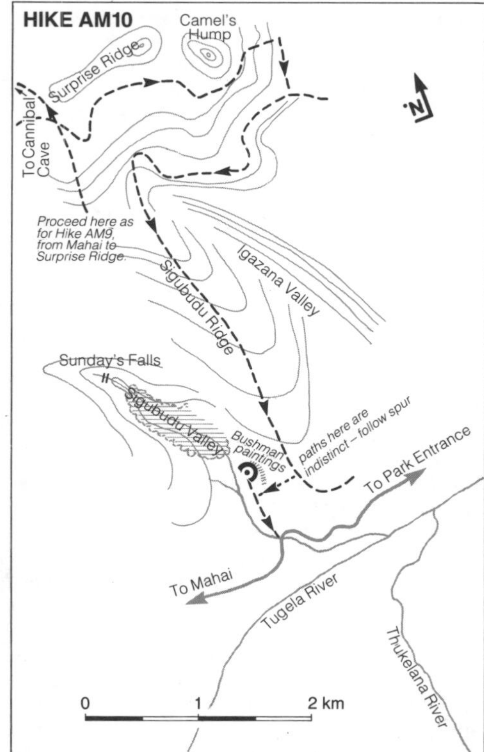

diagonally away from it for about 1,5 km. The path then goes through a 1-km 'S' bend before crossing a second river above the Sunday Falls (Hike AM9).

▶ Continue down this path, veering to the right around a spur, and across the Golide Stream to Fairy Glen. From the Glen the path is obvious: 1 km from the river turn right to the camp site or left to the hotel.

Devil's Hoek Valley *Hike AM11*

Route: *Tugela River car park to Devil's Hoek Valley*
Distance: *3 kilometres*
Duration: *1 hour*
Grade: *Fair*
General: *This hike takes one into the dramatic, often mist-shrouded Devil's Hoek gorge. Where the path peters out, adventure begins. . .*

▶ Walk or drive along the banks of the Tugela River to the car park below the Tendele hutted camp. From the car park follow the river and then a tributary (the Devil's Hoek River) for another kilometre to a junction which is marked by a concrete direction cairn. At the junction follow the Devil's Hoek/Vemvaan path to the right and then to the left up the valley.

▶ After 0,5 km,at the point where a path leads across the river to the left up the Vemvaan Valley, keep to the right-hand bank of the Devil's Hoek River. The path passes through 1st Bush and 1,5 km thereafter into 2nd Bush, from where the going gets progressively more difficult. At a major fork in the river, the path continues up the right-hand tributary; this is near to the end of the path, but not necessarily the end of the hike.

Vemvaan Valley *Hike AM12*

Route: *Tugela River car park to Vemvaan Valley*
Distance: *4,3 kilometres*
Duration: *1 hour 45 minutes*
Grade: *Fair*
General: *The valley walk is short and of fair grade, but more energetic hikers can climb one of the ridges on either side of the river: Policeman's Helmet on the left going upstream is especially rewarding, but it should be scaled from as far down-valley as possible to make it easier on the legs.*

▶ Begin as for Devil's Hoek Valley (Hike AM11), but nearly 1 km after turning right at the junction leading up to Devil's Hoek, the Vemvaan path heads off to the left over the Devil's Hoek River. The Vemvaan stream is reached after about 1,75 km, where the path crosses the stream and heads up the left-hand bank for another 2 km. Recently, a small community of one of the rarest species of protea was found here: *Protea nubigena* (the scientific name means 'borne of clouds') is a hardy, knee-high plant, which, unlike other proteas, has been observed to flower annually.

The Devil's Tooth and its Toothpick.

The Lion Buttress *Hike AM13*

Route: *Tendele Camp car park to Lion Buttress*
Distance: *3,5 kilometres*
Duration: *1 to 2 hours*
Grade: *Moderate*
General: *This is a short but steep hike which affords some excellent views of the Amphitheatre, as well as the Tugela and Thukelana (Little Tugela) valleys. This hike is not for people who prefer well-defined paths.*

▸ From the car park below Tendele camp, cross the Tugela River at a junction with a tributary and head up the zigzag path to the guard hut on the main spur above the tributary. From the guard hut follow the spur to the sandstone cliffs. At the base of the cliffs traverse to the left and you should come to a large cave. To the left of the cave is a steep grassy gully, which leads back uphill to the crest of the ridge. Once on the crest it is possible to continue up to the base of the Outer Tower, from where discretion and valour will determine your progress.

▸ For mountaineers who prefer more vertical outings, there is a number of fine rock routes in this area, but first consult other knowledgeable climbers or the MCSA Journal for route descriptions, and remember to sign to the mountain register before setting out.

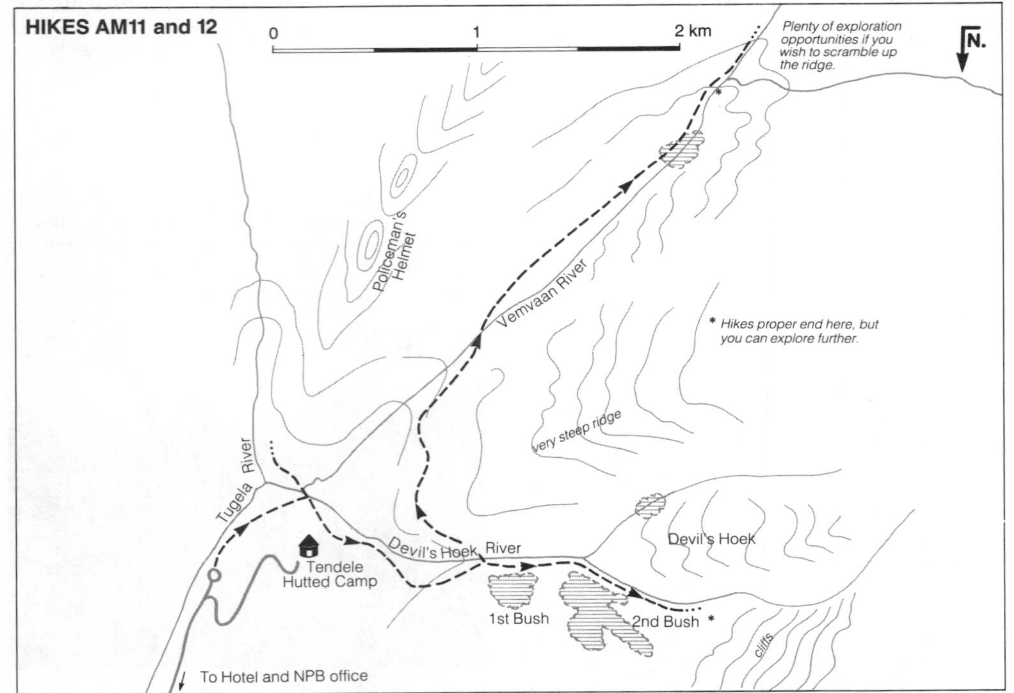

Rugged Glen to Mahai

Hike AM14

Route: *Rugged Glen camp site to Mahai camp site*
Distance: *14 kilometres*
Duration: *5 to 6 hours*
Grade: *Moderate to Severe*
General: *Rugged Glen is a nature reserve in its own right with horse-riding facilities and camp site. This hike is actually circular as the two camp sites are connected by tar road, allowing hikers to arrange transport for the return trip.*

▸ From Rugged Glen camp site, cross the road and head up the ridge, above and on the left of the Zagidhlana Stream, for 1 km. Near a small forest patch, turn left for one steep kilometre, then right for 300 m and right again for 500 m, bringing you to the Surprise Ridge path. Turn left here. For the next 3 km the path climbs and then contours around Camel's Hump, along the southern slope of the ridge.

▸ At a saddle situated at the head of the Sigubudu Valley, there is a four-way junction presenting two alternatives: you can turn left for a short cut across the Sigubudu Valley to the Sunday Falls, Fairy Glen and on to the Mahai camp site; or you can turn right for a 1-km detour to the spectacular Cannibal Cave (Hike AM9), after which I recommend that you continue straight along the ridge for another 3 km.

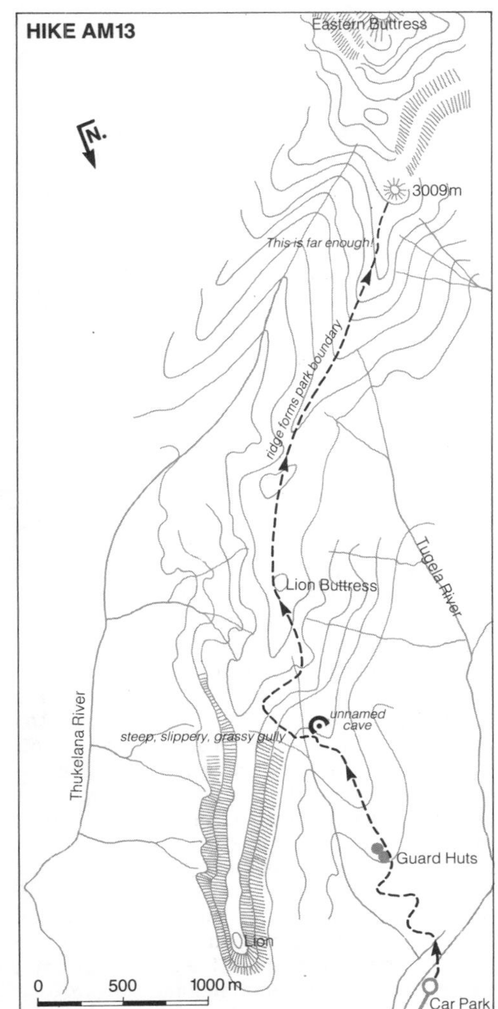

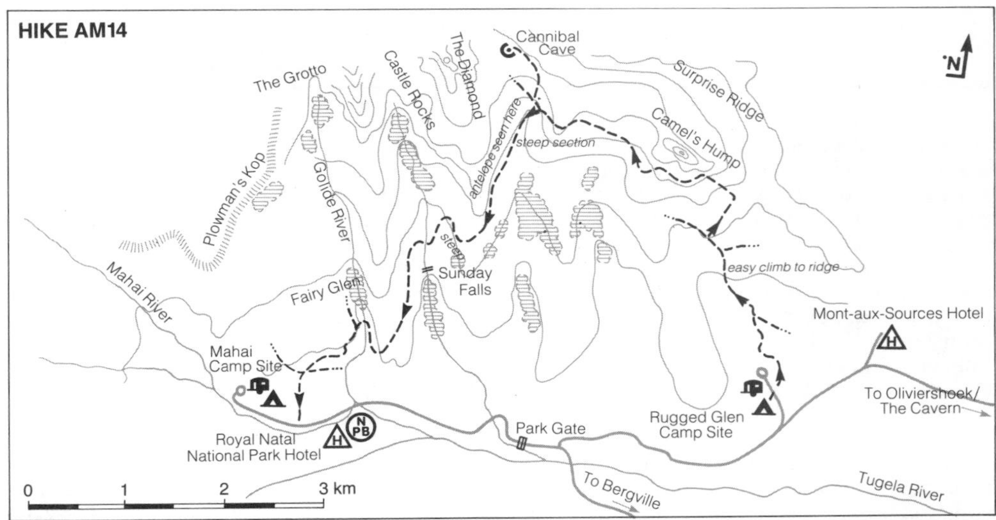

▶ This path winds and undulates around The Diamond and Castle Rocks and between two forest patches in The Grotto, which is well worth another detour (Hike AM8). After crossing the Golide River and proceeding up above the forest, you can turn right to skirt the top of The Grotto. Otherwise turn left for 1,5 km to contour and then zigzag down a steep slope. You will reach a side junction on another steep slope, below a forest. Turn left here to descend to Fairy Glen and right at the T-junction, or carry on straight to Plowman's Kop below the Mudslide and left at another T-junction.

These two routes meet about 600 m above the hotel, and an easy stroll to Mahai follows – if by now your legs haven't waged a campaign of passive resistance against your hiking enthusiasm.

The river lily (Schizostylis coccinea)

MNWENI

Between the popular hiking areas of the Amphitheatre and the Cathedral range lies the remotest and most rugged area of the Drakensberg, frequented only by hardy mountaineers and cattle rustlers. Here, there are no easy hikes, only extreme ones along long, steep paths that lead to the top of the Escarpment. I have called the area Mnweni, but it includes (from north) the Ifidi Pass and Ifidi Buttress, Peak and Pinnacles, Icidi Buttress and Pass, Mbundini Pass, Buttress and Abbey, the Fangs, Rwanqa, Mnweni Pinnacles, Cutback, Pass and Needles, Mponjwane and the Rockeries, the Saddle and finally the valleys of the Ntonjelana River and Ntonjelana Pass. There is no accommodation in the area, which is a KwaZulu 'native location' with only a few poor roads.

All of the hikes begin at the Isandhlwana Police Post; this 'last outpost' keeps the mountain register and serves as a bivouac for tired mountaineers and as scourge against cattle rustling and against the lush dagga fields of the Upper Tugela Location. Although the gravel road carries on past the police post for another six kilometres to Moliva's Store, it may be hazardous to use the road unless you have a four-wheel-drive vehicle. I tried and got my kombi stuck up to its axles in thick clay. The six strong men who helped me out extracted a large donation for their beer club and all my fresh food as payment.

To get to Isandhlwana, take the Rookdale fork at Bergville and then the second turn-off to the left to Woodstock Dam (*not* the first Woodstock/Driel Power Station turn-off). This should lead you, using maps and some imagination, along the Mnweni River to the Isandhlwana Police Post (a 1 : 50 000 map of the area would be a great help if you haven't been there before). From here it is a long haul through clusters of beehive huts and cattle kraals, along ridges of the Little Berg and then into the overwhelming montane cloisters. You will see why this area was first called Cathedral (see the cartographical, Hike AM2): you pass great buttresses which carry the load of millions of years of mountain building; follow basalt colonnades deep into the secluded abbeys of rock and see masonry gargoyles and spires putting the finishing architectural touches to Mnweni.

There are no contour paths here, but many cattle paths crisscross the area, especially in the lower reaches. As you are in a KwaZulu enclave, remember to be polite and take care not to disturb the homes and fields of the local people. The inhabitants of the Mnweni and Ntonjelana valleys are the survivors of once-prosperous people who were butchered by the impis of the Difaqane wars. The Amazizi and Amangwane tribes farm the lower valleys, but higher up among the peaks in the deeper gorges you can recapture a time of the Bushmen: a time before the black and white people arrived with their spears and guns, their cattle, ploughs and tractors; a time when things were wilder and lonelier.

The Mnweni River is fed by the Bhudu, Ifidi, Icidi, Mbundini and Ntonjelana rivers and myriad streams which drain the heavily pleated land. If you want to explore this wonderful area but have no desire to slog it to the top of the Escarpment, then I suggest a trip up the Ntonjelana River and its two main tributaries – the Ntonjelan 'eshonalanga (the 'setting sun', that is the west) and the Ntonjelan 'ephumalanga (the 'rising sun', that is the east). In *Barrier of Spears*, Reg Pearse writes of the days he spent alone exploring and mapping these gorges and ridges, a time he writes of with great conviction and nostalgia. Exactly 40 years later, I repeated his adventures and found myself drifting easily over the rugged countryside, deep in thought about things physical and metaphysical.

While climbing in the area in 1984, an acquaintance of mine was bitten on the finger by a baby berg adder. Within an hour, he began to experience nausea and double vision; a few hours later he could barely walk as the snake's neurotoxin took effect. His companion placed him in a tent on a very steep slopeand headed for the police post, where an Air Force helicopter was requisitioned. Both climbers are experienced and knew that the adder's poison would not be fatal, but that other factors such as exposure could be. The saga ended happily enough with an efficient mountain rescue being carried out, but that was probably due the two climbers' calmness in the face of danger (the incident is related in Reg Pearse's book, *The Dragon's Wrath*). The moral here is three-fold: the Mnweni area is remote and dangers are therefore multiplied; be prepared to cope with possible emergencies, and be wary of poisonous snakes, but not hysterical.

At the time of my visit to the area in 1987, two young hikers were stoned by Lesotho desperados while in their tent; the hikers took flight and one was brought down by a large missile, and then killed and robbed. This does not mean that you need be antagonistic towards the local herdsmen. As a cautionary measure make

camp in a way that allows you to be prepared for such an extreme event; also find out if there is a Police patrol or camp in the area.

This is not the first incident of violence in the area, but it is the first major one involving hikers. Over the last decade tales of aggression by local tribesmen have increased, with hikers being confronted and robbed. (Just consider the wealth you show off to these scantily attired people.) This unfortunate trend may be due to the increased number of hikers or the increased violence and crime generally in the country. If so, it is unfortunate but not without remedy – do not hike alone along the Escarpment, unless you are confident and experienced, but preferably in groups of three or more. Be courteous but do not resort to giving hand-outs – unless as some form of payment – as this is patronizing, undermines the local lifestyle, and may in itself promote crime and violence.

When it comes to rock climbing in the 'Berg, Mnweni is ideal. Mponjwane Tower is among the most exposed and exciting climbing challenges in the Drakensberg, while the Rockeries' eight pinnacles offer unusually firm rock with routes of varying grade. The Fangs, Mnweni Needles and Pinnacles and the Saddle all have exciting routes pioneered by the land's finest climbers.

Standing at the summit of the Mbundini Abbey.

Mnweni via Rockeries and Mnweni Passes *Hike MW1*

Route: *Round trip from Isandhlwana Police Post*
Distance: *48 kilometres*
Duration: *3 days*
Grade: *Extreme*
General: *This hike is extreme to say the least. The 'down' trip is longer than the 'up' one, but you can always return the same way or reverse the route. Although I give three days as the duration, you might reserve a longer period to explore this area more fully, perhaps climb a peak or two. Although I consider the Amphitheatre hike to be scenically the best in the 'Berg, when it comes to solitude and raw excitement, nothing beats Mnweni. If you are concerned about safety, keep in mind that the police mounted patrols prefer to use the Nguza ('backside') Pass to reach the Escarpment, rather than the Rockeries Pass: Nguza Pass branches off from the latter at a junction above Scaly Cave and proceeds up the Ntonjelan' ephumalanga tributary to behind the Saddle's North Peak.*

▶ **Day 1** (16,5 km): Park at the police post and follow the road, across the Isandhlwana River for 2 km. At a store, before a school, follow a footpath on the left up a spur on Scramble Kop. The path leads up and around the right-hand slope of the hill. After 3 km there is a junction and the path that you must take leads down to the right, into the Ntonjelana Valley. Cross the Ntonjelan' ephumalanga and, after 200 m, turn left at a junction to head up a spur between the 'eshonalanga and 'ephumalanga tributaries to Maquela's Kraal. From the kraal one gains majestic views of the Rockeries, Mponjwane and the Mnweni Needles, with grass beehive huts in the foreground.

▶ About 1 km above the kraal the path forks around a steep, narrow spur which leads up to the Saddle, South Peak; take the right-hand fork and continue down to the 'eshonalanga tributary and to a junction on the right-hand bank – this point affords a superb view of the Saddle. Turn left at the junction for 1 km and then zigzag up the gnarled spur which leads to the Saddle's North Peak. After the steep zigzags the path contours around to the left for 700 m and then curves to the right, through a nek. After this the path more or less contours back towards the 'eshonalanga tributary, 3 km from the nek. About 1 km from the river the path passes Scaly Cave, which opens out to give grand views of the Rockeries and Mnweni Needles. The cave lies 17 km from the starting point and makes a good first night's stopover.

▶ **Day 2** (12 km): Cross the river and then follow its right-hand fork, while the Rockeries Pass path follows the left-hand bank of the stream for 3 km. This pass is notoriously steep and rocky in places. Half-way up the pass you come abreast of the Rockeries, from pinnacle A to H. From the top of the pass Mponjwane Cave is 1 km due east (that is, to the right), around the high point and just below the Escarpment edge; it looks out over the gap to Mponjwane. This cave has been a home from home for generations of the country's finest mountaineers and has seen its share of human suffering and triumphs.

Mponjwane was first climbed by the enigmatic George Thomson – of whom I shall say more in the next chapter – and Ken Snelson in 1946. Two years later Thomson and Charles Gloster went on to complete one of the hardest climbs in the Drakensberg, the Outer Mnweni Pinnacle. Although the Inner Pinnacle is more slender and appears to be the more severe challenge, it is in fact the easier of the two but was only conquered in 1949 by Jannie Graaff and party. The two Needles which pierce the sky beyond Mponjwane look more like pyramids than needles. The Outer Needle was first cimbed in 1921 by Ken Cameron and D. Bassett-Smith. A few days after this, they attempted the Inner Needle, only to be turned back some 60 m from the top. Twenty-two years later, this Needle fell to A. Hooper, P. Fenger and E. Burton.

It is only 12 km, albeit steep, from the Scaly Cave to Shepherd's Cave, the two recommended stopovers. This means that with an allotted three-day hike and an early start, most of the second day can be spent taking in the Escarpment's spectacular sights.

▶ **Day 3** (21,5 km): From the top of Rockeries Pass a path leads across the anvil-shaped headland to the Mnweni Pass, but 400 m before this point the path crosses the Senqu River near its source – this is where the mighty Orange River begins. (Turn left at the top of the Rockeries Pass for 4 km to a waterfall on the river.) The Mnweni Pass quickly descends down a very steep section between high cliffs; to the left the path passes Eeny, Meeny, Miny and Mo, and further down the Twelve Apostles can be seen against the skyline, high up and acutely to the left. After 2,2 km the path comes to Chichi Bush Camp on the bank of the Mnweni River. ('Chichi' is a corrupted form of the Zulu name 'itshitshi', the widespread ouhout or *Leucosidea sericea*.)

▶ Cross the river here and proceed for 3 km down the left-hand bank of the river of Shepherd's Cave, which is above the path on the left, just before a junction with the Mbundini Pass path. If you plan to do the hike in three days, this cave is a good spot for the second night's

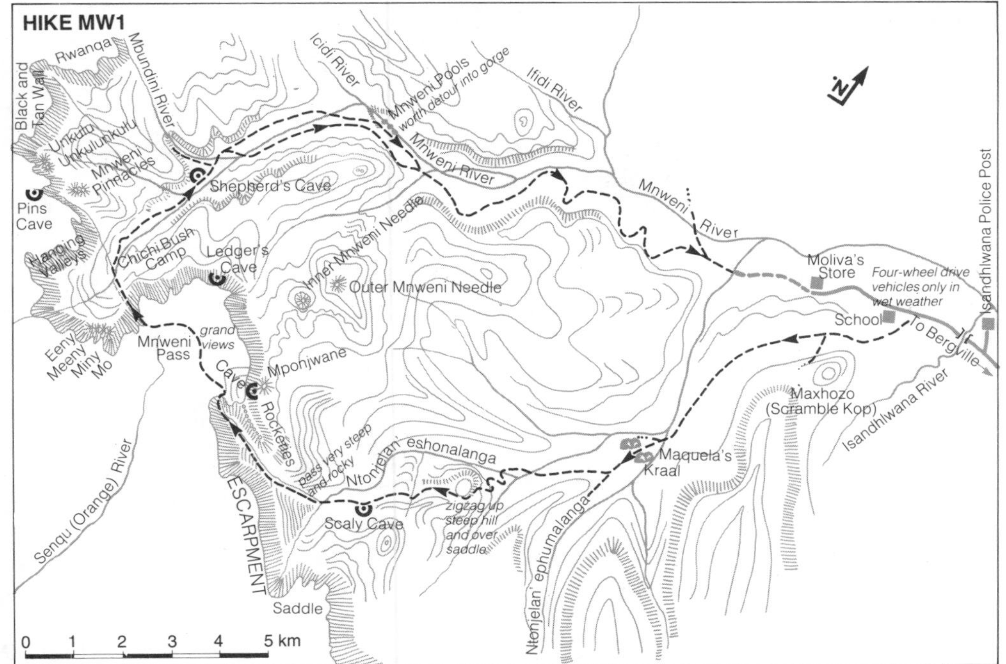

stopover (Chichi Bush Camp being too far upstream for an evenly divided trip). For those who know the spot, or are lucky enough to find it, Five Star Cave nearby offers the luxury accommodation suggested by the name. Cross the Mbundini River and shortly thereafter the Mnweni River, to follow the right-hand bank all the way to Moliva's Store and on to the police post.

▶ If, however, you do choose the longer left-hand route, you will pass what Malcolm Pearse calls one of the 'seven wonders' of the Drakensberg. A little less than 2 km after crossing the Mbundini River below Shepherd's Cave, the path meets the Mnweni River which you can cross or you can continue along the left-hand bank. Here the river plunges through a shallow gorge, cascading down sandstone terraces that form a series of pools, some as big as public swimming pools. Normally they are clear, crisp and ideal for swimming. After summer storms, however, the river becomes an angry torrent bursting through the gorge – swimming at these times is not recommended. The last 20 km, from Shepherd's Cave, are easy going, with only a few fairly steep but short downhill sections.

If this hike has inspired you to explore deeper into the wonders of Mnweni, it is possible to reach the Escarpment via Mbundini Pass which branches off from Mnweni Pass half-way up from the Mnweni River fork; or you can choose Fangs Pass which then branches off to the left half-way up Mbundini Pass. These routes proceed through mountainscapes as dramatic as Mnweni or Rockeries passes, but even less frequented. From the top of the Mbundini and Fangs passes a path leads up a river course parallel to the watershed and then along the watershed itself for about 15 km to Mnweni Pass. Along the way the path passes a number of caves set high up in the Escarpment wall, facing out over the lowlands. Fangs, Rwanqa and Pins caves are all situated in major gullies, and all on the southern slopes, facing true east: Fangs Cave is near the top of Fangs Pass, Rwanqa Cave at the top of the Rwanqa Pass and Pins Cave in a gully which leads directly down to Chichi Bush Camp; the cave looks directly out onto the Mnweni Pinnacles.

SNAKES

Snakes are among the most beautiful of all creatures. They only attack as a last resort, probably being far more afraid of humans than vice versa. The chance of seeing a snake is slight, the chance of being bitten by a poisonous one is remote. Caution, knowledge, ankle-high boots and a walking stick are the best preventative measures against snakebite. Three golden rules in the event of a bite are: don't panic, don't use a tourniquet and do get the victim to a doctor without delay, yet without rushing. Try to positively identify the snake, but never kill one unnecessarily as snakes play an important ecological role.

Lower 'Contour Path' to Cathedral *Hike MW2*

Route: *Isandhlwana Police Post to the Cathedral range*
Distance: *28 kilometres*
Duration: *2 days or 10 hours*
Grade: *Moderate to Severe*
General: *Although this hike does more or less traverse the Little Berg from Mnweni to Cathedral, it is not really part of the Contour Path system. I have not heard of anyone making a traverse of the Little Berg by linking up all the sections of Contour Path, but this could be the starting point for such an epic hike. While it does not match an Escarpment traverse for grand exposure, I believe that longer hikes in the shadow of the high crags are one of the many neglected challenges of the Little Berg.*

▶ Starting from Isandhlwana Police Post where you will have signed the mountain register, cross the Isandhlwana River and continue to the store 1,5 km further on. Take the path through the kraals, up a spur on Scramble Kop (Hike MW1). Pass the summit of the kop on your left and then at a junction continue along the path, which branches off to the left, going up and then even more steeply up a knife-edge spur to a point beyond and higher than Scramble Kop. Once on the Little Berg plateau the path ambles along for about 5 km before reconnecting with the Isandhlwana River. Cross the river at the head of an impressive gorge with forest directly below you. The level area above the river is an appropriate place to make camp as it is close to half-way along the hike.

Looking upstream you can see where the river rises at the base of the Cathedral Range. Given clear weather you should also be able to see the Saddle, Rockeries and Mponjwane and Mnweni Needles to the north, a view that few campsites can rival.

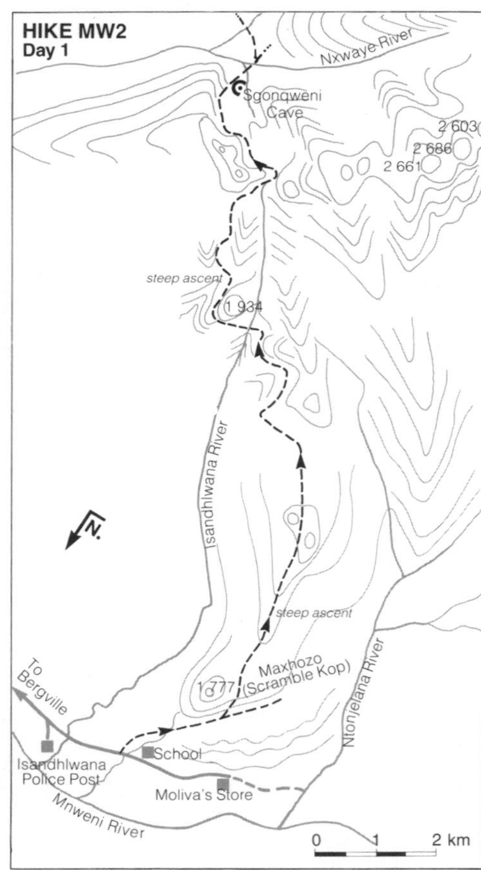

▶ For the next 7 km the path wends its way over the Little Berg, around three hills and then down to Sgonqweni Cave, which overlooks the Nxwaye River. Cross the river and after another 0,5 km turn left at a junction and climb the Ganapu (Ganabu) Ridge for 5 km. The path emerges on top of the Baboon Rock ridge, from where the Cathedral Peak Hotel can be seen in the wide Mlambonja Valley below. From the top of Baboon Rock it is a 3,5 km downhill slog to the hotel gate (from the bottom of the rock, the path next to the plantation has a number of alternative branches, all of which lead to home).

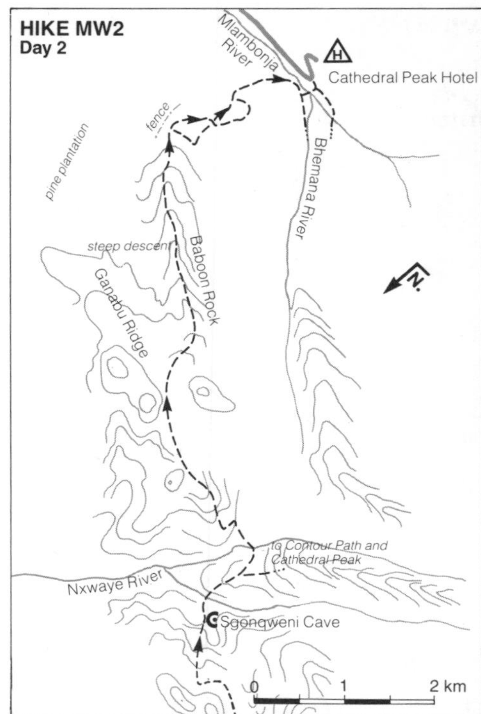

Ntonjelana Pass *Hike MW3*

Route: *Isandhlwana Police Post to Ntonjelana Pass*
Distance: *20,5 kilometres*
Duration: *8 to 9 hours*
Grade: *Extreme*
General: *Although this route is traditionally a trade route between Lesotho and Natal, it is more or less ignored by mountaineers. This is because they only drive to out-of-the-way Isandhlwana in order to reach Mnweni: if getting to the top of the Escarpment were the objective, Cathedral would be the more practical starting point. For people who have discovered the delights of the Little Berg, or who are in search of new hiking routes, Ntonjelana Pass offers an alternative way up the Escarpment, with some special attractions.*

▶ Report in at the Isandhlwana Police Post and then follow the gravel road for 2 km, over the river, to the general store. Take the path up through the kraals to the left and proceed up Scramble Kop, as if heading for the Rockeries Pass (Hike MW1). Pass the peak on your left and then keep along the right-hand slope of the mountain and up to Maquela's Kraal, where grass beehive huts and rondavels stand beneath the looming basalt fingers of Mnweni (the name means 'place of fingers').

▶ The path keeps to the crest of the gentle spur which you have been climbing and comes to a fork after 1 km, where the spur swoops up towards the Saddle. The right-hand path goes up to the Rockeries Pass, but take the left-hand one to follow the 'Ntonjelana of the Dawn'. The path heads easily for 9 km down to the river and then heads up the right-hand bank all the way to its source among the green folds of the Escarpment face. Six kilometres from the fork below the Saddle you will pass a tributary on the right

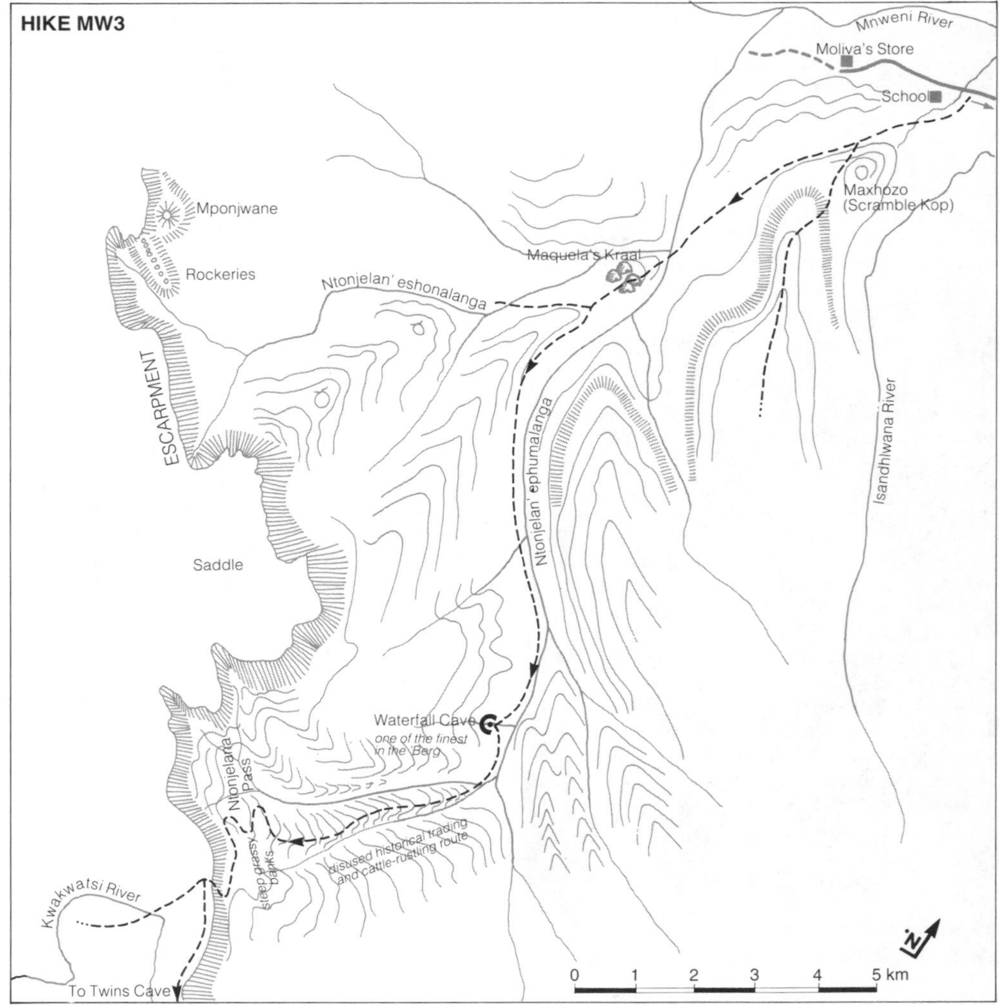

and, high up in this forested gorge, you will find the roomy, appropriately named Waterfall Cave, where a waterfall plunges over its lip.

The trip here is worthwhile if only to sleep in the cave and swim in the stream. Lie in the cave and listen to the fall beating its liquid refrain through the greenery of yellowwoods and wild pear trees, with the Saddle and Cathedral Peak enclosing all around you. It would not be unreasonable if you decided that this, after all, was your destination.

▶ From the cave the path keeps to the right-hand bank of the river, passing a tributary to the left. About 800 m further on there is a fork in the river and the path crosses the right-hand fork to follow the crest of a sharp spur between the two tributaries (the right-hand tributary is the main course of the Ntonjelana River, rising in a deep gully tucked in behind the Saddle's South Peak). At an altitude of 2 400 m, the pass begins at a series of zigzags and then traverses to the left just below the summit ridge for about 1,3 km, before finally levelling out at the watershed.

▶ From here it is only 2 km southwards to the top of the Mlambonja Pass, which leads down, behind the Twins, to Cathedral Peak Hotel; another path leads northwards to the South Peak of the Saddle, but fades out and thereafter it is a 10-km slog to the top of Rockeries Pass. Yet another path heads west into the Lesotho interior.

From the top of the Escarpment, it seems as if one can see forever. The Ntonjelana Valley wends its way below.

CAVES, CAIRNS AND COMPASSES

The rock paintings in the caves of the Drakensberg are all that we have left to remind us of the rich culture of the Bushmen who once lived here. They are internationally acknowledged to be the most skilled and numerous examples of this type of painting in the world; many artists consider them to be one of the most sophisticated art forms ever practised. These paintings are part of our national heritage and hikers are not permitted to camp in any cave that contains such paintings, or to make fires there.

Cairns are traditional route markers in the mountains; they are there essentially to save lives, so don't knock them over. They may seem unnecessary when the path is clear and the grass low, but they are very useful in swirling mists or after a metre of snow has fallen. Cairns are also used traditionally to mark the tops of climbing routes, but excessive cairn building can become an eyesore.

Some hikers swear by, while others scorn the use of a compass. Many people still blunder their way through the bush without a clue as to how a compass actually works. A compass will point to magnetic north which, due to the asymetrical shape and other physical vagaries of the earth, is not the same as true north. Most maps will give the deviation from true to magnetic north; in the Drakensberg, this is approximately 20 degrees west (that is, magnetic north is 20 degrees west of true north). For the purists, this angle changes over time and from place to place, with an annual average rate here of one minute to the west. Remember that any metal you might be carrying affects the compass reading. A compass and 1 : 50 000 map are very useful tools for areas where there are no paths and learning how to use them is fun.

Ifidi Pass *Hike MW4*

Route: *Isandhlwana Police Post to Ifidi Pass*
Distance: *26,5 kilometres*
Duration: *10 hours*
Grade: *Extreme*
General: *If the objective is to reach the summit of Ifidi, then it is easier to hike over from the Chain Ladder. If, however, you wish to explore a new pass then Ifidi should be tempting, as it is seldom used and requires some serious, potentially dangerous, scrambling: a rope may be necessary to climb the final section. This hike should be led only by competent mountaineers with able parties.*

▶ From Isandhlwana follow the road all the way to Moliva's Store and then along the wide track for another 1,5 km to a river crossing. Cross the Ntonjelana River 1 km up from its confluence with the Mnweni River, and then after another 1,5 km cross over to the right-hand bank of the Mnweni River. The path angles away from the river and goes up between numerous kraals, before recrossing the river after 5 km, at the confluence of the Ifidi and Bhudu rivers. The path follows the right-hand bank of the Ifidi River for about 1 km, and then climbs a spur away from the river. It passes numerous kraals for 3 km, before turning to the left to contour along the left-hand side of a major ridge (which leads up to Mount Oompie), back to the Ifidi River.

▶ You are now finally above the reaches of human habitation and from the river crossing the water is fresh and potable. Follow the left-hand bank of the river as the valley becomes narrower and steeper. For the next 7 km the path climbs up the left-hand bank of the Ifidi River and past small forest patches, never venturing far from the river itself. The pass starts where the path crosses a tributary after having climbed steeply up a grassy slope. The tributary gorge leading up between the Ifidi and Icidi buttresses is narrow, steep and wooded. The Ifidi Valley also narrows considerably here to become enclosed on three sides by high folds of green mountainside.

▶ Take a long rest at the river confluence, because after this the going is difficult and often slippery. One and a half kilometres from here the path skirts a large forest patch, crosses the river and crosses back again 200 m further on, following the tree line up a very steep slope, after which it eases off only momentarily. The path moves slowly away from the river to proceed even more steeply up towards the two Ifidi Pinnacles. On the left is the gracious Mount Oompie: the peak, which is known to local tribesmen as Thaba Ndanyazana (the 'little mountain where lightning strikes'), was named in honour of 'Oompie' Liddle who climbed it in 1930. Liddle lived in Kimberley but in his lifetime he seldom missed the MCSA 'Berg climbing meets every July.

▶ The path runs up the inside of a spur, which comes down from the left of the two pinnacles and then cuts back to the right through a shallow gully, around a bulge and into the cleft on the extreme right, following the river's course. It is now necessary to find your own way up the left-hand side of the gully, as the path is indistinct here. Inexperienced mountaineers should consider using a rope under such slippery conditions.

▶ Once at the top of the pass, having recovered from the arduous climb and then having admired the pinnacles and spectacular Little Berg ridges and valleys below, make your

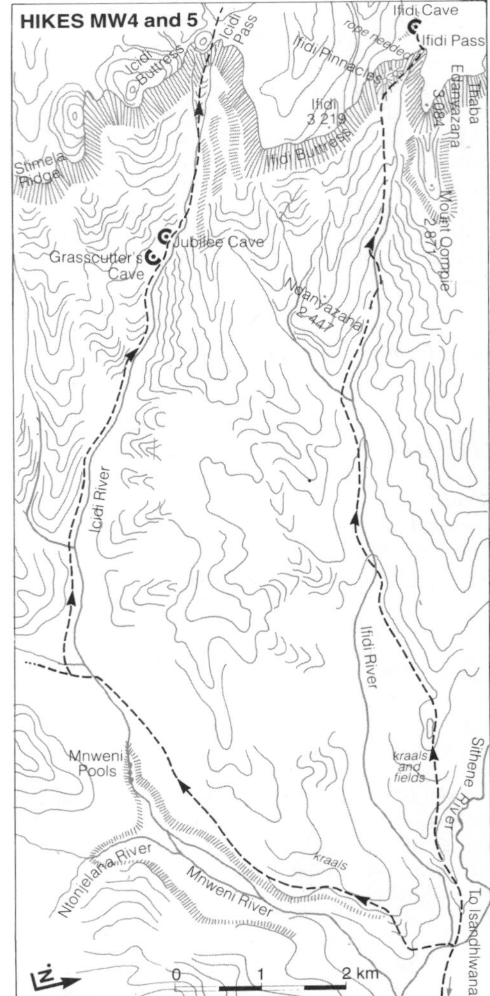

way to the Ifidi Cave up the slope on the left, to a minor rock band. If you have trouble finding the cave, do not despair – there isn't one. It is in fact just a meagre overhang which in no way deserves the title of 'cave'. From here it is about 8 km up the course of a stream to a vlei, and then over a ridge into the Tugela basin, past the old MCSA hut and on to the Chain Ladder. To the south it is a 3-km slog over a ridge to Icidi Pass, another 6 km to Mbundini Pass and then a further 2,5 km down and along to the Mnweni Pass.

Icidi Pass *Hike MW5*

Route: *Isandhlwana Police Post to Icidi Pass*
Distance: *27 kilometres*
Duration: *2 days or 11 to 12 hours*
Grade: *Extreme*
General: *Another seldom-used path to the top of the 'Berg, but an easier ascent than the Ifidi Pass. The valley of the Icidi River, a tributary of the Mnweni, is a superb contrast to the lower, tree-littered valley floor and lush slopes leading into the dramatic mountainous cloister beyond Icidi Buttress. The top of this pass is situated close to Ifidi and, with the right preparation, these two passes would make an excellent three-day circular hike – remote, rugged and sustained.*

▸ From Isandhlwana proceed down the road to Moliva's Store and continue for another 1,5 km along the wide track to a junction next to the Mnweni River. Take the left-hand fork, which rises gently up above the river, to a junction 9 km further on, winding up and down, in and out of kraals along the way. At the junction take the right-hand fork and make for the Mnweni Baths 2,5 km away: these baths are among the finest attractions of the Drakensberg, so plan to spend some time here (Hike MW1).

▸ Cross the Mnweni River and head back downriver for 1 km to the Icidi River, where you turn left to proceed up the left-hand bank. You will find yourself in one of the loveliest valleys in the Drakensberg: guarded by high sandstone cliffs, this wide valley floor narrows and steepens as it climbs up towards the towering volcanic donjons, with the river racing and tumbling down. The path goes up the left-hand bank of the river most of the way to the summit plateau, which is 8 km from where it joins the Icidi River. After 4,5 km the route takes you past the large Jubilee Cave, and, 500 m back above the path, you will find Grasscutter's Cave.

▸ Two kilometres above Jubilee Cave the path crosses the river, and then crosses back again after another 1,2 km. Tucked away in this cut-back is the thin spire of the Ifidi Pencil. The pass reaches the summit at a high 3 100 m, to the left of which is a wide, shallow bowl-like swampy area where *Kniphofia* (red-hot poker) and *Moraea* blooms add splashes of colour to the drab summit plateau in spring and late into summer.

Mbundini and Fangs Passes *Hike MW6*

Route: *Isandhlwana Police Post to Mbundini and Fangs Passes*
Distance: *27 kilometres*
Duration: *2 days or 11 to 12 hours*
Grade: *Extreme*
General: *These two passes are like the nave aisles in a Gothic cathedral, terminated by Mbundini Abbey, while in front of the high altar stands Madonna and her Worshippers. The religious metaphor of this area would have been well served had the original Cathedral not been substituted by Mponjwane as the name for the soaring Rockeries Tower to the south. More than any other area of the Drakensberg this one is suggestive of the architecture of Europe's mediaeval cathedrals.*

▶ Begin at Isandhlwana police post and then proceed past Moliva's Store, as for Hike MW5, to the Mnweni Baths (not on Slingsby's map). Cross the stream here but then turn left to continue up the right-hand bank of the Mnweni River for 1,5 km and cross the Mbundini (Nqingili) River just above its confluence with the Mnweni. Half a kilometre further on, traverse the river-levelled terrace to a junction and take the right-hand fork, which heads up the Mbundini River's left-hand bank.

Shepherd's Cave is set at the top of the grassy ramp, at the base of the sandstone cliffs that point into the 'V' of the junction of the path. The two river valleys here are thickly matted with ouhout and wild sage bushes, while proteas are scattered on the grassy slopes below the sandstone cliffs. On the south-facing slope of the Mbundini Valley (the right-hand slope facing upstream), taller Afro-montane trees, such as yellowwood and cabbage trees, grow in the wetter gullies. From this low perspective you should just be able to identify the Fangs and some of the spires around Mbundini Abbey.

▶ The path up Mbundini Valley proceeds from the river junction upstream and then climbs steeply up through the sandstone band above the flood plain. After 1 km the valley narrows considerably and steepens. At 3 km from the junction there is a fork in the path, where Fangs Pass heads off up the gully of a tributary to the left and reaches the summit; the Mbundini Pass route is only 3 km from this junction to the summit. From the top of the Mbundini Pass you can look out over the Mnweni Cutback, to Mponjwane peeping over the far side of the Escarpment. The only blots on the landscape are the cattle paths which have become heavily eroded, multi-laned scars.

What I would do from the outset is to decide which pass to take on the upward trip, and then to take the other one down again. One kilometre inland of Fangs Pass a path leads for 14 km to Mnweni Pass. This would make an ideal one-day outing, taking in some of the finest scenery the Drakensberg has to offer. The Icidi Pass is a shorter 8-km hike from the top of Mbundini Pass, but there is no path between the Mnweni and Mbundini passes. Ideally, four days is needed to complete a round trip of the two passes, stopping over first at Shepherd's Cave, then on to the summit – depending on which pass is chosen for the ascent – and back to Shepherd's Cave again on the third night. Between the cave and the police post it is a moderately graded 20-km slog, while the distance from the cave around the passes is 27 km (give or take a few), but divided over two days.

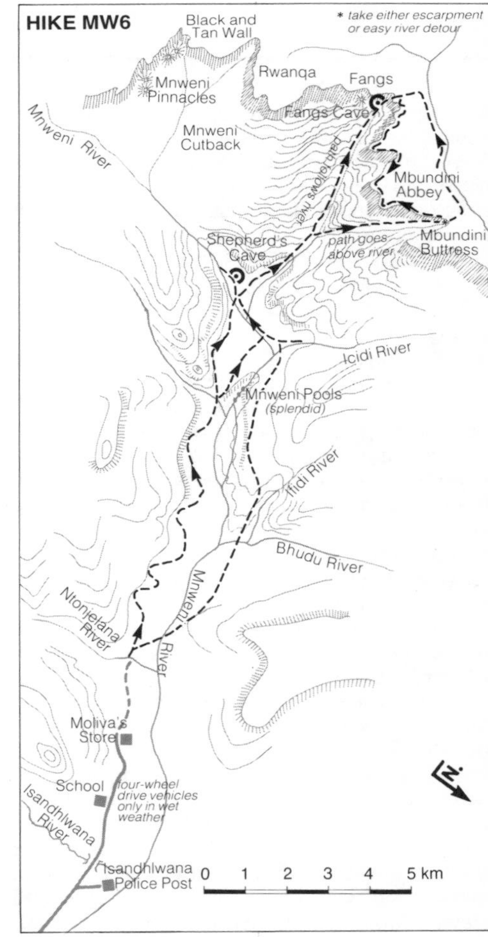

On reach the summit of the Ifidi Pass (3 100 metres), one can gaze upon the larger of the two Ifidi Pinnacles at close quarters.

CATHEDRAL RANGE

Since the Van der Riet family built the Cathedral Peak Hotel in 1939, this resort has become a favourite among mountaineers and is one of the country's best-known hotels. The area was developed much later than the other main resort areas of Champagne Castle, Cathkin Peak and the Amphitheatre, as it is more remote – direct access was along a wagon track even when the hotel was new. In 1937 Philip van der Riet bought the farm on which the hotel stands and a year later his son, Albert, chose the site for the hotel so close to the mountains that by sitting on the patio under the shadow of the prominent Cathedral Peak, one experienced the sense of venturing among the high peaks. In 1940 a young bricklayer from New Zealand, one George Thomson, found work at the hotel doing alterations. Thomson had never climbed before and at first had no interest in the mountains surrounding the hotel: soon, however, his sensational climbing career was to begin.

Like that of Giant's Castle, the Cathedral range is formed by a high corridor of basalt, which juts out from the Escarpment for four kilometres, eroded over millions of years to form well-known peaks like the Chessmen and the Horns, the Bell, and finally the impressive Cathedral Peak itself (which does not, however, resemble a cathedral). From the summit of Cleft Peak, at 3 281 metres the tenth highest peak in the country, one gains a view to the north over the Cathedral Range, the Saddle and Mnweni and all the way to the Eastern Buttress and Devil's Tooth, silhouetted against the sky and fading like cut-outs into the blue distance. To the south you look over Ndedema Dome to Sterkhorn and mighty Cathkin Peak. Standing out from the Escarpment, between Cleft Peak and Cathedral, two imposing pinnacles guard the head of the Tseketseke Valley – the Column and the Pyramid. The Pyramid projects furthest from the Escarpment and is a sensational, yet standard rock climb of E grade – it was also Thomson's first climb. The Column is closer to the Escarpment wall, and is as sheer and daunting as the Devil's Tooth, Mponjwane or the Injasuti Triplets further south.

The Column is one of the most thrilling rock climbs in the Drakensberg, of about F3 standard; but George Thomson didn't know about grades or using ropes for protection and abseiling when he set off for a stroll up the Tseketseke Pass in 1945. At the base of the terrifying precipices of the Column his companion turned back in fright, but Thomson climbed on undaunted, as he had done on several occasions by now. He reached the top without too much difficulty – in itself a remarkable achievement – but during the descent he became stuck on a narrow ledge with 500 metres of vertical rock below and no way down. Three and a half metres below him was a narrow ledge leading into a chimney – he jumped for the ledge, bounced off and slid into the chimney with the help of a small erica bush. Several hours later he arrived, unscathed, at the hotel. (This incident did motivate him to learn how to use a rope, and after that there was no holding him back.)

Year after year, peak by peak, he climbed the most formidable routes in the Drakensberg. In 1949 Reg Pearse unknowingly met him in Twins Cave and asked the 'stranger' whether he had done much climbing in the area. Thomson replied, 'Oh, just a bit. Not very much.' In the next chapter (see page 102) we will again meet up with the remarkable George Thomson on the face of Cathkin Peak, where he enacted another, even more incredible epic of South African mountaineering.

The second major renovations of the Cathedral Peak Hotel have recently been completed, this time adding a conference centre in Swiss chalet style. During peak holiday times the hotel tends to be congested with non-residents, much to the chagrin of the management: this spoils the hotel's traditional relationship with mountaineers, so avoid going there unless to make straight for the delights of Harry's Bar, or perhaps the fare and flair of the legendary Saturday night dinner-dance. The only other accommodation in the area is the small Forestry camp site opposite the Mike's Pass guard house, where a permit to drive up Mike's Pass, as well as camping, day-hiking and overnight wilderness permits can be bought. This is also where the mountain register is kept. The nearby Forest Station is one of the most advanced hydrological research stations in the world, and as you hike through this lovely area you are likely to see the weirs and gauges used to measure river flow.

Apart from the official 1:50 000 map of the area by Peter Slingsby, the hotel also sells area maps drawn by Reg Pearse, the compiling of which is discussed in *Barrier of Spears*. These maps are especially useful for the shorter walks. Armchair hikers can follow routes over the mountains on Pearse's scale model, built for the hotel and displayed in the shop. Where differences in spelling exist between the two maps, I have preferred to use the more correct

Zulu names from Slingsby's map than the common English corruptions on Pearse's. Many of the present names in this area were coined by the MCSA on various climbing meets, and one Professor Sweeny was the most prolific of name givers. I think it is a pity that the original Zulu names have not been retained throughout, and that more careful thought was not given to the naming of peaks, consistent with other names and traditions. For instance, Cathedral Peak was first known as Mponjwane ('the little horn on a heifer's head'). During the mid-1800s it was renamed Zikhali's Horn, after Chief Matiwane's son and heir, who settled here and started a dynasty following the slaying of his father by Dingane for his war crimes during the Difaqane. Mponjwane to the north would be better known by its earlier name of Cathedral, or better still as Ntabamabutho, 'the mountain of the warriors', considering the Zulu name for the Drakensberg is Quathlamba, or 'barrier of spears'.

The Column and the Pyramid, seen here from the Organ Pipes Pass, form part of the Cathedral range.

Cathedral Peak *Hike CR1*

Route: *Cathedral Peak Hotel to Cathedral Peak*
Distance: *10 kilometres*
Duration: *4 to 5 hours*
Grade: *Severe to Extreme*
General: *This hike is thrilling and affords the experienced hiker or climber a chance to stand on top of one of the major free-standing peaks in the Drakensberg. I must emphasize, however, that the path from the top of the Orange Peel gap to Twins Cave is dangerous. It is a C-grade rock scramble to the summit and should only be attempted by experienced climbers. The first ascent of the peak was made in 1917 by the prolific climbing team of D. Bassett-Smith and R. Kingdon. The summit is a breathtaking vantage point from which to assess the full grandeur of 100 km of the Drakensberg's finest face.*

▶ The driveway from the hotel gate makes a tight U-bend, from which a path leads up the left-hand bank of the Mlambonja River to a trout hatchery. Take this path and cross the river about 500 m upstream. Continue for another 500 m to a junction at the base of a short ascent, to the right of which is a pine plantation. Take the left-hand path up across a grassy area to the first band of sandstone cliffs. The path is wide but has eroded in places, so keep to the track and try not to damage the erosion barriers.

▶ On reaching the sandstone cliffs the path zigzags to the right-hand side of the main Cave Sandstone escarpment, where it contours for a short distance before ascending diagonally up through the cliff line to the top of a gully: Gurney's sugarbirds and malachite sunbirds flit among the protea trees. The path crosses a small stream to emerge on top of a wide plateau, marking a dramatic change in the vegetation on the Little Berg summit. At the base of the main cliffs a path continues along the contour into the wooded gorge where a delightful cascade forms a small gorge and falls into a pool surrounded by the familiar riverine companions – yellowwood, mountain hard pear, African holly and Cape ash trees. Near the pool is the overhang known as Barker's Chalet.

▶ The Little Berg here either gives one a sense of freedom or of agoraphobia, as it sweeps southwards all the way past Ntunja (Gatberg) to Cathkin Peak. Redwing francolin and common quail are flushed out virtually at one's feet and disappear over the nearest slope, while small, brown cisticolas sing from their grass perches. The path crosses the wide plateau towards a steep ridge between here and Cathedral Peak. Half-way up the ridge, where the summer or autumn clouds hang threateningly, the Contour Path proper begins, going to the left around the Oqalweni Valley. I encountered two fat puff adders on the path here, but they were so bloated with their winter store that I had to shove them gently out of the way.

▶ After another 700 m the path heads into a steep gully between the second and third of five prominences and climbs over to the northern side of the ridge – attempt this gully with caution when wet. Once over the ridge, the path contours to the left for about 1 km into the upper Nxwaye River valley, passing the source of another river on the way, where a vague path heads down a spur towards Sgonqweni Cave in the Nxwaye Valley. Once in the upper Nxwaye gully the going is steep and as badly eroded as a path can be – use your discretion so as to minimize any further damage (I called this section Desperation Gully).

▶ At the top of the gully you will reach a level shoulder and this makes for a good spot to break for tea. From this shoulder the path climbs through a steep chute known as the Orange Peel Gap, which can be seen from the hotel. This is the end of the hike for all but experienced hikers or climbers. At the top of the gap it is possible to follow a well-used but treacherous and eroded 'contour' path in and out of the gullies past the Bell, over to the northern side of the range past the Horns, Chessmen and Mitre to Twins Cave. The path from the top of the gap to the summit of

CLOTHING

There are two basic considerations to bear in mind when deciding on what clothing to take along:

- the number of changes of clothing required
- the size of your pack

I decide according to a 'layer' system: I take a change or two of underwear and a T-shirt or two, a winter shirt and a jersey, one pair of shorts and one pair of jeans, a lightweight but warm jacket, and then a good rain jacket, preferably of gortex material which 'breathes'. A tracksuit is also useful. As the weather changes, so one can strip off or put on layers – in this way you will be prepared for all types of weather.

Socks are something you must not skimp on. I carry three light cotton pairs and three heavy woollen ones, always wearing two pairs with boots to avoid blisters. On long hikes my underwear, socks and T-shirts are washed *en route* and dried on top of my pack.

Finally, a peaked cap or sun hat and sun glasses complete the image.

Cathedral Peak is steep and winding but marked by beacons. Enjoy the view, but beware of fickle weather which can make the descent back to the gap dangerous.

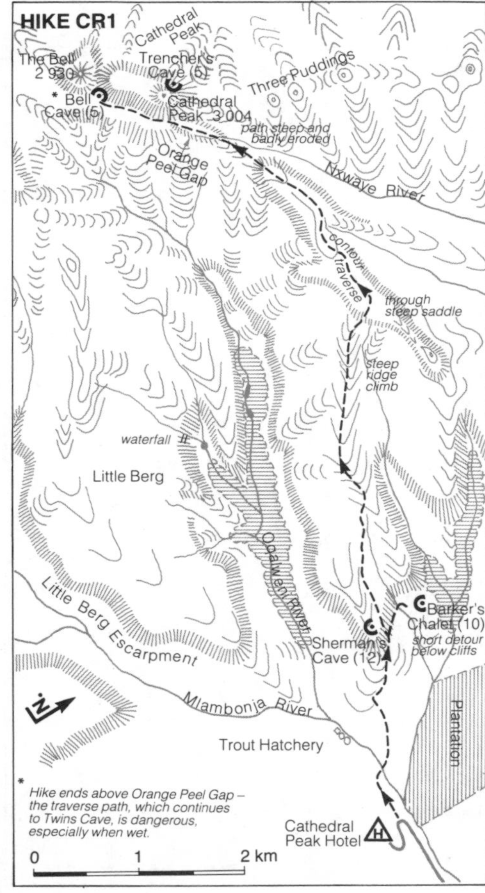

Mlambonja Pass to Twins Cave *Hike CR2*

Route: *Cathedral Peak Hotel to Twins Cave*
Distance: *11 kilometres*
Duration: *5 to 6 hours*
Grade: *Extreme*
General: *This is one of the most unrelenting passes in the 'Berg and, with all the rests one needs along the way, may take a lot longer than the prescribed five to six hours. George Thomson would have had no trouble in leaving the hotel at dawn, reaching the cave by noon and then heading over to Mnweni to sleep in Mponjwane Cave the same night and climb a peak the next day – but then there was only one George Thomson. If you are carrying a heavy load and do not make an early start, consider spending the first night at the Contour Path level, where the path meets the river. (The name Mlambonja means 'hungry dog', and refers to the scarcity of game here that left the early hunters' dogs hungry.)*

▶ This hike begins behind the hotel, up a wide track which goes gently uphill to the west, diagonally away from the Mlambonja River. After 2 km a path branches off to the left towards Tarn Hill, but carry on straight to cross the Tseketseke River near its confluence with the Mlambonja, then follow the latter's course for about 1 km to where the path comes to the Xeni River. On the approach bank of the Xeni River a cul-de-sac heads off to the left and winds up for 1,5 km to the magnificent Xeni Cave; but beware, this path has already claimed the lives of two hikers.

▶ Cross the Xeni River to follow the course of the Mlambonja River for about 800 m, where the path veers to the left and zigzags steeply up a

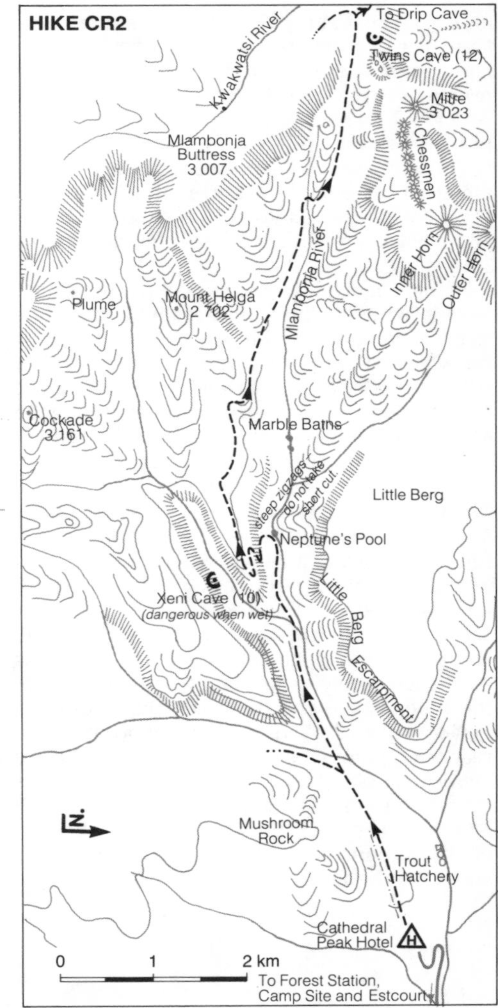

grassy slope and then cuts back to a ridge. Erosion has been caused here by people taking short cuts across the zigzags and unless this practice ceases, we will all soon have to walk on concreted paths across the Drakensberg. Once at the ridge take a few deep breaths and then begin climbing the 1,5 km section to a junction, which is really a T-junction with the Contour Path. Follow the Contour Path to the right for about 2,5 km where it meets the Mlambonja River.

▶ There is a number of small pools around here in which to swim, and level spots can be found among the boulders and ouhout bushes on which to lay out a groundsheet or pitch a tent. (The Contour Path continues along the opposite side of the river, cutting back along the same level.) From here the pass starts and follows the steep left-hand bank above the river, where several small tributaries are crossed. The ground can be soggy in places and hikers should be careful to keep their footing, both in the lower boggy areas where legs easily disappear down holes, and on the higher slope where it is easy to slip on the scree.

▶ If by now you aren't exhausted you will enjoy the 3-km climb past Mlambonja Buttress on the left, while to the right one passes under the Inner Horn, and then past the Chessmen half-way up to the Twins Cave turn-off. The path reaches a point where the Escarpment and the Twins are joined by a saddle. Cross over this saddle to the right and proceed slightly uphill and to the right to Twins Cave, set at the bottom of a basalt band below the Twins. The cave looks across to the Escarpment and up towards the Saddle.

The Mlambonja Valley *Hike CR3*

Route: *Cathedral Peak Hotel to the lower Mlambonja Valley, Neptune's Pool and Marble Baths*
Distance: *1,5 to 5 kilometres*
Duration: *30 minutes to + 2 hours*
Grade: *Easy to Moderate*
General: *The Mlambonja Pass route bypasses most of the lower river valley which is well worth a visit, especially if you are staying in the hotel from where access is easy, indeed inviting. A number of paths can be taken upriver to various scenic spots and may be linked to form a 5-km hike. It is easy to amble upstream and find your own variation, but I will describe three hikes of varying length. Take along binoculars and field guides, for this is a good place to identify birds and plants.*

Lower Valley round trip: 1,5 km

Begin at the U-bend on the hotel driveway and follow the path to the river. Cross the river via the stepping stones, but be prepared to get your feet wet when the river is high. The path makes its way through high reeds and grass for about 500 m, continuing gently uphill to a junction; the left-hand path goes up a steeper slope, but take the right-hand fork to cross the Bhemana River. Head back down the left-hand bank for 1 km and cross the river opposite the hotel.

Neptune's Pool: 4,2 km

Starting behind the hotel take the Mlambonja Pass path for 300 m and then turn right, continuing high above the river on the left-hand bank. After 1 km the path reaches the Mlambonja River just above its confluence with the Oqalweni River. Cross the river and then turn sharp right to follow the right-hand bank for 1 km, where you cross the river again to meet up with the Mlambonja Pass route. The route follows the

(Opposite.) The form and motion of a stream in the one of the many Drakensberg forests.

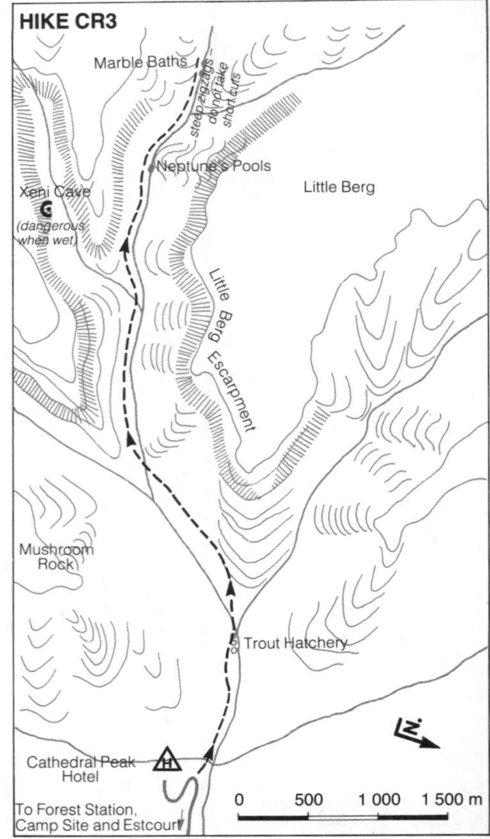

river for 1 km, crosses the Xeni River and ascends a steep slope before the path eases off. Another 800 m onwards you must leave the main path, which zigzags steeply up to the left, and carry on along the river. Neptune's Pool is another 800 m upstream, in a narrow section of the valley. The path is indistinct but not difficult.

Marble Baths: 5,2 km

From Neptune's Pool the valley opens out and Marble Baths is 1 km upstream, where the river has scoured out and polished the underlying sandstone to form smooth, marbled pools. For the more adventurous there is a tributary halfway between Neptune's Pool and Marble Baths that heads off to the right. Follow the valley for 1,2 km to a waterfall. The first half of the detour is fairly easy going, but the last 0,5 km is steep and awkward. The return trip should take four to four and a half hours, not including swimming, drying and picnicking time. The common tree with small, silvery, serrated leaves along the river banks is the ouhout (*Leucosidea sericea*); the other common bush, with long, drooping leaves is the mountain sage (*Buddleja salviifolia*); less obvious is the common spike thorn (*Maytenus heterophylla*), the specific name of this bush giving a clue as to its confusing variability, and various *Rhus* species which are characterized by their trifoliate branch ends.

Oqalweni Forest Walk

Hike CR4

Route: *Round trip from Cathedral Peak Hotel via Oqalweni Forest*
Distance: *5,5 kilometres*
Duration: *2 hours*
Grade: *Easy*
General: *The path to the forest is not shown on Slingsby's map, but it is on Pearse's. This seldom-used route is ideal for hikers who prefer secluded outings.*

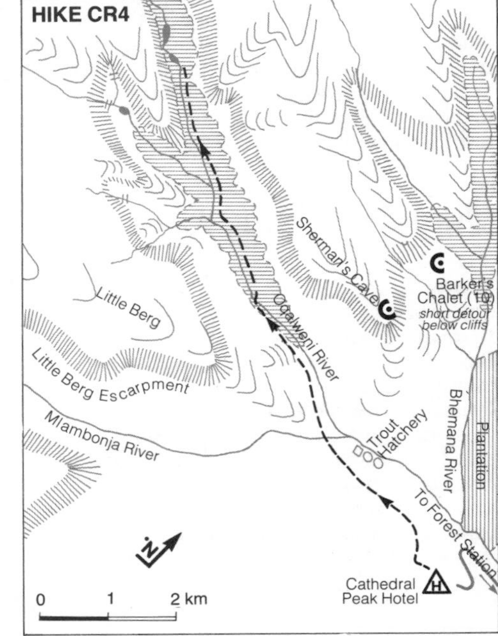

▶ Begin either behind the hotel along the Mlambonja Pass route and then branch off down towards the river after 200 m, or from the U-bend on the hotel driveway, following the left-hand bank of the Mlambonja River past the trout hatchery to a river, which crosses above the Oqalweni confluence. From the crossing (at which both paths converge) take neither the path up the Mlambonja River nor the other up to One Tree Hill, but go to the right around the bottom of the hill, following the left-hand bank of the Oqalweni River to enter the forest.

▶ About 1,5 km into the forest you will come to a waterfall and pool. Here the route crosses the river and returns down the opposite bank, below the guard hut and past the confluence with the Mlambonja River, then past the trout hatchery across the river to the crossing over a boulder causeway 700 m downstream of the hatchery. Cross the river and follow the jeep track back to the hotel driveway.

Oqalweni Valley *Hike CR5*

Route: *Round trip from Cathedral Peak Hotel via Oqalweni Valley*
Distance: *16,5 kilometres*
Duration: *+ 5 hours*
Grade: *Moderate*
General: *This hike gives you a grand tour of the valley, circumnavigating at the Little Berg level. The path passes through a number of macro- and micro-habitats (see page 15) and skirts a few more, so take along whatever field guides you fancy. The more habitats you encounter the greater the variety of things you will see.*

▶ Start at the U-bend in the hotel driveway, taking the Cathedral Peak path (Hike CR1), and cross the Mlambonja River, keeping left up a hill and crossing a grassy plain to the broken sandstone cliffs ahead. The path zigzags up through the cliffs and then continues uphill towards the right-hand side of the larger sandstone cliffs now ahead. At the base of the cliffs a path contours to the right, into a gorge, but avoid this path and keep going upwards to the head of the gorge, where the path emerges on a wide expanse of the Little Berg plateau. Follow the path across the plateau towards the sharp ridge between you and Cathedral Peak. Half-way up the ridge the Contour Path begins, leading off to the left: below you on the left is the heavily wooded valley of the Oqalweni River and from here, weather permitting, you can see the entire route around the valley.

At the head of the valley you cross the river and reach a camp site; the area around here abounds with cycads (*Encephalartos ghellenckii*). The common name for these fascinating plants is the breadfruit or breadtree, as Hottentots used the pineapple-like cones for making baked cakes. Only the outer pulp around the seeds is pounded into meal as the hard kernel is extremely poisonous. Baboons and birds also eat the outer pulp but avoid the kernel. Cycads have changed little since the earliest days of plant life on earth and are therefore often referred to as living fossils, having first made their appearance some 200 million years ago. The genus *Encephalartos* is restricted to a few species in tropical Africa and about 20 species in South Africa, where they are protected plants.

▶ After a short climb the path follows the 2 100 m contour line, until 3,5 km past the camp site where it meets the One Tree Hill path, going down the spur on the left. Take this path down One Tree Hill, first gently and then very steeply down the Little Berg escarpment to the valley where the Oqalweni joins the Mlambonja River. Cross the river and head straight on to the hotel. From the One Tree Hill path junction it is possible to keep to the Contour Path as it winds in and out of two prominent gullies to descend the Mlambonja Pass path, 6 km further on.

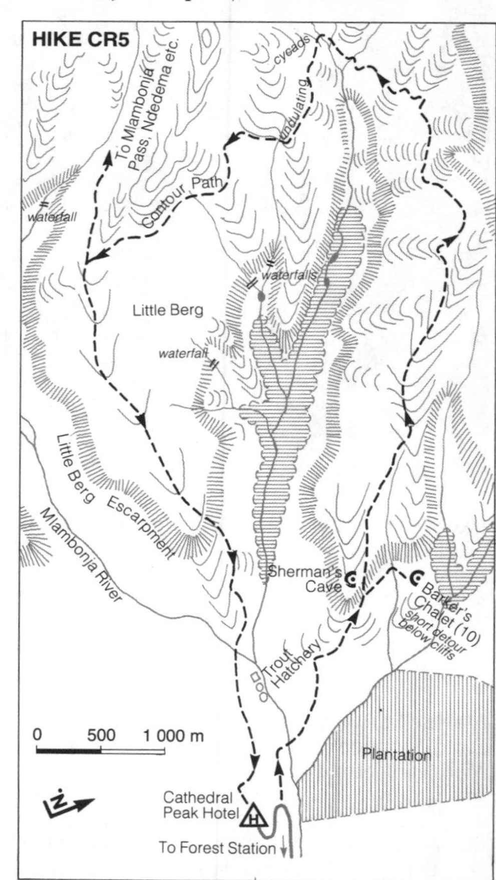

Ganabu Ridge and Baboon Rock Hike CR6

Route: *Round trip from Cathedral Peak Hotel via Ganabu Ridge*
Distance: *15 kilometres*
Duration: *6 hours*
Grade: *Severe*
General: *This hike starts on the Cathedral Peak route and then branches off to the right, going down into the Nxwaye Valley, up the Ganabu Ridge and down Baboon Rock.*

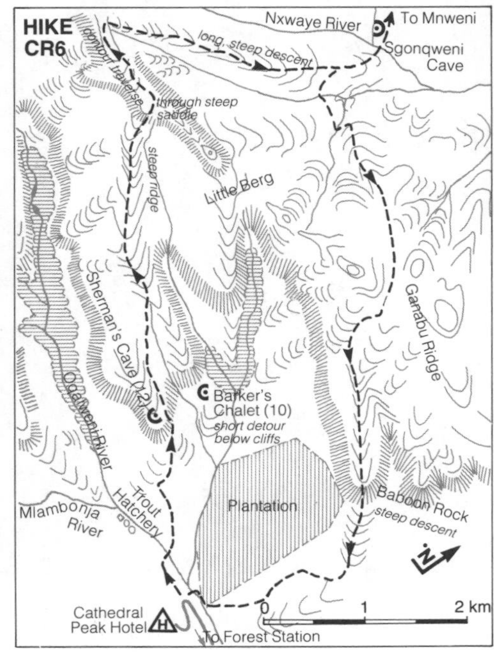

▶ Proceed up towards Cathedral Peak (Hike CR1), passing the Contour Path half-way up a steep ridge (Hike CR5). Continue to the top of the ridge and into a steep gully, passing over between the second and third of five prominences, then contour along the northern side of the ridge for 1,5 km to the top of a river source. Just past the river (a tributary of the Nxwaye) a little-used path heads down a ridge between the river's two main tributaries for 2,5 km. The descent starts off steeply but veers towards a junction on a level shoulder.

▶ At the junction take the right fork to cross three streams and then head up the Ganabu Ridge (the left fork at the previous junction leads across the Nxwaye River to Sgonqweni Cave). Once on top of the ridge – the Little Berg plateau – the path veers slightly to the right and begins its descent to Baboon Rock. This rock is a narrow promontory, where the path turns sharply to the left and begins its descent on the northern side of the rock, before working its tenuous way down and back onto the front ridge. At the bottom of Baboon Rock the path goes through a large plantation before coming to the Mlambonja River. Cross the river and within 100 m you will be at the hotel driveway.

From Cathedral to Cathkin, the view in the vicinity of Baboon Rock extends across the Little Berg plateau.

Rainbow Gorge *Hike CR7*

Route: *Cathedral Peak Hotel to Rainbow Gorge*
Distance: *5,5 kilometres*
Duration: *2 hours*
Grade: *Fair*
General: *This is probably the most picturesque short hike in the area and is certainly a photographer's delight: coloured fungi and lichens, mosses and ferns in the forest, and the many pools, rapids and falls along the Ndumeni River should keep you enthralled for hours. Once in the gorge itself the path follows the river, where filtered light throws spectra of colour on the soft veils of spray. The path is easy to follow, but don't wear your best shoes for they will get wet and muddied. In many ways this trip resembles the Tugela Gorge walk (Hike AM3).*

▶ The main part of this hike follows the Ndumeni River, which rises below the Organ Pipes. It starts at the hotel on the Ndumeni path, crossing the stream directly behind the hotel and turning sharp left. After 500 m you come to a fork where you must turn left again and then skirt around the base of Tryme Hill, through tall grass and over numerous streams for about 3 km where the path curves around to the south towards the river. From here Mike's Pass can be seen on the hillside opposite you. The path continues curving to the right, around the southern side of Tryme Hill, and then slowly descends into the forested valley of the Ndumeni River. Collared sunbirds may be seen on the proteas which grow alongside the isolated yellowwoods and other trees on the forest margin. Some of the trees are marked by numbers corresponding to the National Tree List.

▶ One kilometre into the forest the path comes to an enchanting pool which is fed by two waterfalls as they cascade around a large, moss-covered boulder. From here the going gets progressively wetter, with numerous river crossings: each crossing is marked by stepping stones but these may be underwater and very slippery. A few hundred metres upstream you come to the gorge where the path ceases, the vertical sandstone walls dropping straight into the river bed. It is possible to walk to the head of the gorge, under a large chockstone wedged between the walls of the gorge (earlier writers refer to two chockstones).

▶ At the top of the gorge large boulders block the way – this is the end of the hike, but for those who still have some breakfast kilojoules to work off, clamber over the boulder and continue onward and upward. Climb the steep bank on your right to the top of Tryme Hill where you will meet a path. Turn right and descend the hill back to the hotel. This return trip is only 4,5 km on the map, but it is a third longer than the route that turns back in the gorge.

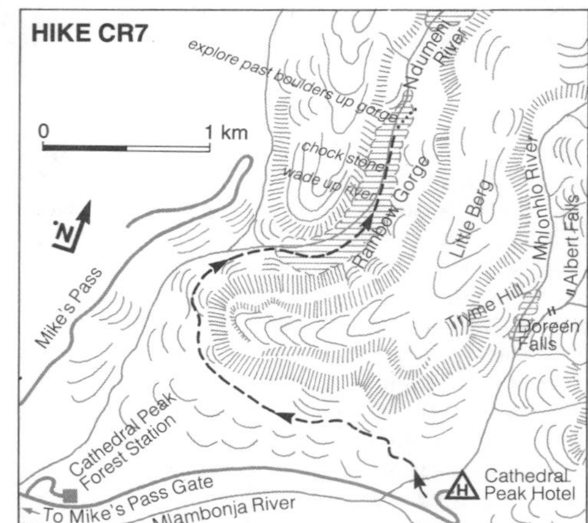

In Rainbow Gorge, one should beware of the slippery path, while absorbing the picturesque surroundings.

Masongwana Gorge

Hike CR8

Route: *Cathedral Peak Hotel to Masongwana Gorge*
Distance: *8 kilometres*
Duration: *2 hours 45 minutes*
Grade: *Moderate*
General: *Masongwana Gorge lies between Rainbow Gorge on the Ndumeni River and the incomparable Ndedema Gorge: in terms of size it also falls between these two gorges but is probably the least explored of the three – consequently the path up the gorge is not shown on Slingsby's map. It is possible to make this a short, 3-km hike by driving up Mike's Pass to the paper maché display model of the mountains in the area, about 1,5 km up from the guardhouse, and then past the Gewaagd homestead where a path leads down into the valley.*

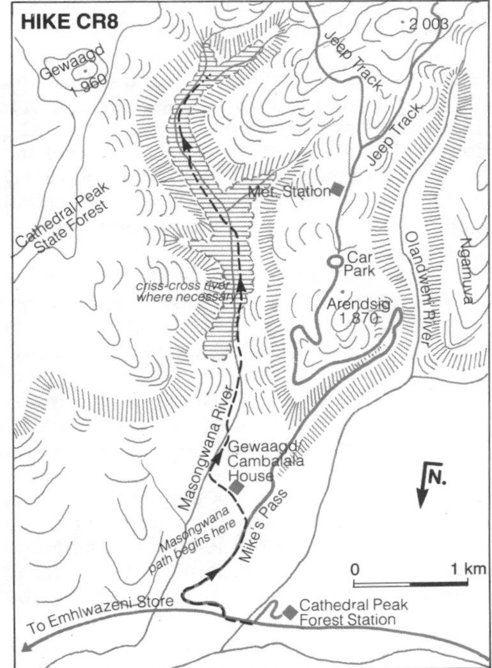

▶ From the hotel walk down the main road to the Forestry guardhouse and then head up Mike's Pass to the display model and Gewaagd homestead. From the homestead a path leads down into the gorge and thence upstream. The path criss-crosses the river for about 3 km to where the river splits into two tributaries. It is not possible to hike to the top of the gorge as both tributaries terminate under high waterfalls, but it is possible to explore a lot further up the longer left-hand tributary and then climb out via one of the side gullies on the left-hand side of the gorge, going upstream. This will take you up to a track used by the Forestry Department, connecting the various measuring weirs in the area. This track leads back to the main jeep track at the head of Mike's Pass, next to the meteorological station.

Ndedema Gorge

Hike CR9

Route: *Round trip from Emhlwazeni Store via Ndedema Gorge*
Distance: *26,5 kilometres*
Duration: *3 days*
Grade: *Moderate*
General: *This gorge is also known as the Valley of the Bushmen, and it is possible that it was the last refuge for the little San hunter-gatherers in these mountains. Some of the finest Bushman rock paintings are situated in the Cave Sandstone cliffs in and around the valley. The return trip will take two days, but, if planning to camp out, three days are needed to appreciate all that the gorge has to offer. With the Cathedral range becoming more and more popular, Ndedema Gorge is developing into a popular hiking and camping area with good paths and easy gradients (except for a few steep zigzags). There are two well-known caves (Leopard and Schoongezicht caves) to use as bases, as well as numerous excellent camping spots and a gorge-full of pools and cascades. Of my list of the 'seven wonders of the Drakensberg', Ndedema Gorge is the first. Ndedema and its side gorges shelter the largest natural forest in the Drakensberg, so an abundance of game and birds will be seen. One can begin this hike either from the top of Mike's Pass or from the Emhlwazeni Store: the distance from the former to the top of the gorge or from the latter to the bottom of the gorge is about the same (the distance between these two points, which are connected by a road, is 12 km). I will describe a round trip of about 25 km, beginning at the trading store, a hike that should take three carefree days to complete. How to arrange transport at the beginning and end of the hike is up to you, but it would be expedient to have a vehicle waiting for your tired legs at the top of Mike's Pass, where it is safe to park.*

▶ **Day 1** (11 km): From the Emhlwazeni Trading Store on the Cathedral/Estcourt road, 2 km before the bridge over the Mhlwazini River, take the jeep track to the right for 4 km, parallel to the river, crossing it just past the Forestry guard huts on the Solar Cliffs farm. Cross the river upstream from a waterfall which is situated on a side tributary. Turn right to follow the left-hand bank upstream for another 3 km and cross the river at its confluence with the Ndedema River at the mouth of the Ndedema gorge. There is a camp site here near an old ruin.

▶ Three paths branch off from the camp site,

but keep to the main, right-hand path following the river and gaining about 300 m in altitude over a 2-km stretch. Where the path turns abruptly to the left to zigzag up through the sandstone crags, you would do well to continue straight up the gorge for another 1 km, for here you will find the Sebaaieni (Poacher's) Cave, which is considered to be one of the greatest Bushman art galleries. The internationally renowned rock art expert and author, Harold Pagar, spent two years in the Ndedema area recording the rock paintings: he considered it to be the world's richest storehouse of rock art, in both quantity and quality. It is therefore not surprising that camping and fires are prohibited in caves housing such treasures.

▶ Return to the zigzag and proceed to climb the only really strenuous section of the hike, crossing a stream half-way up to the level section which runs like a platform between two main bands of sandstone. From this platform a contour path heads upstream for an easy 5-km stretch above the gorge, allowing you to take in all of its splendour. It is also possible at this point to take a lesser path to the right, cross a stream after about 800 m and then make your way up the zigzags to Leopard Cave, just below the Little Berg summit plateau. This large cave is a good spot for a first night's stopover and affords a fine view across the gorge.

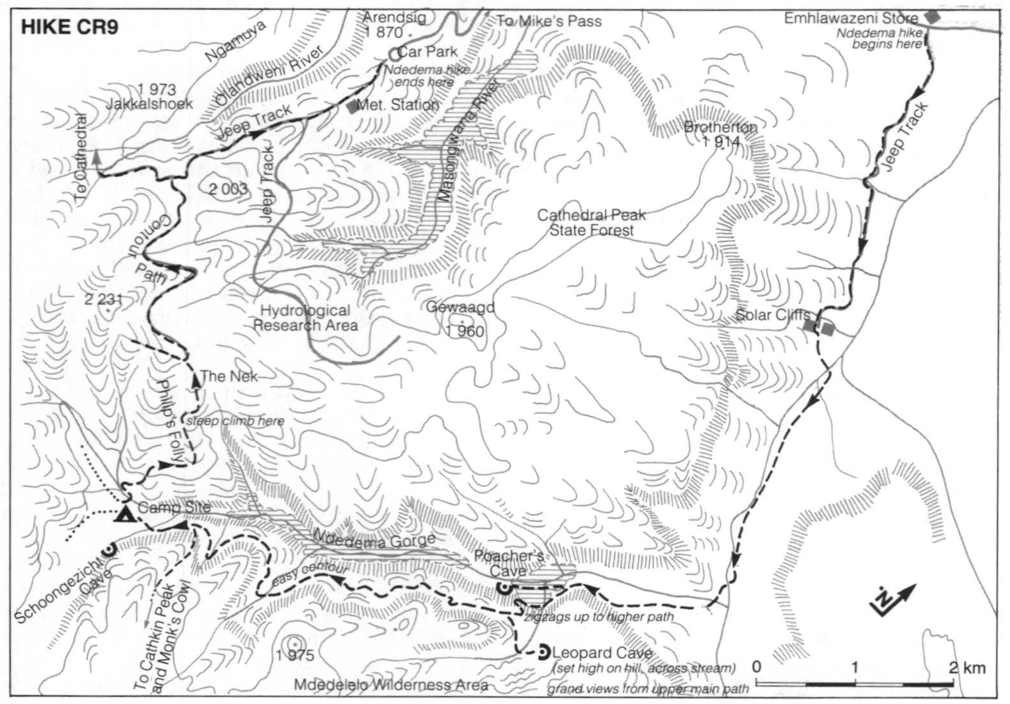

▶ **Day 2/3** (15,5 km): After rising in the embrace of primeval wilderness here, I always run down to the stream and plunge in – no matter what the weather. Head back down to the contour path and hike the five exhilarating kilometres to a junction with the main Contour Path, near the head of the gorge. Turn right along the Contour Path, cross one of two tributaries at the head of the gorge and after 500 m you will come to a camp site at the base of Eastman's Ridge. Less than a kilometre up the left-hand bank of the stream (the one crossed before coming to the camp site), Schoongezicht Cave can be found at the base of the cliffs. Beware of the ground in wet conditions as it can become very slippery. This area is suitable for a second night's stopover, or a tea spot if you are planning a two-day hike.

▶ From the camp site the path heads up Philip's Folly to the Nek, above the northern branch of the Ndedema Gorge, gaining 370 m over this stretch. A jeep track is reached at the Nek and from here you leave the wonderland of Ndedema. Skirting high above the Masongwana Gorge, the track undulates for 3,5 km through old pine plantations, now reverting to natural bush. Below the Forestry lookout, turn right at a junction on the jeep track and from here it is another 3 km to the car park at the top of Mike's Pass. A scale model of the area can be found here and in clear weather it is interesting to compare it to the lie of the land beyond. If you have only one day in which to see the gorge, start early from the car park at the top of Mike's Pass and make for the camp site below the Nek and down Philip's Folly. Do not attempt a 'short cut' along a lower jeep track down to the Masongwana Gorge, as there are more jeep tracks in the area than are shown on the map, and only one is the right one.

Mushroom Rock Hike CR10

Route: *Cathedral Peak Hotel to Mushroom Rock*
Distance: *2 kilometres*
Duration: *1 hour*
Grade: *Fair*
General: *This is a fairly steep hike, which leads up behind the hotel to a large mushroom-shaped rock.*

▶ From the car park behind the hotel, take the Mushroom Rock path which follows the right-hand bank (upstream) of the Mhlonhlo River and then veers right up the grassy slope to where it forks at the base of the first sandstone band. Take the left-hand path and continue for about 100 m where an arrow painted on a rock shows the way sharply to the right and up through the rocky bank to the Mushroom Rock. This section of the path is difficult and dangerous when wet.

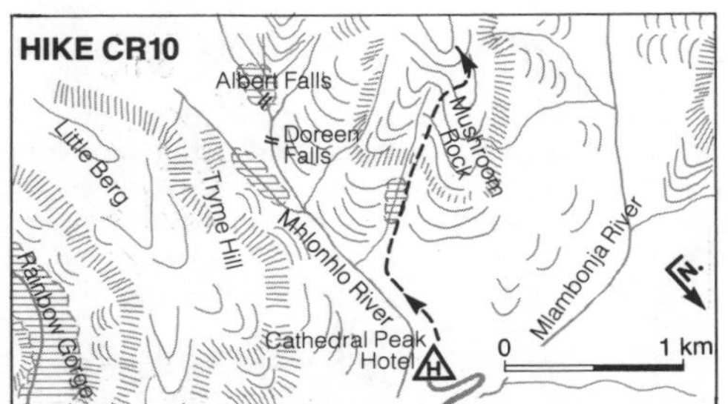

Tseketseke Camp Site Hike CR11

Route: *Cathedral Peak Hotel to Tseketseke camp site*
Distance: *9,5 kilometres*
Duration: *4 hours*
Grade: *Moderate to Severe*
General: *This hike takes one into the awesome embrace of the mountains directly below the mighty Cleft Peak which dominates the area between Cathedral Peak and Champagne Castle. At one time Cleft Peak was thought to be the highest peak in the Drakensberg. The Tseketseke camp site is the base from which the Pyramid, Column and Cleft Peak are climbed; the mountain hut has been condemned but, unlike all the other huts in Wilderness Areas, has not been removed. Directly west of the camp site stand the formidable twin spires of the Pyramid (2 914 m) and the Column (2 926 m). The latter is the peak on which George Thomson inscribed the first episode of the legend that he was to become.*

▶ From Mushroom Rock (Hike CR10), continue up to Tarn Hill on a 'peninsula' of the Little Berg and along this narrow strip of plateau past a small tarn, which is usually dry in winter. About 1,2 km past the tarn and 4,5 km from the hotel, the path becomes a jeep track which, after 1,5 km, climbs gently to meet the main Contour Path jeep track. Turn right here, below Castle Buttress and the Camel, heading into the wooded gully of a stream. After climbing up the other side, veer away from the gully for 2 km to arrive at the camp site on the near bank of the Tseketseke River, where cycads (*Encephalartos ghellinckii*) abound.

From the camp site the Contour Path continues for 14,5 km in a north-easterly direction through the Mlambonja Wilderness Area to its starting point below Cathedral Peak. Another path heads up the left-hand bank of the river, past the Pyramid and Column, and then ascends the Tseketseke Pass, which is seldom used. For rock climbers the Column offers two extremely exposed F3 routes (Thomson's route and one up the Escarpment Arête), while the Pyramid is an easier E-grade climb, most of which consists of slogging up steep grassy slopes. It is possible to reach the saddle between these two peaks without the use of ropes, threading your way across the slope around the base of the Column.

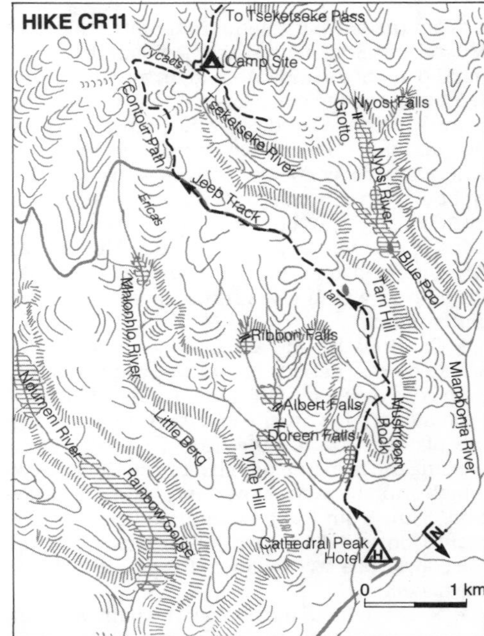

Tarn and Tryme Hills *Hike CR12*

Route: *Round trip from Cathedral Peak Hotel via Tarn and Tryme Hills.*
Distance: *10 kilometres*
Duration: *4 hours*
Grade: *Moderate*
General: *This pleasant, half-day outing to the top of the Little Berg affords grand views of the Escarpment and close-up encounters with some high spires and buttresses, as well as the possibility of exploring the sylvan cloisters around the Ribbon, Albert and Doreen falls, all on the same stream.*

▶ From the car park behind the hotel, take the Mushroom Rock path (Hike CR10) up the right-hand bank of the Mhlonhlo River and then veer right to climb the steep grassy bank to the base of the sandstone band. Here the path forks: take the left-hand alternative for about 100 m to where an arrow shows the way sharply to the right and up through the cliffs – this section is difficult and may be dangerous in wet conditions. This will bring you to the Mushroom Rock, a sandstone protruberance with a hole through it, which gives it the appearance of a giant fungus.

▶ Continue up the steep slope to Tarn Hill, situated on a 'peninsula' of the Little Berg. The path goes over Tarn Hill and past the small tarn – usually dry in winter – and then ambles along the plateau towards the Camel. Shortly after passing the tarn, the path becomes a jeep track which soon begins a slow climb. At a side junction, 5 km from the hotel and 500 m from the main Contour Path, turn sharp left, following the course of a stream down the gentle slope of the plateau.

▶ Near the lip of the plateau the path veers to the right away from the stream before descending Tryme Hill towards the wooded valley below. Ribbon Falls is situated on this stream some 70 m below the Little Berg: it can be reached by some imaginative traversing to the left, for about 500 m. The path continues down what becomes a spur and then cuts across to the right to meet the Mhlonhlo River, which is crossed a little way downstream. Both Albert and Doreen falls are situated at about the same level as this crossing, on the tributary that you followed up the Little Berg. This stream now runs parallel to and to the left of where you are: to reach the falls, veer diagonally left away from the Mhlonhlo River at the level of the crossing. Alternatively, carry on down the right-hand bank of the Mhlonhlo River and then cross it again just before reaching the hotel.

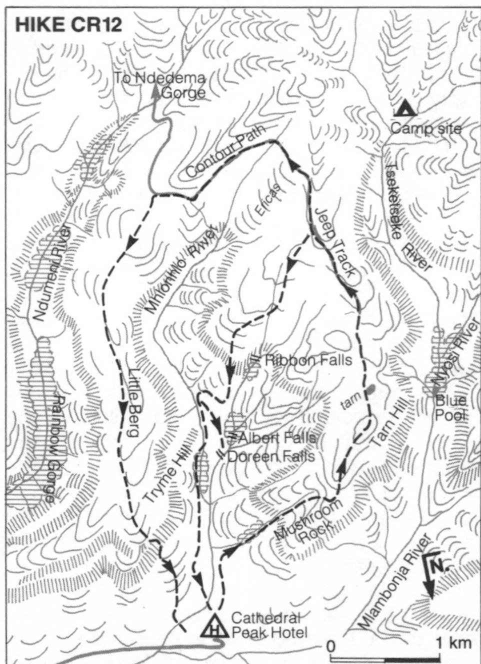

Continued on page 97

EQUIPMENT

Once again, your choice of equipment will be dictated by your pocket.

• **Stoves**
Essential for cooking food and making the endless cups of tea which one's body seems to crave in the mountains. Gas cartridge cookers are convenient and popular, but they are less efficient than benzine or paraffin stoves. A brass, benzine-fired primus stove has served me well for many years.

• **Tents**
Compare the mechanics and the internal space of all models for the best you can afford. Beware of cheap versions of the real thing, as the material and stitching may be inferior and you will be uncomfortably wet and cold.

• **Containers**
Keep all plastic household containers to carry things like sugar, powdered milk, butter, rice and muesli. Matches, toilet paper, maps, permits and passport should be sealed in plastic bags. Never carry liquids in glass bottles, which may break. Plastic or aluminium bottles are ideal.

Don't forget a torch, a trowel, spare batteries and your Swiss army knife.

GOLDEN GATE

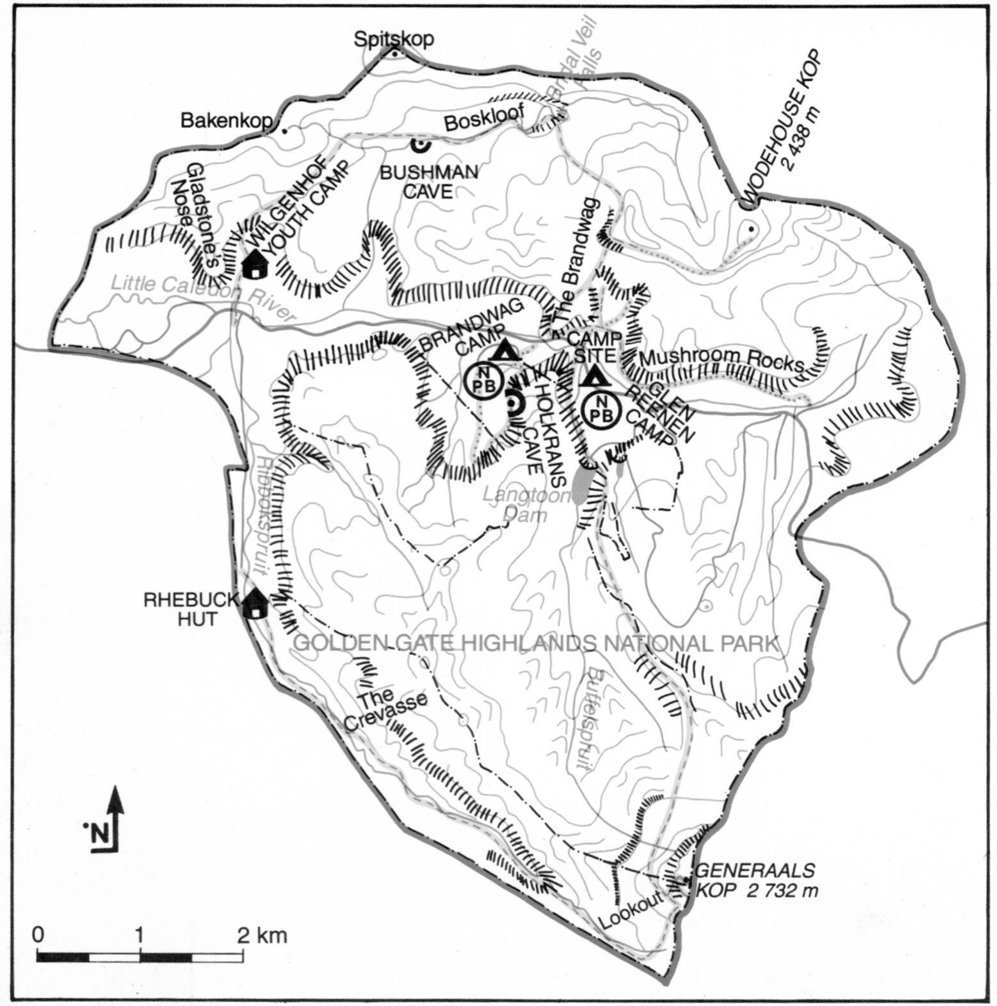

KEY TO DRAKENSBERG REGIONAL MAPS

- Park boundaries
- Roads – minor and major
- Rivers with falls
- Contour lines (not to scale)
- Hiking path with junction – minor and major
- •2212 Peak beacons and spot heights
- Caves
- Hotel and entry point (permit required)
- Camp site and caravan park
- Natal Parks Board Office
- Hut
- Natural forest
- Plantation
- Game fence

1. (Previous page.) The setting sun plays on the creamy Cave Sandstone layer and the coppery Red Beds of the Golden Gate, bathing the cliffs in range of different hues. **2.** *The mouth of the Holkrans Cave overlooks the mountains and valleys of the Golden Gate Highlands National Park (see Hike GG7).* **3.** *The hike to Holkrans Cave begins at the Brandwag camp site (right). The Brandwag, a massive sandstone rampart, can be seen on the left of the picture.* **4.** *The honeycombed sandstone formation to be found in the Holkrans Cave.* **5.** *The Mushroom Rocks are so named due to the mushroom-like shape formed by many thousands of years of erosion. An easy, 30-minute stroll to visit the rocks begins at the Glen Reenen camp site (Hike GG3).* **6.** *Mountain zebra (*Equus (Hippotigris) zebra zebra*) feed on the grasses of the* Themeda-Festuca *community.*

2

3

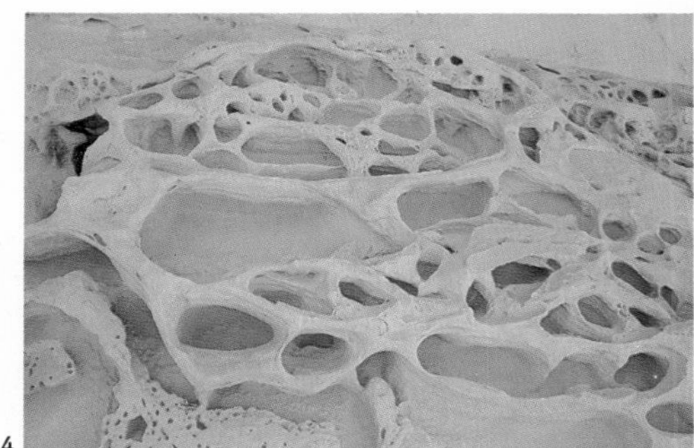
4

5

6

7

8

9

10

7. The Rhebuck Trail is a two-day round trip from the Glen Reenen camp site. At the end of the first day the weary hiker is greeted by the welcome sight of the Rhebuck Hut. ***8.*** *Generaals Kop is the highest point in the Golden Gate area and affords splendid views of the undulating hills and valleys.* ***9.*** *Massive overhanging sandstone walls line the road near the north-east gate of the Park. These walls form a terrace between the top of the Little Berg and the Little Caledon River Valley.*
10. *Its bright colours acting as a warning to predators, this grasshopper (*Dictyophorus spumans*) emits a foul-smelling foam when disturbed.*

1

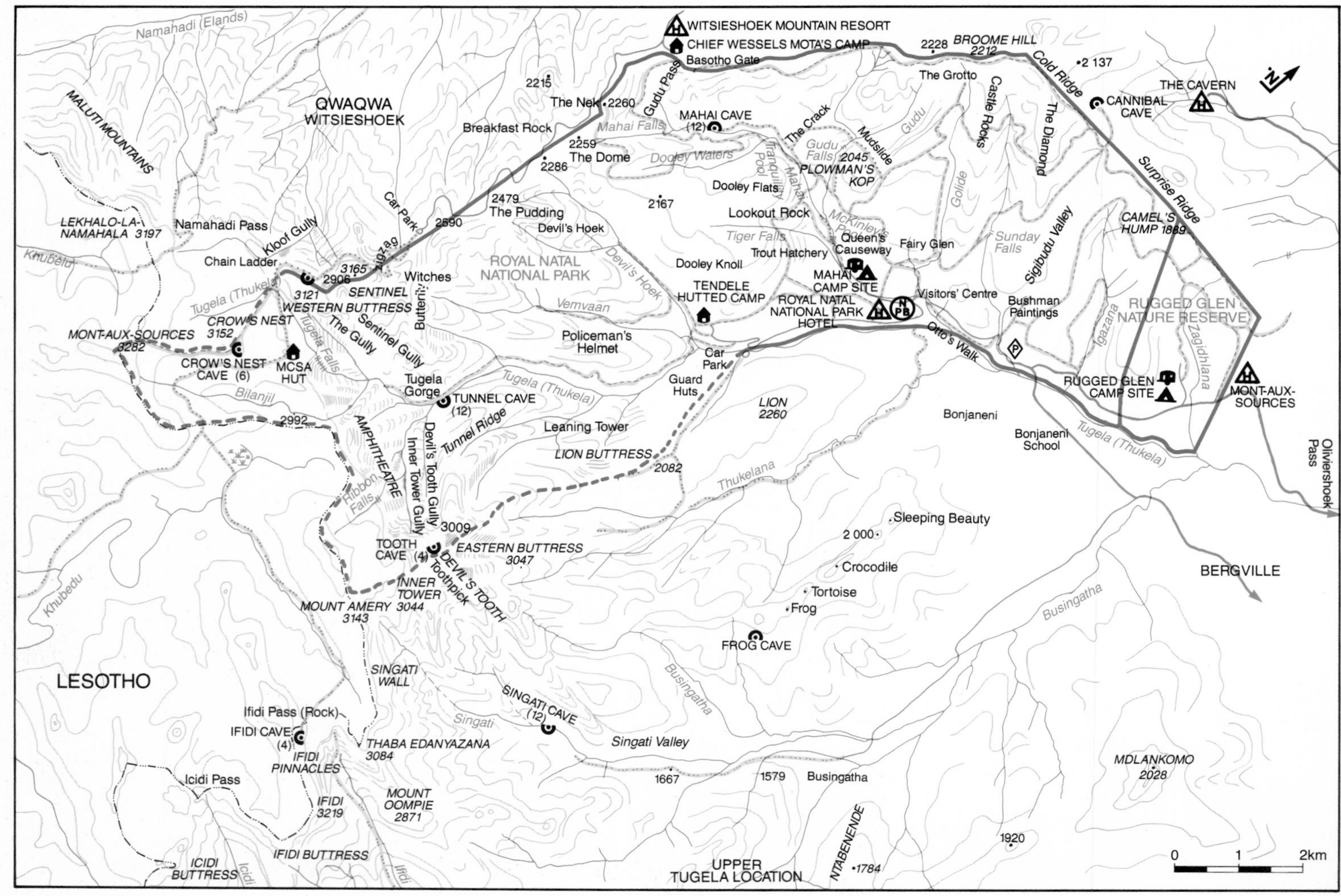

WITSIESHOEK MOUNTAIN RESORT
CHIEF WESSELS MOTA'S CAMP
Basotho Gate
BROOME HILL
2228
2212
Cold Ridge
2 137
THE CAVERN
CANNIBAL CAVE
The Grotto
Castle Rocks
The Diamond
Namahadi (Elands)
MALUTI MOUNTAINS
QWAQWA
WITSIESHOEK
2215
The Nek
2260
Gudu Pass
Breakfast Rock
MAHAI CAVE (12)
Mahai Falls
The Crack
Mudslide
Gudu
Gudu Falls
2045
PLOWMAN'S KOP
2259
The Dome
2286
Dooley Waters
Tranquility Pool
Mahai
Dooley Flats
Golide
Surprise Ridge
2479
The Pudding
2167
Lookout Rock
McKinley's Pool
Car Park
2590
Devil's Hoek
Tiger Falls
Queen's Causeway
Fairy Glen
Sunday Falls
Sigubudu Valley
CAMEL'S HUMP 1889
LEKHALO-LA-NAMAHALA 3197
Namahadi Pass
Kloof Gully
Khubedu
Chain Ladder
Zigzag
3165
2906
3121
Witches
ROYAL NATAL NATIONAL PARK
Trout Hatchery
Dooley Knoll
MAHAI CAMP SITE
SENTINEL
WESTERN BUTTRESS
Tugela (Thukela)
Buttress
Vemvaan
TENDELE HUTTED CAMP
ROYAL NATAL NATIONAL PARK HOTEL
Visitors' Centre
Bushman Paintings
RUGGED GLEN NATURE RESERVE
Igazana
Zagidhlana
MONT-AUX-SOURCES 3282
CROW'S NEST 3152
Tugela Falls
The Gully
Sentinel Gully
Policeman's Helmet
Otto's Walk
CROW'S NEST CAVE (6)
MCSA HUT
Car Park
Guard Huts
RUGGED GLEN CAMP SITE
MONT-AUX-SOURCES
Bilanjil
Tugela Gorge
TUNNEL CAVE (12)
Tugela (Thukela)
LION 2260
Bonjaneni
2992
AMPHITHEATRE
Devil's Tooth Gully
Inner Tower Gully
Tunnel Ridge
Leaning Tower
Bonjaneni School
Tugela (Thukela)
Oliviershoek Pass
LION BUTTRESS
2082
Ribbon Falls
Thukelana
Sleeping Beauty
3009
2 000
TOOTH CAVE (4)
EASTERN BUTTRESS 3047
DEVIL'S TOOTH
Toothpick
Crocodile
BERGVILLE
INNER TOWER 3044
Tortoise
MOUNT AMERY 3143
Frog
Khubedu
Busingatha
FROG CAVE
LESOTHO
SINGATI WALL
SINGATI CAVE (12)
Busingatha
Ifidi Pass (Rock)
IFIDI CAVE (4)
Singati
Singati Valley
IFIDI PINNACLES
THABA EDANYAZANA 3084
MDLANKOMO 2028
Icidi Pass
1667
1579
Busingatha
MOUNT OOMPIE 2871
IFIDI 3219
NTABENENDE
1920
ICIDI BUTTRESS
Icidi
IFIDI BUTTRESS
Ifidi
UPPER TUGELA LOCATION
1784
0
1
2km

2

1. *(Previous page.) A classic view of the long sweep of Amphitheatre from the Eastern Buttress on the left to the Sentinel, with the Tugela River in the foreground.* **2.** *The Royal Natal National Park does not offer just idyllic views: the Eastern Buttress and the Devil's Tooth loom threateningly above the gorge over the valley of the Tugela River.* **3.** *Just a short distance from the Mahai camp site (Hike AM5), the path takes the hiker along the Mahai River to the Cascades, where the British Royal Family once walked in 1947. Above the rapids stands Plowman's Kop and Gudu Bush.* **4.** *A magnificent bird found only in mountainous or hilly country, the black eagle (Aquila verreaux) usually nests on a ledge of a cliff and will return to the same nest year after year. In spite of many of their number being killed by farmers, these large raptors are still common in the 'Berg.* **5.** *A refreshing end to an hour's hike, Gudu Falls is icy cold even in mid-summer.* **6.** *Pink river lilies (Schizostylis coccinea) grace the banks of a river in the Royal Natal National Park.*

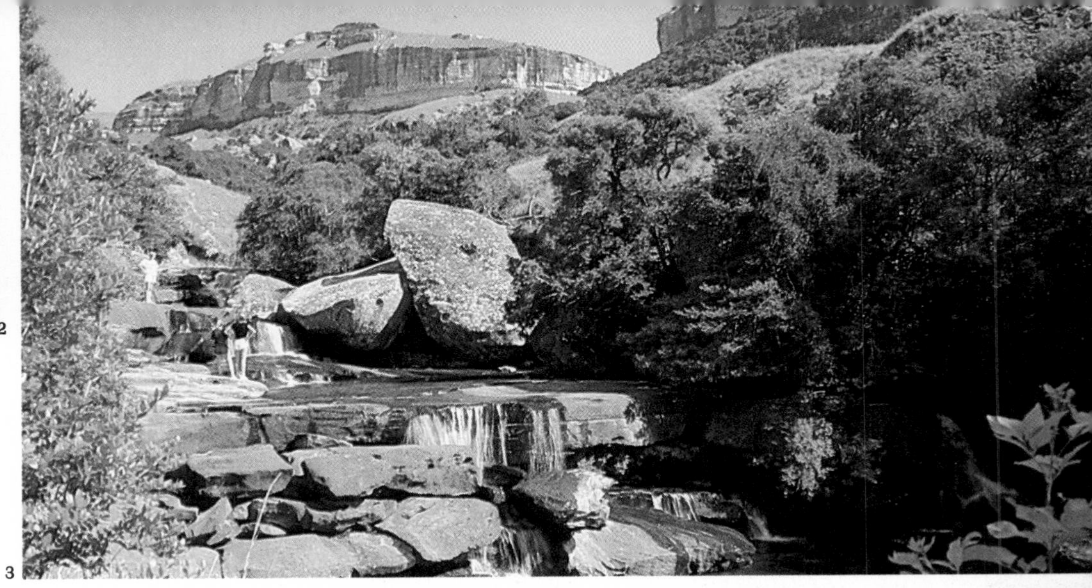

3

4

5

6

MNWENI

2

3

1. (Opposite.) Mnweni, 'the place of fingers'. (View from the summit of Cleft Peak). *2. In winter, the streams which cascade down the Mnweni Pass turn to ice, creating the impression of 'ice' falls. In recent years, local climbers have discovered the sport of scaling walls of ice, using all the techniques of Alpine climbing.* *3. On reaching the top of the Mnweni Pass, the hiker is presented with views of row upon row of mountain peaks.* *4. There are no easy hikes in the Mnweni area, as the paths are long and steep and certainly treacherous when icy.* *5. It is a Zulu custom to use the smoke of burning Helichrysum flowers, which they call 'ipepa', to invoke the spirits of their ancestors.*

4

5

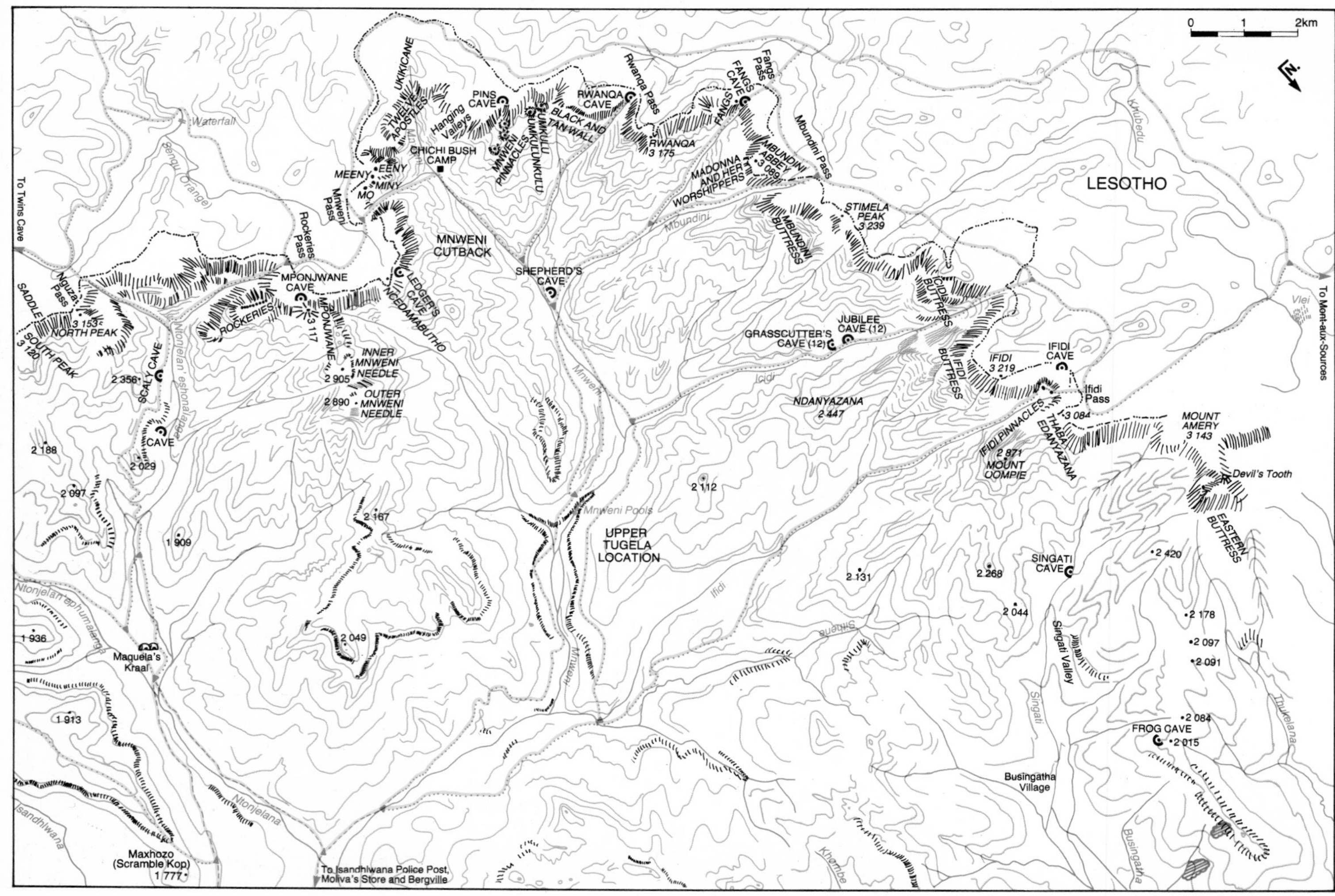
0 1 2km
LESOTHO
To Twins Cave
To Mont-aux-Sources
To Isandhlwana Police Post, Moliva's Store and Bergville
UKIKICANE
TWELVE APOSTLES
Hanging Valleys
PINS CAVE
RWANQA CAVE
Rwanqa Pass
FANGS CAVE
Fangs Pass
FANGS
BLACK AND TAN WALL
RWANQA 3 175
CHICHI BUSH CAMP
MNWENI PINNACLES
UMKULUNKULU
MADONNA AND HER WORSHIPPERS
MBUNDINI ABBEY 3 089
Mbundini Pass
MEENY
EENY
MINY
MO
Mnweni Pass
Waterfall
Rockeries Pass
MNWENI CUTBACK
STIMELA PEAK 3 239
MBUNDINI BUTTRESS
Mbundini
SHEPHERD'S CAVE
MPONJWANE CAVE
LEDGER'S CAVE
NCEDAMABUTHO
Nguza Pass
SADDLE
3 153
NORTH PEAK
SOUTH PEAK 3 120
ROCKERIES
MPONJWANE
3 117
ICIDI BUTTRESS
JUBILEE CAVE (12)
GRASSCUTTER'S CAVE (12)
Vlei
INNER MNWENI NEEDLE
2 905
OUTER MNWENI NEEDLE
2 890
SCALY CAVE
2 356
IFIDI BUTTRESS
IFIDI 3 219
IFIDI CAVE
Ifidi Pass
3 084
NDANYAZANA 2 447
Icidi
Mnweni
CAVE
2 188
2 029
2 097
IFIDI PINNACLES
THABA EDANYAZANA
2 871
MOUNT OOMPIE
MOUNT AMERY 3 143
Devil's Tooth
2 112
Mnweni Pools
2 167
1 909
UPPER TUGELA LOCATION
EASTERN BUTTRESS
2 420
SINGATI CAVE
2 268
2 131
Ifidi
2 044
Ntonjelan' eshonalanga
Ntonjelan' ephumalanga
1 936
Maquela's Kraal
2 049
Sihlene
Singati Valley
2 178
2 097
2 091
1 913
Singati
Thukelana
2 084
FROG CAVE
2 015
Busingatha Village
Ntonjelana
Isandhlwana
Maxhozo (Scramble Kop)
1 777
Khombe
Busingatha
Sengu (Orange)

6

7

9

10

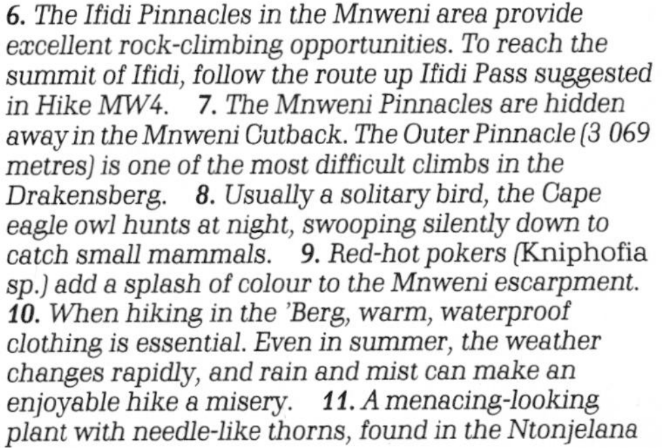

6. The Ifidi Pinnacles in the Mnweni area provide excellent rock-climbing opportunities. To reach the summit of Ifidi, follow the route up Ifidi Pass suggested in Hike MW4. ***7.*** *The Mnweni Pinnacles are hidden away in the Mnweni Cutback. The Outer Pinnacle (3 069 metres) is one of the most difficult climbs in the Drakensberg.* ***8.*** *Usually a solitary bird, the Cape eagle owl hunts at night, swooping silently down to catch small mammals.* ***9.*** *Red-hot pokers (Kniphofia sp.) add a splash of colour to the Mnweni escarpment.* ***10.*** *When hiking in the 'Berg, warm, waterproof clothing is essential. Even in summer, the weather changes rapidly, and rain and mist can make an enjoyable hike a misery.* ***11.*** *A menacing-looking plant with needle-like thorns, found in the Ntonjelana area.*

8

11

CATHEDRAL RANGE

2

4

3

5

1. (Opposite.) The mist-shrouded Cathedral Peak. **2.** *A highveld protea (Protea caffra) graces the view above the splendid Ndedema Gorge. The three-day Contour Path route to Ndedema is described in Hike CR16.* **3.** *The Organ Pipes are basalt columns which can be seen above the Organ Pipes Pass path. Once called Bushman's Pass, this was a route used by Bushman cattle thieves during the last century.* **4.** *From left to right: the Inner and Outer Horns (both 3 005 metres), the Bell (2 930 metres) and Cathedral peak (3 004 metres).* **5.** *Everlastings (Helichrysum spp.) are also commonly known as strawflowers as they look as though they are made of straw and in earlier days were used as stuffing for mattresses.*

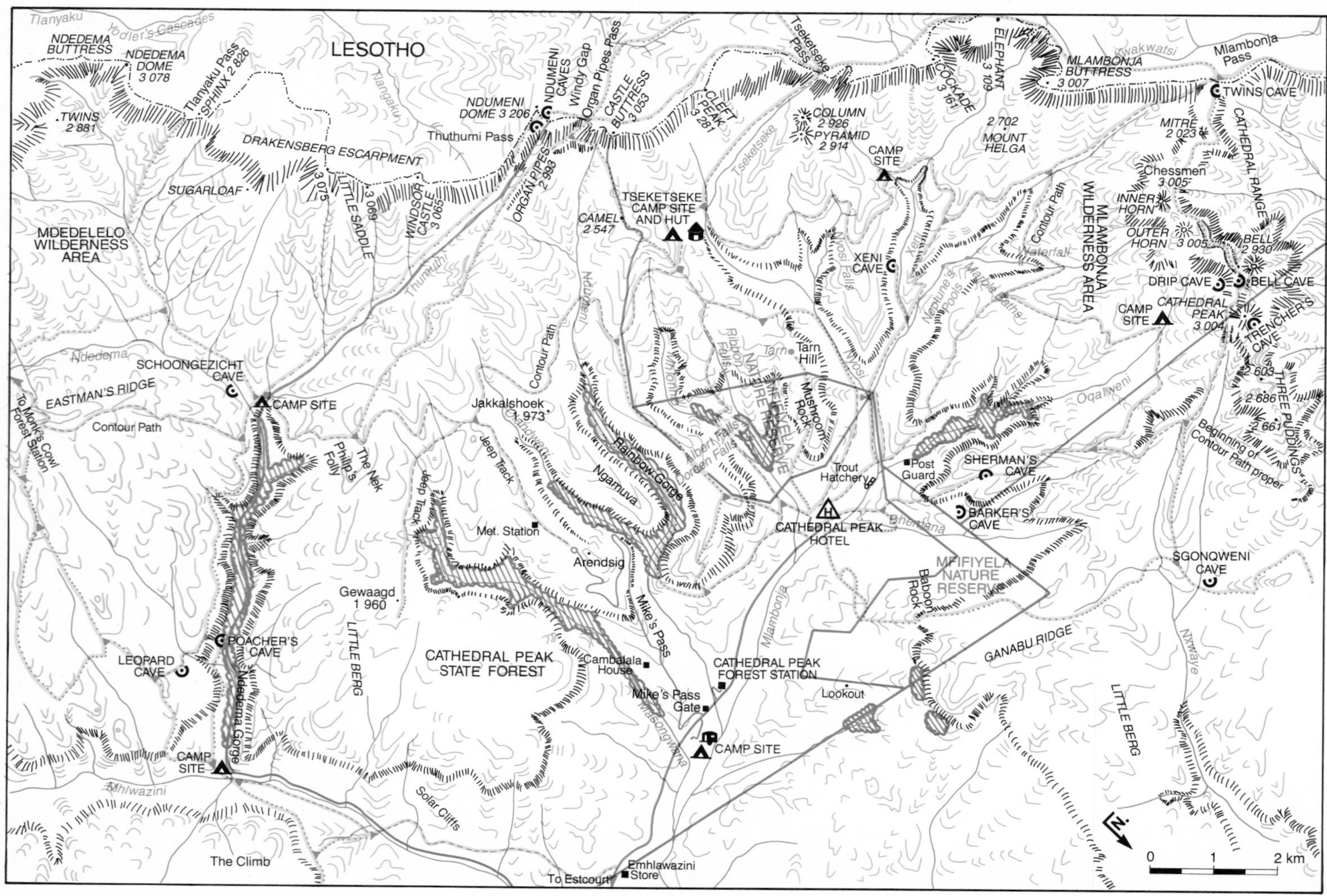

LESOTHO
NDEDEMA BUTTRESS
NDEDEMA DOME 3 078
Tlanyaku Pass
SPHINX 2 826
TWINS 2 881
DRAKENSBERG ESCARPMENT
SUGARLOAF
3 075
LITTLE SADDLE 3 069
WINDSOR CASTLE 3 065
ORGAN PIPES 2 993
NDUMENI DOME 3 206
NDUMENI CAVES
Windy Gap
Organ Pipes Pass
Thuthumi Pass
CASTLE BUTTRESS 3 053
CLEFT PEAK 3 281
Tseketseke Pass
COCKADE 3 161
ELEPHANT 3 109
MLAMBONJA BUTTRESS 3 007
Mlambonja Pass
TWINS CAVE
COLUMN 2 926
PYRAMID 2 914
CAMP SITE
2 702 MOUNT HELGA
MITRE 2 023
CATHEDRAL RANGE
Chessmen 3 005
INNER HORN
OUTER HORN 3 005
BELL 2 930
DRIP CAVE
BELL CAVE
CATHEDRAL PEAK 3 004
TRENCHER'S CAVE
CAMP SITE
MLAMBONJA WILDERNESS AREA
TSEKETSEKE CAMP SITE AND HUT
CAMEL 2 547
XENI CAVE
MDEDELELO WILDERNESS AREA
SCHOONGEZICHT CAVE
EASTMAN'S RIDGE
CAMP SITE
Contour Path
To Monk's Cowl Forest Station
Jakkalshoek 1 973
Philip's Folly
The Nek
Jeep Track
Rainbow Gorge
Ngamuva
Tarn Hill
Mushroom Rock
NATURE RESERVE
Trout Hatchery
Post Guard
SHERMAN'S CAVE
BARKER'S CAVE
2 603
2 686
2 661
THREE PUDDINGS
Beginning of Contour Path proper
CATHEDRAL PEAK HOTEL
Met. Station
Arendsig
Gewaagd 1 960
MFIFIYELA NATURE RESERVE
Baboon Rock
SGONQWENI CAVE
POACHER'S CAVE
LEOPARD CAVE
Ndedema Gorge
LITTLE BERG
CATHEDRAL PEAK STATE FOREST
Cambalala House
Mike's Pass
Mike's Pass Gate
CATHEDRAL PEAK FOREST STATION
Lookout
GANABU RIDGE
LITTLE BERG
CAMP SITE
CAMP SITE
Solar Cliffs
The Climb
To Estcourt
Emhlawazini Store
N
0 1 2 km

6

8

9

10

6. and *8.* *The Rainbow Gorge is probably one of the most picturesque spots in the Cathedral Range area. The coloured fungi and lichens, the mosses and ferns and the many rapids and pools provide a delightful setting for this walk along the Ndumeni River (Hike CR7).*
*7. Another resident of the mountains, the jackal buzzard (*Buteo rufofuscus*) is so named, because its call resembles that of the black-backed jackal.* *9. Twins Cave is large and comfortable and is perfect for the second night's stopover on the Cleft Peak Escarpment Hike (Hike CR14).* *10. The view from Cleft Peak.*
11. Fungi play an important role in forest ecosystems, aiding the decomposition of the wood of dead trees and thus returning the nutrients to the soil.

7

11

MDEDELELO

2

3

4

5

6

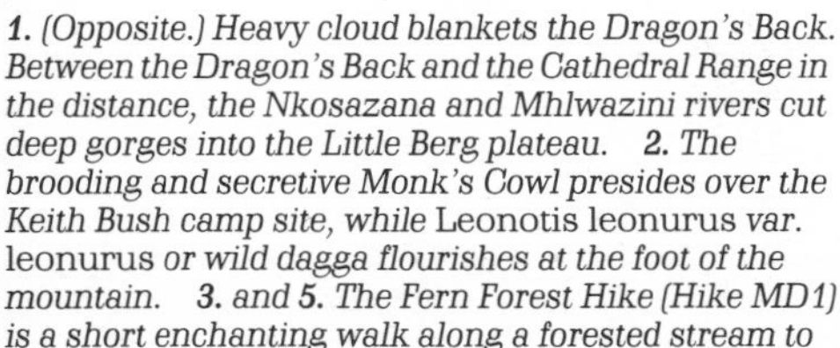

1. (Opposite.) Heavy cloud blankets the Dragon's Back. Between the Dragon's Back and the Cathedral Range in the distance, the Nkosazana and Mhlwazini rivers cut deep gorges into the Little Berg plateau. ***2.*** *The brooding and secretive Monk's Cowl presides over the Keith Bush camp site, while* Leonotis leonurus var. leonurus *or wild dagga flourishes at the foot of the mountain.* ***3.*** *and* ***5.*** *The Fern Forest Hike (Hike MD1) is a short enchanting walk along a forested stream to waterfall and picnic site surrounded by verdant coolness.* ***4.*** *Between Champagne Castle and the Dragon's Back on the right and Cathkin and Monk's Cowl on the left, the long slog up Gray's Pass is rewarded by the beauty of the Mhlwazini Valley.*
6. *Cathkin Peak or Mdedelelo (3 149 metres) is guarded on each side by precipitous cliffs which defied all attempts by climbers until 1912, when George Amphlett and party reached the summit via the South Gully.*

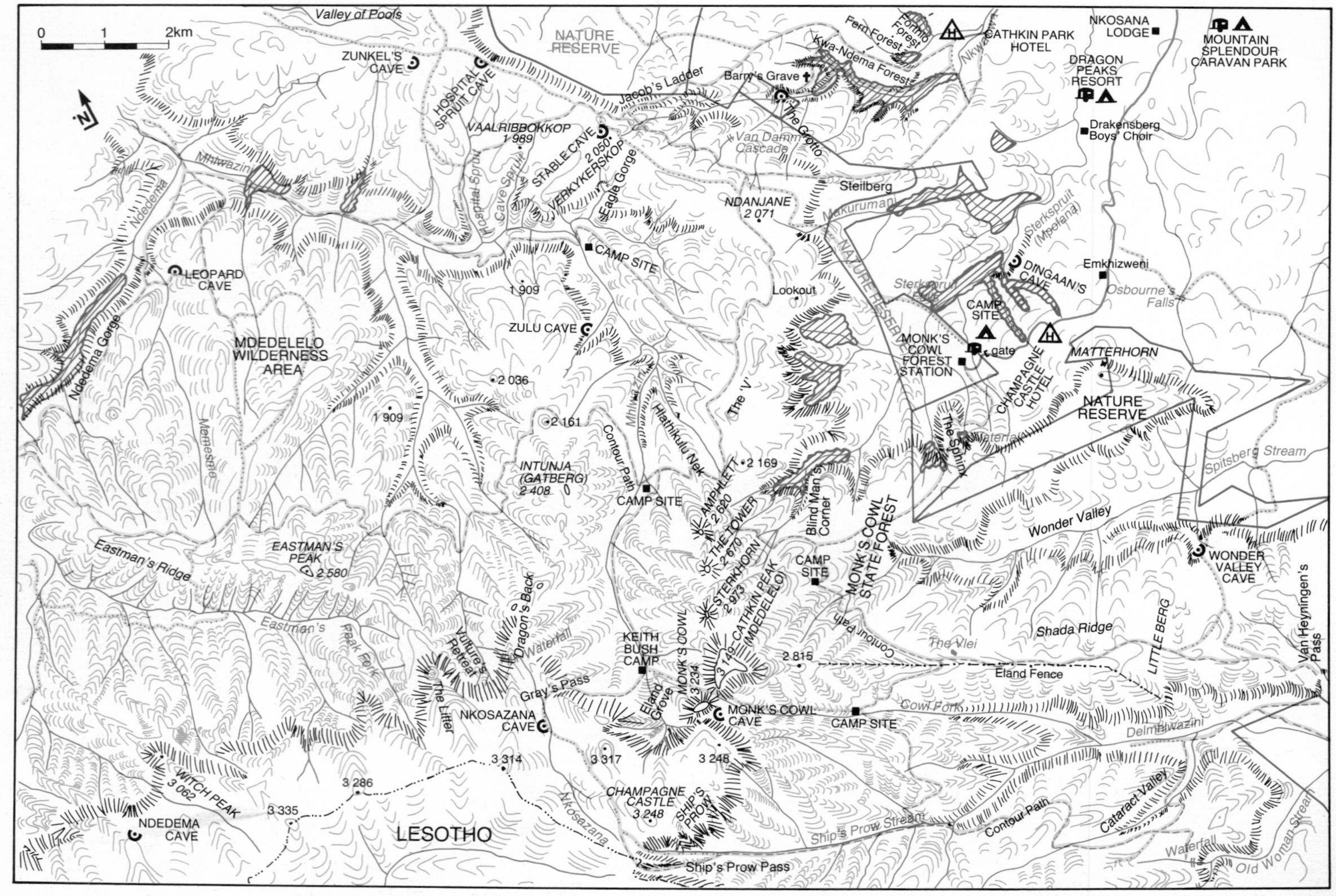

0 1 2km
Valley of Pools
NATURE RESERVE
ZUNKEL'S CAVE
HOSPITAL SPRUIT CAVE
Fern Forest
Forth Forest
Kwa-Ndema Forest
CATHKIN PARK HOTEL
NKOSANA LODGE
MOUNTAIN SPLENDOUR CARAVAN PARK
DRAGON PEAKS RESORT
Barry's Grave
Jacob's Ladder
The Grotto
Van Damm Cascade
Drakensberg Boys' Choir
VAALRIBBOKKOP 1 989
STABLE CAVE
2 050
VERKYKERSKOP
Eagle Gorge
Hospital Spruit
Cave Spruit
Mhlwazini
Ndedema
Steilberg
Makurumani
NDANJANE 2 071
Sterkspruit (Mpofana)
DINGAAN'S CAVE
Emkhizweni
Osbourne's Falls
CAMP SITE
LEOPARD CAVE
1 909
Lookout
NATURE RESERVE
Sterkspruit
CAMP SITE
ZULU CAVE
MDEDELELO WILDERNESS AREA
MONK'S COWL FOREST STATION
gate
MATTERHORN
Ndedema Gorge
2 036
The 'V'
CHAMPAGNE CASTLE HOTEL
NATURE RESERVE
1 909
2 161
Hlathikulu Nek
Contour Path
The Sphinx
Waterfall
Memeshne
INTUNJA (GATBERG) 2 408
2 169
Spitsberg Stream
CAMP SITE
AMPHLETT 2 620
Blind Man's Corner
MONK'S COWL STATE FOREST
Wonder Valley
THE TOWER 2 670
Eastman's Ridge
EASTMAN'S PEAK 2 580
STERKHORN 2 973
CAMP SITE
WONDER VALLEY CAVE
Dragon's Back
CATHKIN PEAK (MDEDELELO) 3 149
Van Heyningen's Pass
Eastman's
Peak Fork
Vulture's Retreat
Waterfall
MONK'S COWL 3 234
Contour Path
Shada Ridge
The Vlei
LITTLE BERG
KEITH BUSH CAMP
2 815
Eland Fence
Gray's Pass
Eland Grove
The Litter
MONK'S COWL CAVE
CAMP SITE
Cowl Fork
NKOSAZANA CAVE
Delmhlwazini
3 314
3 317
3 248
WITCH PEAK 3 062
3 286
CHAMPAGNE CASTLE 3 248
SHIP'S PROW
Cataract Valley
Contour Path
3 335
Nkosazana
Ship's Prow Stream
NDEDEMA CAVE
LESOTHO
Waterfall
Old Woman Stream
Ship's Prow Pass

INJASUTI

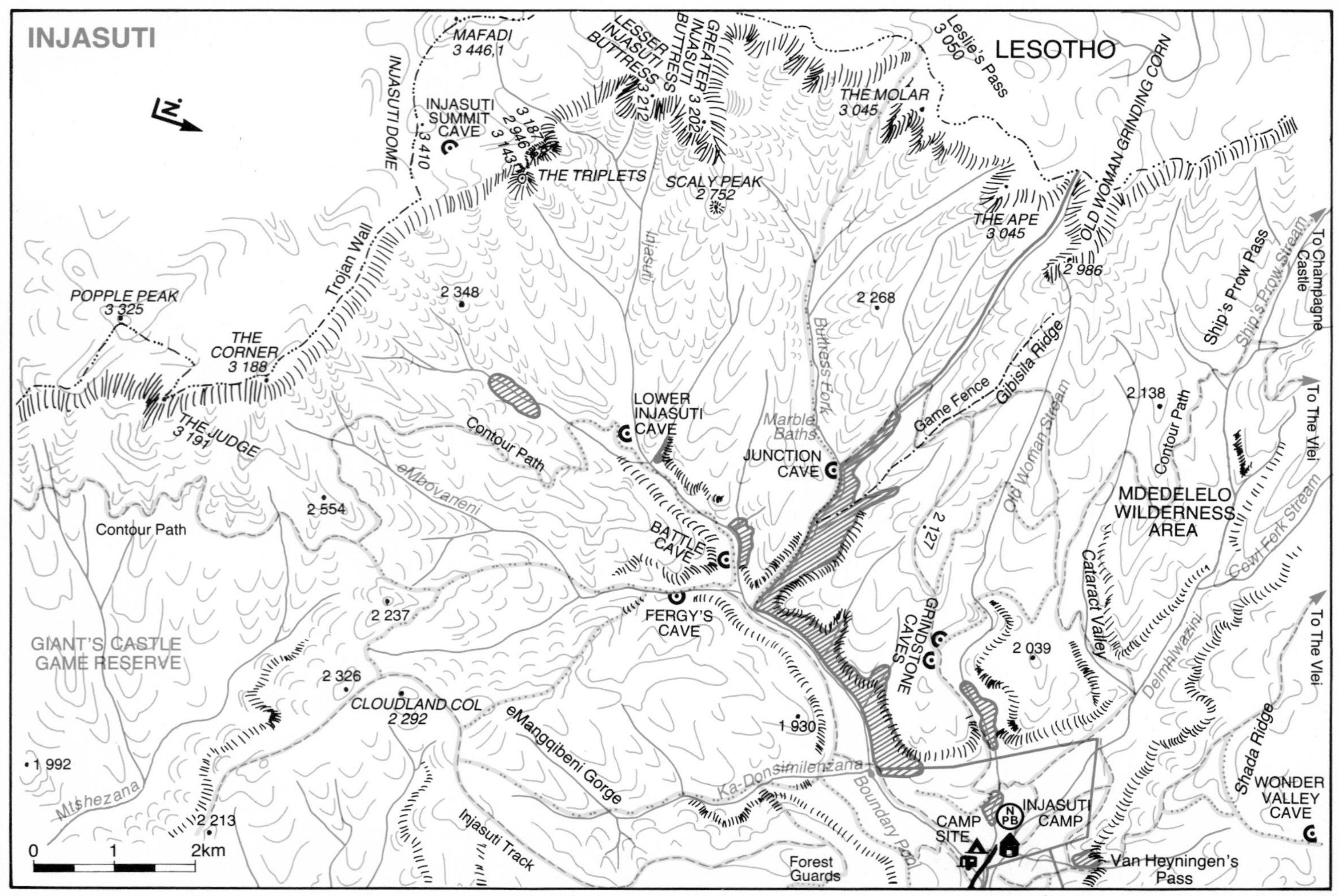
INJASUTI
MAFADI 3 446,1
INJASUTI DOME
INJASUTI SUMMIT CAVE
3 410
LESSER INJASUTI BUTTRESS 3 212
GREATER INJASUTI BUTTRESS 3 202
Leslie's Pass 3 050
LESOTHO
THE MOLAR 3 045
3 187
2 946
3 143
THE TRIPLETS
SCALY PEAK 2 752
THE APE 3 045
OLD WOMAN GRINDING CORN
2 986
Injasuti
Trojan Wall
POPPLE PEAK 3 325
2 348
2 268
Buttress Fork
Ship's Prow Pass
Ship's Prow Stream
To Champagne Castle
THE CORNER 3 188
Game Fence
Gibisila Ridge
LOWER INJASUTI CAVE
Marble Baths
2 138
Contour Path
To The Vlei
THE JUDGE 3 191
JUNCTION CAVE
Old Woman Stream
eMbovaneni
MDEDELELO WILDERNESS AREA
2 554
Contour Path
BATTLE CAVE
2 127
Cataract Valley
Cowl Fork Stream
FERGY'S CAVE
2 237
GRINDSTONE CAVES
GIANT'S CASTLE GAME RESERVE
2 039
To The Vlei
2 326
CLOUDLAND COL 2 292
eMangqibeni Gorge
Delmhlwazini
1 930
Shada Ridge
1 992
Ka-Donsimilenzana
Boundary Pool
WONDER VALLEY CAVE
Mtshezana
INJASUTI CAMP
N PB
CAMP SITE
2 213
Injasuti Track
0 1 2km
Forest Guards
Van Heyningen's Pass

2

3

4

5

6

1. (Page 83) Monk's Cowl from Injasuti. The beautiful river valley was named by early hunters after the bountiful game they found there. They called the area Injasuti, meaning the 'well-fed dog', for their hounds never went hungry for the want of left-overs. ***2.*** *The right clothing is essential in snowy conditions (seen here on the Injasuti Pass). Jackets made of gortex material 'breathe', keeping one warm and dry. It is advisable to wear waterproof gaiters to protect boots, keeping one's socks and feet dry, and to take along a pair of running shoes in case boots get wet.* ***3.*** *Pink, red and white Cosmos (*Bidens formosa*) carpet the Injasuti Valley (the common name is derived from the Greek* kosmos*, meaning beautiful). These flowers flourish along roadsides and wherever ground has been disturbed.* ***4.*** *At the Marble Baths, the river has polished the sandstone to a shiny white as it flows through a series of narrow pools below the Injasuti Triplets.* ***5.*** *The author at the end of Hike IN7, taking a rest in the Lower Injasuti Cave.* ***6.*** *An easy stroll from the Hillside camp site, the Forest Walk (Hike IN13) can be arranged to coincide with a guided tour given by one of the game rangers.*

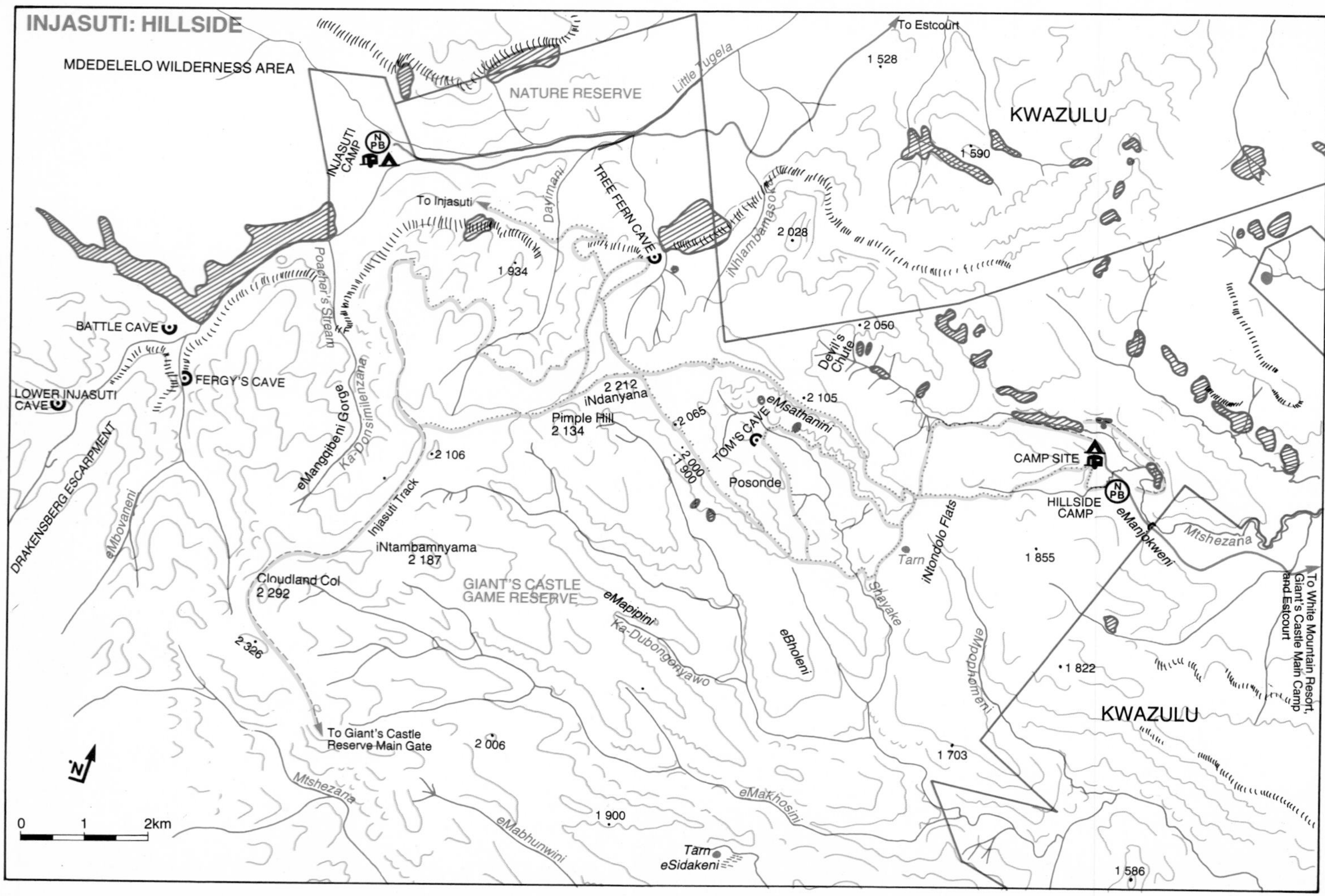

INJASUTI: HILLSIDE
MDEDELELO WILDERNESS AREA
NATURE RESERVE
Little Tugela
To Estcourt
1 528
KWAZULU
1 590
INJASUTI CAMP
NPB
To Injasuti
Dayimani
TREE FERN CAVE
iNhlambamasoka
2 028
1 934
Poacher's Stream
BATTLE CAVE
2 050
Devil's Chute
FERGY'S CAVE
LOWER INJASUTI CAVE
Ka-Donsimilenzana
eMangqibeni Gorge
2 212
iNdanyana
2 105
Pimple Hill
2 134
2 065
eMsathanini
TOM'S CAVE
2 000
1 900
Posonde
CAMP SITE
HILLSIDE CAMP
DRAKENSBERG ESCARPMENT
eMbovaneni
2 106
Injasuti Track
iNtambamnyama
2 187
Cloudland Col
2 292
GIANT'S CASTLE GAME RESERVE
eMapipini
Ka-Dubongonyawo
eBholeni
Shayake
iNtondolo Flats
Tarn
eManjokweni
Mtshezana
1 855
To White Mountain Resort, Giant's Castle Main Camp and Estcourt
eMpophomeni
1 822
2 326
To Giant's Castle Reserve Main Gate
2 006
1 703
KWAZULU
N
Mtshezana
eMakhosini
0
1
2km
eMabhunwini
1 900
Tarn
eSidakeni
1 586

GIANT'S CASTLE

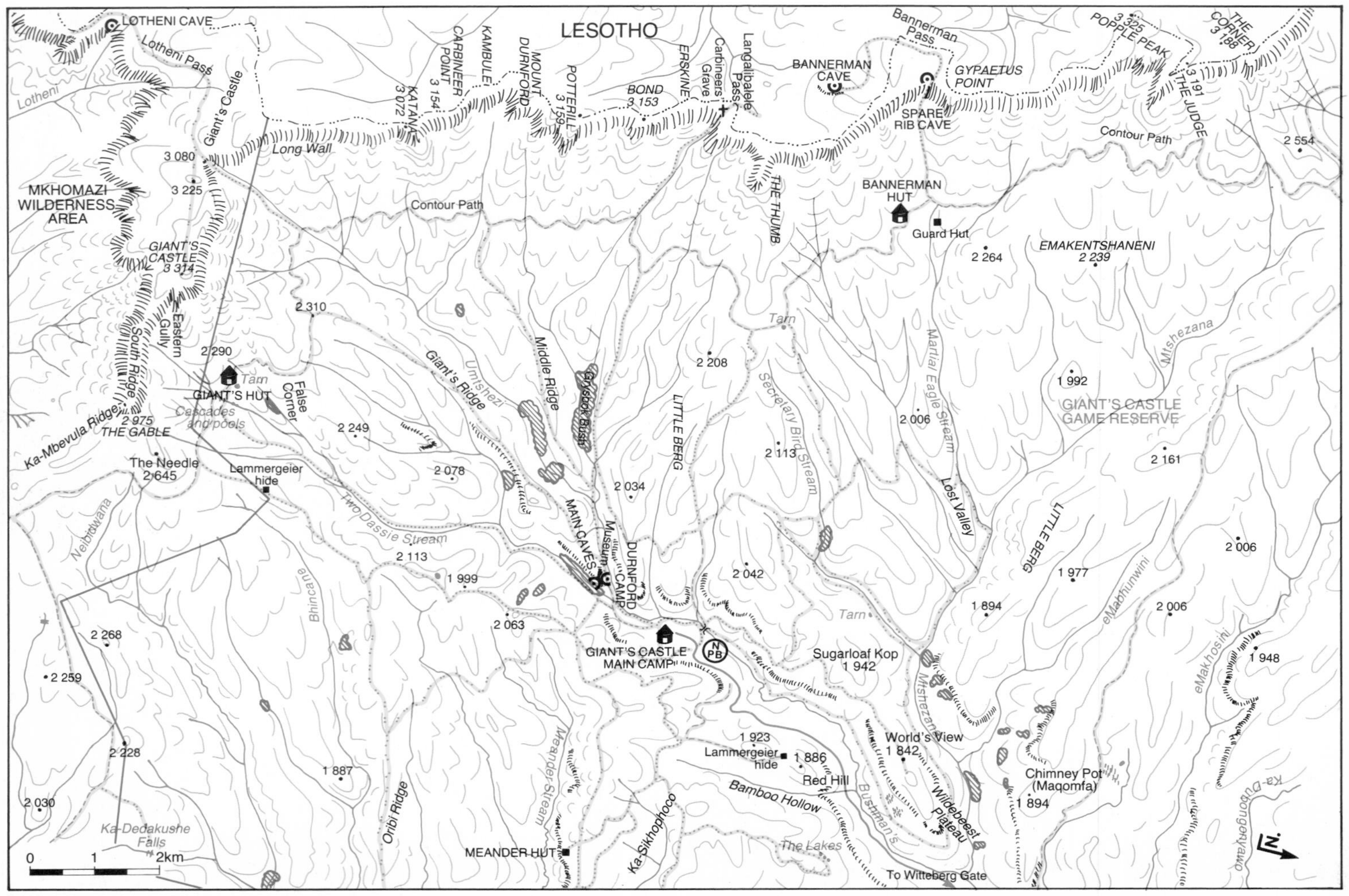
LESOTHO
LOTHENI CAVE
Lotheni Pass
Lotheni
Giant's Castle
Long Wall
KATANA 3 072
CARBINEER POINT 3 154
KAMBULE
MOUNT DURNFORD
POTTERILL 3 159
BOND 3 153
ERSKINE
Carbineers' Grave
Langalibalele Pass
BANNERMAN CAVE
Bannerman Pass
GYPAETUS POINT
SPARE RIB CAVE
3 325 POPPLE PEAK
THE CORNER 3 188
3 191 THE JUDGE
Contour Path
2 554
3 080
3 225
MKHOMAZI WILDERNESS AREA
Contour Path
THE THUMB
BANNERMAN HUT
Guard Hut
2 264
EMAKENTSHANENI 2 239
GIANT'S CASTLE 3 314
2 310
Eastern Gully
South Ridge
2 290
Tarn
GIANT'S HUT
False Corner
Cascades and pools
Ka-Mbevula Ridge
2 975 THE GABLE
The Needle 2 645
Lammergeier hide
Giant's Ridge
Umtshezi
Middle Ridge
Grysbok Bush
LITTLE BERG
Tarn
2 208
Secretary Bird Stream
Martial Eagle Stream
Mtshezana
1 992
GIANT'S CASTLE GAME RESERVE
2 006
2 249
2 078
2 034
2 113
Lost Valley
2 161
Two Dassie Stream
Neibidwana
2 113
1 999
MAIN CAVES
Museum
DURNFORD CAMP
2 042
LITTLE BERG
1 977
2 006
Bhincane
2 063
Tarn
1 894
eMadhlunwini
2 006
2 268
2 259
GIANT'S CASTLE MAIN CAMP
N PB
Sugarloaf Kop 1 942
Mtshezana
eMakhosini
1 948
2 228
1 887
1 923
Lammergeier hide
1 886
Red Hill
World's View 1 842
Chimney Pot (Maqomfa)
1 894
Wildebeest Plateau
Bamboo Hollow
Bushman's
Ka-Dubongonyawo
2 030
Oribi Ridge
Meander Stream
Ka-Sikhophoco
Ka-Dedakushe Falls
The Lakes
MEANDER HUT
To Witteberg Gate
0 1 2km
N

3

4

6

1. (Opposite.) An escarpment view in the Giant's Castle Game Reserve. Two passes – Bannerman and Langalibalele – ascend this section of the Drakensberg. It was here that Chief Langalibalele fled with his people while being pursued by colonial forces in 1873. **2.** *A stream in the vicinity of Giant's Hut.* **3.** *A mountain hut is always a welcome sight at the end of a day's hard slog. Before leaving on a hike, always check with the relevant authorities as to whether you have to book your hut – you may find another party occupying your night's shelter.* **4.** *Tarn, Giant's Castle.* **5.** *The lush floor of the* Podocarpus *forest along the banks of the Bushman's River. The Forest Walk (Hike GC3) takes one past enchanting sights such as this one.* **6.** *The delicate grasslike* Dierama *is commonly found on the moist grasslands of the Little Berg slopes.*

MKHOMAZI

2

3

4

5

6

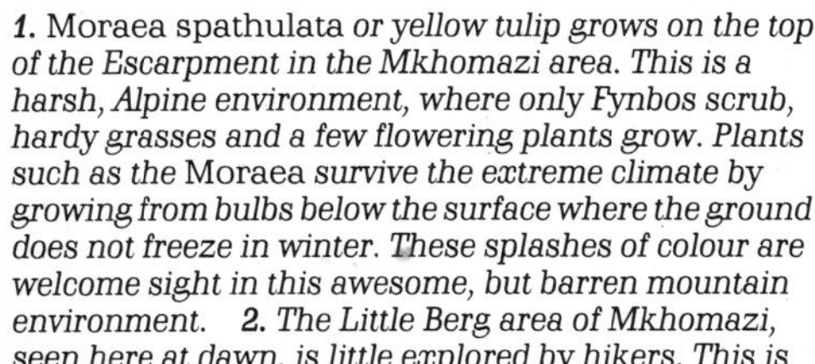

1. Moraea spathulata *or yellow tulip grows on the top of the Escarpment in the Mkhomazi area. This is a harsh, Alpine environment, where only Fynbos scrub, hardy grasses and a few flowering plants grow. Plants such as the* Moraea *survive the extreme climate by growing from bulbs below the surface where the ground does not freeze in winter. These splashes of colour are welcome sight in this awesome, but barren mountain environment.* **2.** *The Little Berg area of Mkhomazi, seen here at dawn, is little explored by hikers. This is fortunate for the lucky few who go there, as it offers excellent wilderness opportunities.* **3.** *On the Mkhomazi Trail. Each year a few lucky hikers will be able to see the lammergeiers that use the Ka-Malungana Ridge as a seasonal roosting site.* **4.** *A tranquil valley in the Mkhomazi Wilderness Area, rich in wildlife.* **5.** *The male gaudy commodore butterfly (*Junonia octavia sesamus*) in its violet-blue winter form.* **6.** *Delicious mountain water: these crystal clear streams are one of the many attractions of hiking in the 'Berg.*

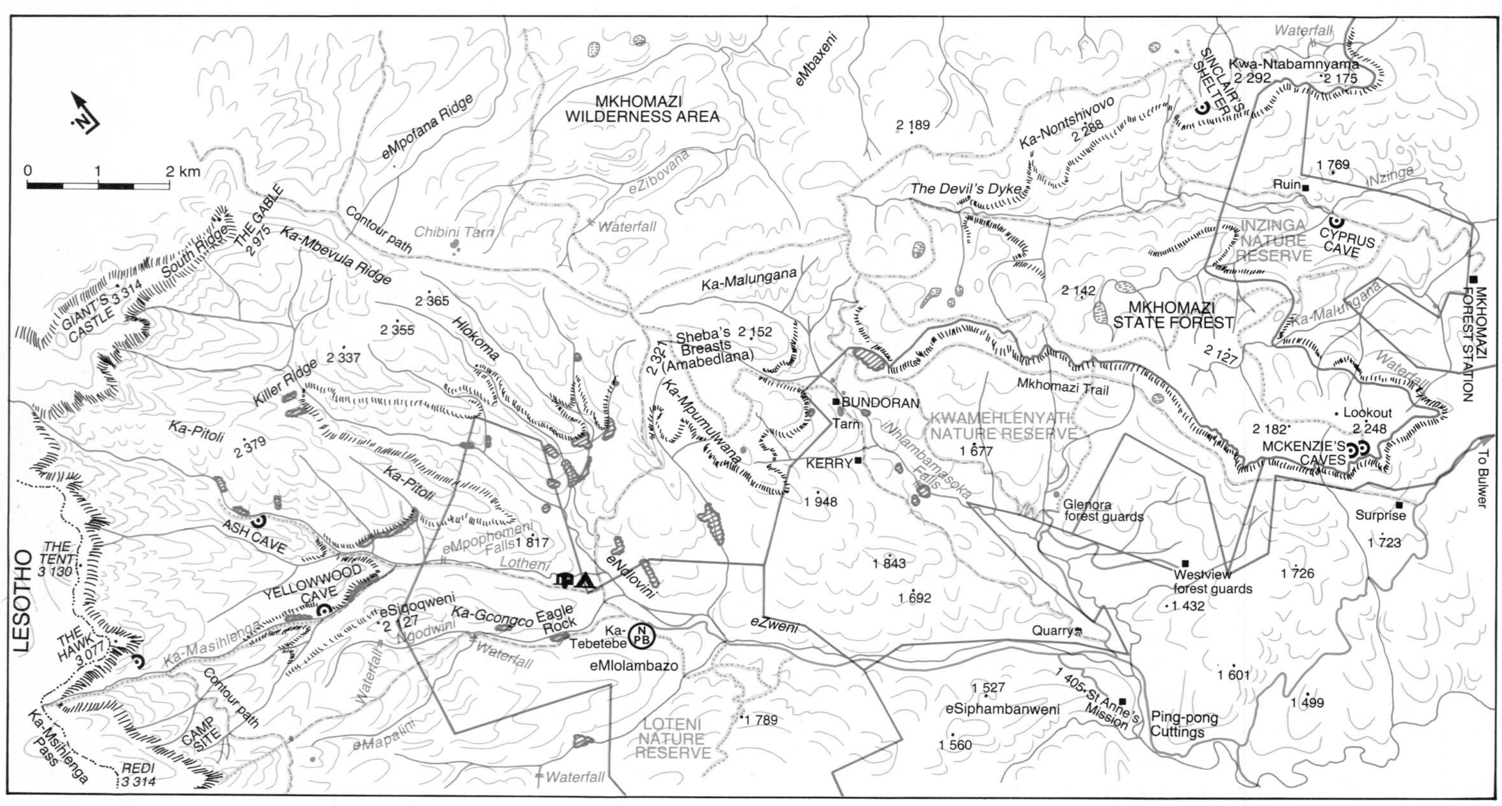

N
0 1 2 km
MKHOMAZI WILDERNESS AREA
eMpofana Ridge
eMbaxeni
eZibovana
Waterfall
Chibini Tarn
Contour path
THE GABLE 2 975
South Ridge
GIANT'S CASTLE 3 314
Ka-Mbevula Ridge
2 365
2 355
2 337
Hlokoma
Killer Ridge
Ka-Pitoli
2 379
Ka-Pitoli
ASH CAVE
THE TENT 3 130
LESOTHO
YELLOWWOOD CAVE
THE HAWK 3 077
Ka-Masihlenga
Ka-Msihlenga Pass
REDI 3 314
Contour path
CAMP SITE
eMpophomeni Falls
1 817
Lotheni
eSiqoqweni 2 127
Ngodwini
Ka-Gcongco
Eagle Rock
Waterfall
Waterfall
eMapalini
Waterfall
Ka-Tebetebe
NPB
eMlolambazo
LOTENI NATURE RESERVE
1 789
eNdlovini
eZweni
Ka-Malungana
Sheba's Breasts (Amabedlana)
2 152
2 321
Ka-Mpumulwana
BUNDORAN
Tarn
KERRY
1 948
1 843
1 692
KWAMEHLENYATHI NATURE RESERVE
1 677
iNhlambamasoka Falls
Mkhomazi Trail
2 189
Ka-Nontshivovo 2 288
The Devil's Dyke
SINCLAIR'S SHELTER
Kwa-Ntabamnyama 2 292
2 175
Waterfall
1 769
Ruin
iNzinga
INZINGA NATURE RESERVE
CYPRUS CAVE
2 142
MKHOMAZI STATE FOREST
Ka-Malungana
2 127
Waterfall
MKHOMAZI FOREST STATION
Lookout
2 248
2 182
MCKENZIE'S CAVES
To Bulwer
Glenora forest guards
Surprise
1 723
Westview forest guards
1 726
1 432
Quarry
1 601
1 499
1 527
eSiphambanweni
1 405
St Anne's Mission
Ping-pong Cuttings
1 560

MZIMKHULU

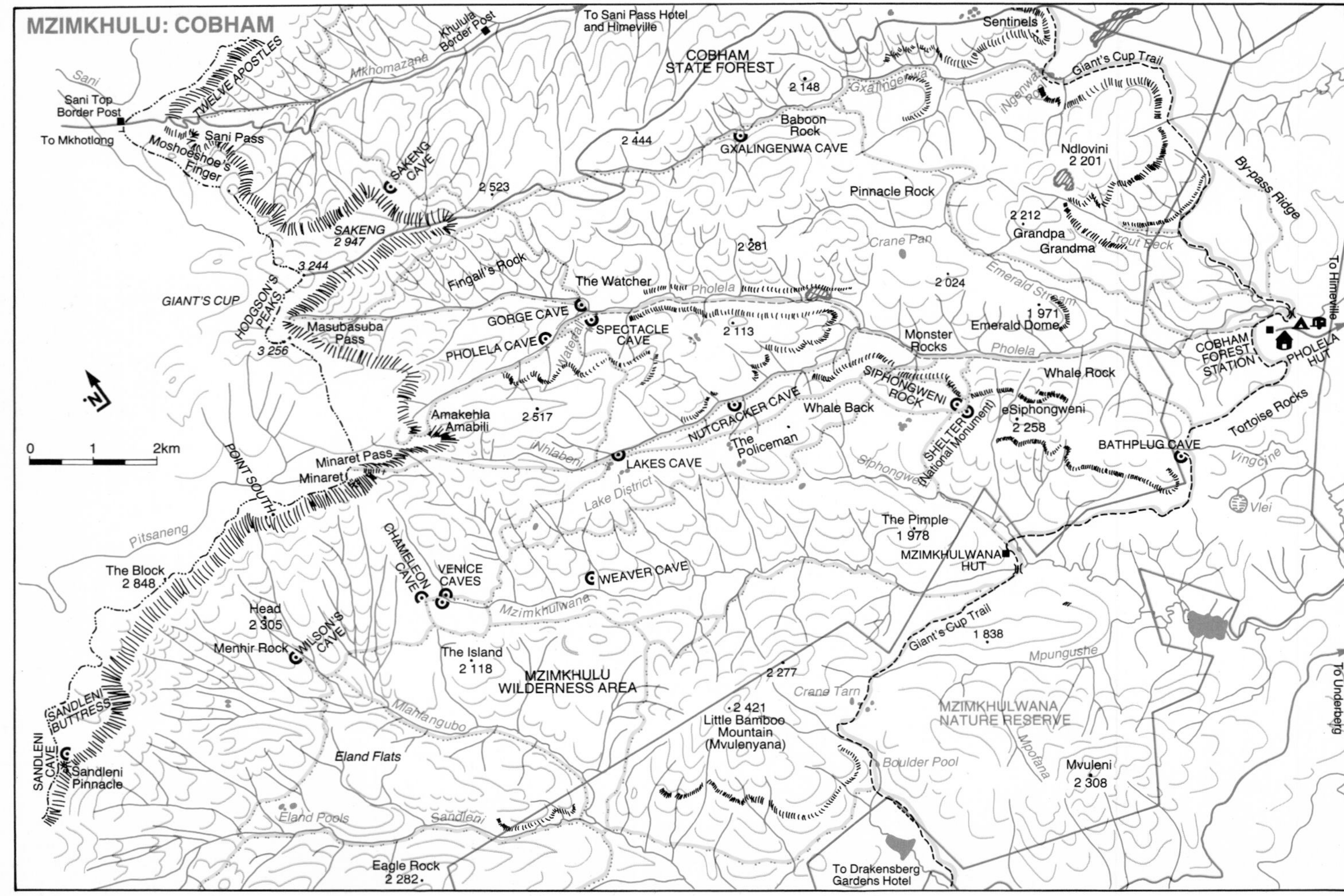
MZIMKHULU: COBHAM
To Sani Pass Hotel and Himeville
Khulula Border Post
Mkhomazana
Sani
Sani Top Border Post
To Mkhotlong
TWELVE APOSTLES
Sani Pass
Moshoeshoe's Finger
SAKENG CAVE
SAKENG 2 947
3 244
GIANT'S CUP
HODGSON'S PEAKS
Masubasuba Pass
3 256
COBHAM STATE FOREST
2 148
Gxalingenwa
Baboon Rock
2 444
GXALINGENWA CAVE
2 523
Pinnacle Rock
2 281
Fingall's Rock
The Watcher
Pholela
GORGE CAVE
SPECTACLE CAVE
PHOLELA CAVE
Waterfall
2 113
Sentinels
Giant's Cup Trail
iNgenwa Pool
Ndlovini 2 201
By-pass Ridge
2 212
Grandpa
Grandma
Trout Beck
Crane Pan
2 024
Emerald Stream
1 971
Emerald Dome
Monster Rocks
Pholela
To Himeville
COBHAM FOREST STATION
PHOLELA HUT
Whale Rock
SIPHONGWENI ROCK
eSiphongweni 2 258
Tortoise Rocks
Amakehla Amabili
2 517
0 1 2km
Minaret Pass
Minaret
POINT SOUTH
Nhlabeni
LAKES CAVE
NUTCRACKER CAVE
The Policeman
Whale Back
SHELTER (National Monument)
Siphongweni
BATHPLUG CAVE
Vingcine
Vlei
Lake District
Pitsaneng
The Block 2 848
CHAMELEON CAVE
VENICE CAVES
WEAVER CAVE
The Pimple 1 978
MZIMKHULWANA HUT
Mzimkhulwana
Head 2 305
Menhir Rock
WILSON'S CAVE
The Island 2 118
MZIMKHULU WILDERNESS AREA
Giant's Cup Trail
1 838
Mpungushe
To Underberg
2 277
Crane Tarn
SANDLENI BUTTRESS
Mlahlangubo
2 421
Little Bamboo Mountain (Mvulenyana)
MZIMKHULWANA NATURE RESERVE
Mpofana
SANDLENI CAVE
Sandleni Pinnacle
Eland Flats
Boulder Pool
Mvuleni 2 308
Eland Pools
Sandleni
Eagle Rock 2 282
To Drakensberg Gardens Hotel

2

3

4

5

6

1. *One of the many tarns above the Cobham Forest Station that gives the 'Lake District' its name. These tarns are situated on the Little Berg plateau with the Giant's Castle as a magnificent backdrop.* ***2.*** *Thaba-Ntsu, meaning 'mountain of the lammergeier', is also known as the Devil's Knuckles. This cluster of peaks is generally considered to be the tip of the dragon's tail, although the Drakensberg basalt formation continues into the north-eastern Cape.* ***3.*** *The Caves Tranverse (Hike MZ18) is a four-day hike, covering 35 kilometres. The hikers seen here are en route to Lammergeier Cave in the Bushman's River area.* ***4.*** *The water falling into Bathplug Cave, on the Giant's Cup NHW trail, disappears through a hole in the floor of the cave.*
5. *Bushman rock paintings near Sehlaba-Thebe.*
6. *Like the 'Lake District' near Cobham, the exceptionally high and extensive plateau of the Sehlaba-Thebe National Park is bejewelled with glistening mountain tarns.*

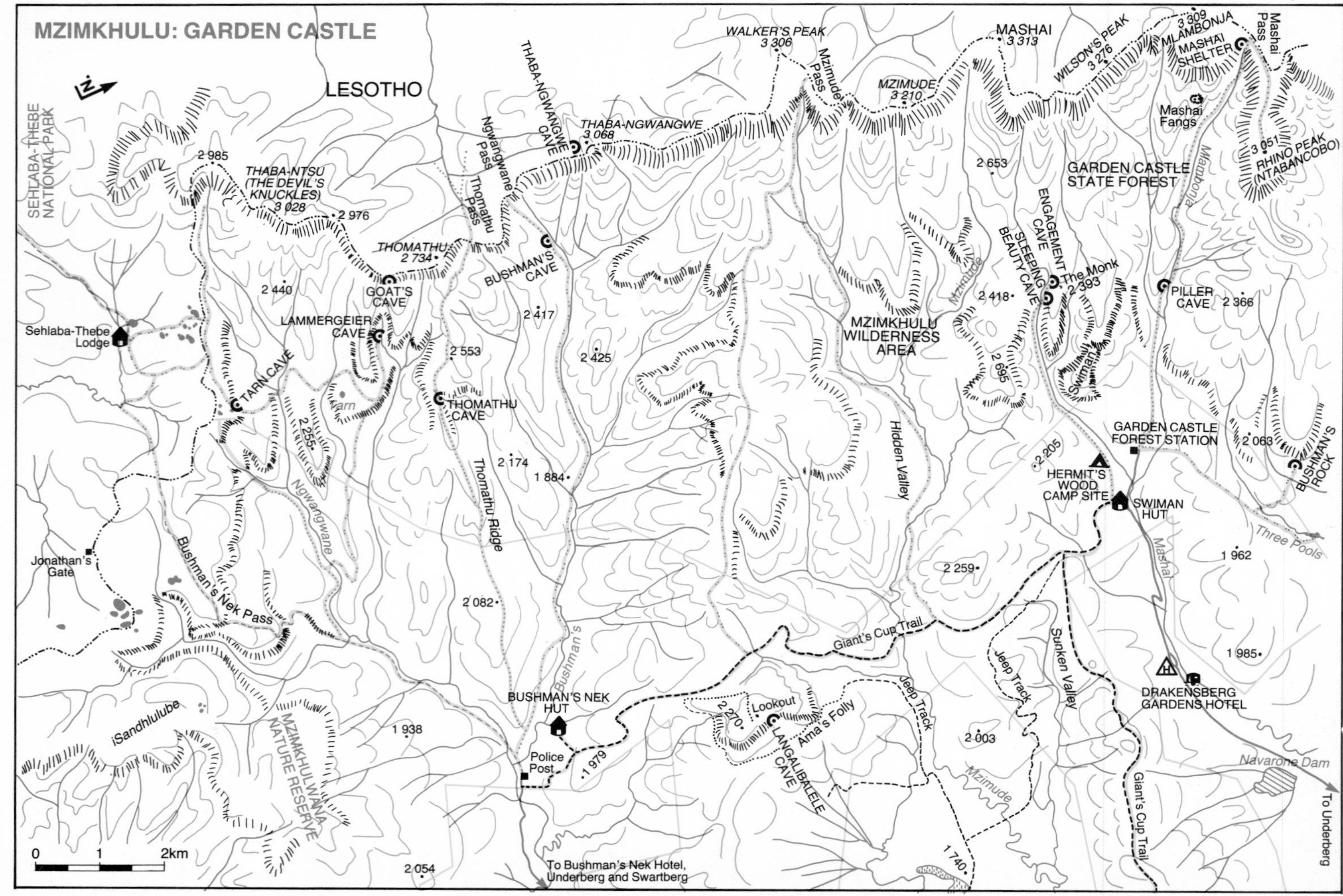
MZIMKHULU: GARDEN CASTLE
LESOTHO
SEHLABA-THEBE NATIONAL PARK
Sehlaba-Thebe Lodge
Jonathan's Gate
THABA-NTSU (THE DEVIL'S KNUCKLES) 3 028
2 985
2 976
THOMATHU 2 734
GOAT'S CAVE
LAMMERGEIER CAVE
TARN CAVE
Tarn
THOMATHU CAVE
Thomathu Pass
Ngwangwane Pass
THABA-NGWANGWE CAVE
THABA-NGWANGWE 3 068
BUSHMAN'S CAVE
WALKER'S PEAK 3 306
Mzimude Pass
MZIMUDE 3 210
MASHAI 3 313
WILSON'S PEAK 3 276
3 309
MLAMBONJA
MASHAI SHELTER
Mashai Pass
Mashai Fangs
RHINO PEAK (NTABANCOBO) 3 051
GARDEN CASTLE STATE FOREST
Mlambonja
ENGAGEMENT CAVE
SLEEPING BEAUTY CAVE
The Monk 2 393
PILLER CAVE
2 366
2 653
2 418
2 695
Swiman
MZIMKHULU WILDERNESS AREA
Mzimude
Hidden Valley
2 440
2 417
2 553
2 425
2 255
2 174
1 884
Thomathu Ridge
Ngwangwane
Bushman's Nek Pass
2 082
GARDEN CASTLE FOREST STATION
2 063
BUSHMAN'S ROCK
2 205
HERMIT'S WOOD CAMP SITE
SWIMAN HUT
Three Pools
Mashai
1 962
2 259
Giant's Cup Trail
Jeep Track
Sunken Valley
1 985
DRAKENSBERG GARDENS HOTEL
Bushman's
BUSHMAN'S NEK HUT
Police Post
1 979
Lookout
2 270
Ama's Folly
LANGALIBALELE CAVE
2 003
Mzimude
Navarone Dam
To Underberg
1 938
iSandhlulube
MZIMKHULWANA NATURE RESERVE
2 054
1 740
0 1 2km
To Bushman's Nek Hotel, Underberg and Swartberg

Continued from page 64

Blue Pool and Nyosi Grotto *Hike CR13*

Route: *Cathedral Peak Hotel to Nyosi Grotto*
Distance: *5,5 kilometres*
Duration: *2 hours*
Grade: *Easy*
General: *This is an undemanding outing from the hotel for a picnic and a swim. Stop at the Blue Pool on the Tseketseke River 3,5 km from the hotel, or venture another 1,5 km up a tributary to a small waterfall and overhang.*

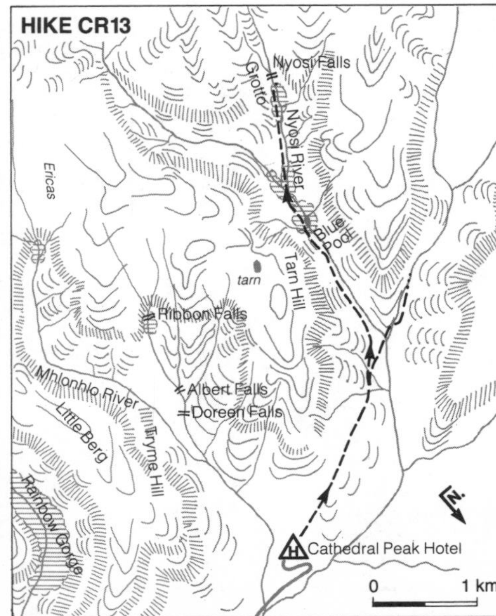

▶ Any one of three paths can be used to reach the confluence of the Mlambonja and Tseketseke rivers, but for hikers not staying at the hotel it is suggested that you follow the left-hand bank of the Mlambonja River upstream, past the trout hatchery to the river junction. Cross over to the right-hand bank of the Tseketseke River and head upstream for about 1,5 km to the delightful Blue Pool, where the picnic spot is marked by a fireplace and where you can enjoy a swim before resuming your walk.

▶ If you wish to continue on to the Nyosi Grotto, find the path running up the left-hand bank of the river and follow it for about 2 km to the junction with the Nyosi Stream, which comes in from the right. Follow the Nyosi Stream for about 1,5 km to the Nyosi Falls where the grotto will be found.

Two Passes and Cleft Peak Escarpment Hike *Hike CR14*

Route: *Mike's Pass to Cathedral Peak Hotel via Organ Pipes and Mlambonja Passes*
Distance: *37,5 kilometres*
Duration: *3 days*
Grade: *Extreme*
General: *This hike is the most popular multi-day excursion in the Cathedral area and it may be tackled from either end: the easier ascent, and the route described here, is up the Organ Pipes Pass. Unless an early start is made each day, the three days allotted for this hike will easily draw out to four days – so unless you are fit and an early riser, give yourself four days for the round trip. This is a spectacular hike with breathtaking vistas for most of the route – but keep alert for the onset of bad weather. On my first trip to the Drakensberg, while still a schoolboy, I was caught with my companions in an unexpected three-day April blizzard on Cleft Peak, an experience I shall never forget. We scarcely made it back alive and since then I have always been prepared for the worst conditions possible.*

▶ **Day 1** (13,5 km): From the top of Mike's Pass follow the jeep track for 3 km to the Contour Path. Turn left along the Contour Path for 3 km to the Nek, above Ndedema Gorge, where a path goes up the long ridge on the right to the Forestry lookout (a small, white, disused building). Take the path up the ridge and from here it is 2 km to the lookout, which is often used as an emergency bivouac. Carry on up the knife-edged ridge, first on the left-hand side and then crossing over to the other side. Be sure always to keep to the path, even though it can be tricky to follow, especially on the top of the rocky ridge or when going through rock scrambles: the exposure is at times quite exhilarating for a 'mere' hike.

▶ The Organ Pipes Pass is reached about 3 km from the lookout, and the path traverses across some boggy areas below the Organ Pipes themselves – basalt columns which stand vertically to the left and above the path. This pass was originally called Bushman's Pass (along with quite a few others), for it had long been used as a route over the Escarpment and was the site of numerous conflicts between Bushman cattle thieves and white commandos and bounty hunters. Only the last 500 m are really steep, but caution is required for most of the 5-km climb from the lookout to the top of the pass.

▶ The pass heads out at Windy Gap into a wide valley between Ndumeni Dome on the left and Castle Buttress obscuring Cleft Peak on the

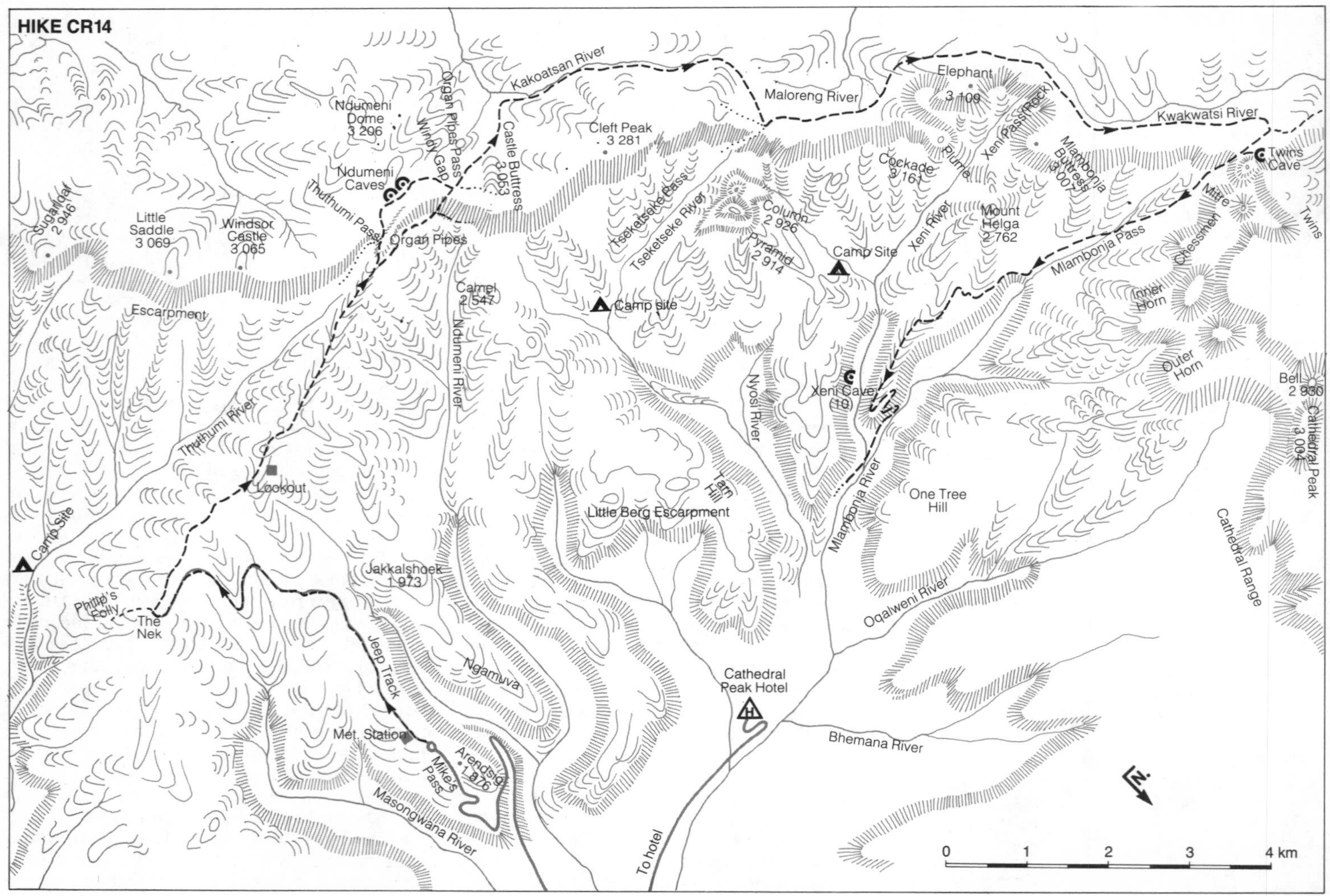
HIKE CR14
Kakoatsan River
Maloreng River
Elephant
3 109
Kwakwatsi River
Ndumeni Dome
3 206
Organ Pipes Pass
Windy Gap
Castle Buttress
3 053
Cleft Peak
3 281
Xeni Pass (Rock)
Mlambonja Buttress
3 007
Twins Cave
Ndumeni Caves
Cockade
3 161
Plume
Sugarloaf
2 946
Thuthumi Pass
Little Saddle
3 069
Windsor Castle
3 065
Organ Pipes
Tseketseke Pass
Tseketseke River
Column
2 926
Pyramid
2 914
Xeni River
Mount Helga
2 762
Mitre
Twins
Camp Site
Mlambonja Pass
Chessmen
Camel
2 547
Camp site
Escarpment
Inner Horn
Outer Horn
Ndumeni River
Xeni Cave
(10)
Bell
2 930
Thuthumi River
Nyosi River
Cathedral Peak
3 004
Lookout
Tarn Hill
One Tree Hill
Little Berg Escarpment
Mlambonja River
Camp Site
Cathedral Range
Jakkalshoek
1 973
Oqalweni River
Phillip's Folly
The Nek
Jeep Track
Ngamuva
Cathedral Peak Hotel
Met. Station
Bhemana River
Arendsig
1 876
Mike's Pass
Masongwana River
To hotel
N
0
1
2
3
4 km

Looking towards Cleft Peak, where fast-descending mist often proves hazardous to hikers.

right. This will have been a stiff 13-km hike and more than enough for one day's walking with a heavy pack, so pitch your tent in the valley and hope Ndumeni Dome does not brew up one of its notorious storms: appropriately, Ndumeni means 'the mountain of storms'. High up on the Dome there are two caves, which many people struggle to find: basically they are higher up than would be expected on the Thuthumi Pass path which comes up behind the Organ Pipes. One cave faces to the north-east and the other to the south-east, giving alternative views across the Cathedral and Cathkin areas from high vantage points.

▶ **Day 2** (12,5 km): From Windy Gap one can follow the watershed over Castle Buttress and Cleft Peak, or continue up the Kakoatsan Valley, heading out to the right, and then skirt the bases of the upward-sloping 'peaks' to rejoin the watershed on the far side of Cleft Peak. Either way no-one should miss the opportunity of scaling Cleft Peak, the highest point between Mont-aux-Sources and Champagne Castle, for the spectacular views in all directions. From here the path hugs the watershed all the way past Tseketseke and Xeni passes and on to Mlambonja Pass, 12 km from Windy Gap but a more strenuous hike than a map suggests with long, up-and-down hauls. Your hard work is rewarded, however, by the view from the path, which looks over the edge of the Escarpment.

The views are breathtaking, as Pearse describes in *Barriers of Spears*: '. . . a vast panorama of toppling crags, battlement spires, ruined towers and impregnable fortresses. Dark clefts fall sheer into valleys a thousand metres below. Peak on peak stands clearly etched against blue horizons. And everywhere there are clouds. Sometimes they sail in solemn splendour, slowly and ponderously across the sky. Sometimes they lift and curl and boil around the indifferent peaks, opening up to reveal brief, tantalising glimpses of yawning black abysses and shadowed gorges, only to close in again with their clinging white veils. And sometimes their anger boils over in a fury of storm and tempest, and the earth trembles.'

▶ From Xeni Pass the last 3 km of this section follow the right-hand bank of the Kwakwatsi River. It is easy to miss the path to Mlambonja Pass and Twins Cave as it leads off unexpectedly to the right on an upward slope; the path leads off a few hundred metres beyond the Twins, but at the imaginary hinge or saddle between the main Escarpment and the Cathedral range. To find Twins Cave, take the path to the right and descend a short way down the grassy slope. Pass over the saddle between the Escarpment and the Twins. Situated up to the right, in a band of basalt cliffs, Twins Cave is large and comfortable and should adequately suffice for the second night's stayover.

▶ **Day 3** (11,5 km): From the cave head back over the saddle and turn right, to descend the steep slope that alternates between slippery grass and crumbling scree past the Twins, the Mitre, Chessmen and the Inner Horn which appear to slip into the sky as you get lower and lower. After 2,5 km in this gully, the path crosses the Mlambonja River proper and after another 500 m it heads to the right, away from the river on a general contouring line for 2 km, and then at a side junction it begins to descend a steep spur, eventually taking in wide zigzags back to the river. The Xeni tributary is crossed where the path reaches the valley floor and thereafter it is a more gentle, 3-km downhill haul back to the hotel.

Valley of Pools *Hike CR15*

Route: *Round trip from Emhlwazeni Store via the Valley of Pools*
Distance: *29 kilometres*
Duration: *10 hours*
Grade: *Severe*
General: *This valley really lies in the Mdedelelo area and could therefore belong in the next chapter; the easiest access is, however, from Cathedral. It can also be approached from Cathkin, via Jacob's Ladder and Hospital Spruit Cave. It is described here as a round trip that should ideally be tackled over two days, or even longer if the area it to be more fully appreciated, for there are many attractions that beckon.*

▶ Start at the Emhlwazeni Store and follow the jeep track for 4 km, past the guard huts at Solar Cliffs, and crossing over the Mhlwazini River just upstream from a waterfall. At a junction you must take the left-hand fork, which curves around first left and then right to proceed up a hill known as The Climb, following a stream's course. At the base of the cliffs the path reaches a T-junction where you take the left-hand branch once again. This leads into the valley of the Nkwazi River, or the Valley of Pools.

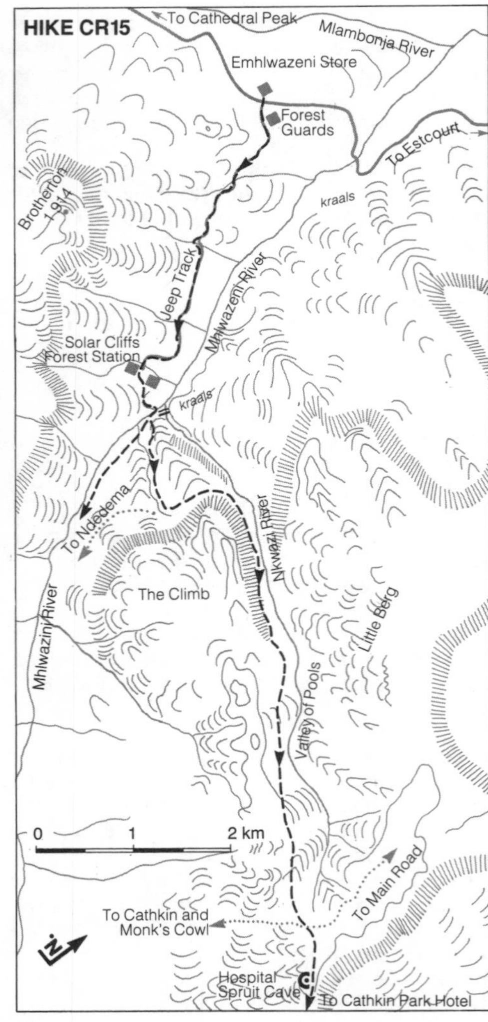

▶ The path follows the right-hand side of the valley, but always climbs above the river for 6 km, with a few steep sections along the way. Finally the path climbs out of the valley and up to the Little Berg where a four-way junction is reached. Turn sharply right here along a peninsula-like plateau for 2 km and then head down to the left into the Hospital Spruit valley and down to the river. On reaching the river, turn right and head down the right-hand bank of the river, curving around to the right where the Hospital Spruit joins the Mhlwazini River. From the path the vista stretches out across the Little Berg, past the eye-of-the-needle peak of Intunja to the Dragon's Back sweeping up to Champagne Castle and the imposing Cathkin Peak. At the four-way junction above the Valley of Pools, the path off to the left heads for 3 km along the Little Berg, where a path to the left leads down to the Crystal Beds and The Maze.

▶ The path then heads down the right-hand side of the Mhlwazini Valley for 5 km, crossing the river after 3 km, to the camp site where Ndedema Gorge branches off to the left. From the camp site, cross the river and head down the right-hand river bank for 3 km to another crossing, meeting the path which leads up The Climb. From this point the path leads away from the river to the left and it is 4 km back to the Emhlwazeni Store.

Contour Path – Cathedral to Ndedema *Hike CR16*

Route: *Cathedral Peak Hotel to Ndedema Gorge*
Distance: *35 kilometres*
Duration: *3 days*
Grade: *Moderate to Severe*
General: *This hike starts where the constructed Contour Path begins. The original Contour Path was built in 1937 by J. van Heynigen, the then forester at Monk's Cowl, to link up the Cathkin and Cathedral areas, keeping roughly to the 2 000 m level, curving in and out of the valleys and over the spurs. Since then, the path has been extended, and in some places its course has been changed. The Natal Parks Board, too, has extended its Contour Path northwards from Giant's Castle to meet the Forestry path on the border of Injasuti at, appropriately, Van Heynigen's Pass. This section of the path traverses the most rugged terrain in the area and is therefore more strenuous and tortuous: as far as I know, this section of the Contour Path is seldom tackled as a complete hike; nevertheless, it is most dramatic and challenging.*

▶ From the hotel take the Cathedral Peak path (Hike CR1) up to the 2 100 m contour level as this is where the Contour Path begins. From this point you can see the path as it winds its way around the Oqalweni Valley above the tree line. There is a camp site among the cycads at the spot where the path crosses the Oqalweni River and from here it carries on to above One Tree Hill, 7 km from the start where it joins another path coming uphill. The path then cuts back sharply to the right heading into a deep gully where the squat Drakensberg protea (*Protea dracomontana*) is encountered. After crossing a tributary of the Mlambonja River the path again heads out around a ridge coming down from the Inner Horn and then it turns sharply back again to enter the Mlambonja Valley.

▶ After crossing the river the Contour Path forms a 2-km section of the Mlambonja Pass path, before turning sharply around a spur while the pass heads off down the same spur toward Xeni Cave. From this point begins a 7,5-km stretch, which wriggles in and out of the contorted landscape, up over ridges and down to cross streams and gullies, past cycads, protea thickets and boggy areas, to emerge at the Tseketseke camp site, below Cleft Peak where there is a hut with a vaulted corrugated iron roof. From the camp site the path heads into another valley and then out around what might be called the hump on the Camel's back.

▶ From here the path becomes a well-defined jeep track, and it takes a wide loop around the Camel's second hump, where a lesser path heads off down the ridge towards Tryme Hill. Then, it's back towards the Escarpment, with a tight 'S' bend on the way to the Ndumeni River below the Organ Pipes Pass. From the river it is a 4-km hike to meet the jeep track coming up from Mike's Pass car park, between the Ofandweni and Masongwana gorges. Follow the main, high jeep track and do not be tempted into taking a lower 'short cut', essentially leading nowhere.

▶ The Contour Path heads more or less uphill from the Mike's Pass path junction, through the burnt-out remains of an old pine plantation, to the Nek at the base of the long ridge which leads up past the old Forestry lookout to the Organ Pipes Pass. At the Nek, turn left to descend down the grassy slope of Philip's Folly towards a side branch of Ndedema Gorge. The path heads down for a few hundred metres, then contours off to the right, turns back down for another few hundred metres and then does a 1-km deviation off to the right again before descending finally to the camp site at the head of the main Ndedema Gorge. From the camp site there is a grand view down the full length of this magnificent gorge, where the rushing waters reverberate as they gush down between the sandstone cliffs and gurgle along its floor (in Zulu, Ndedema means 'the place that reverberates').

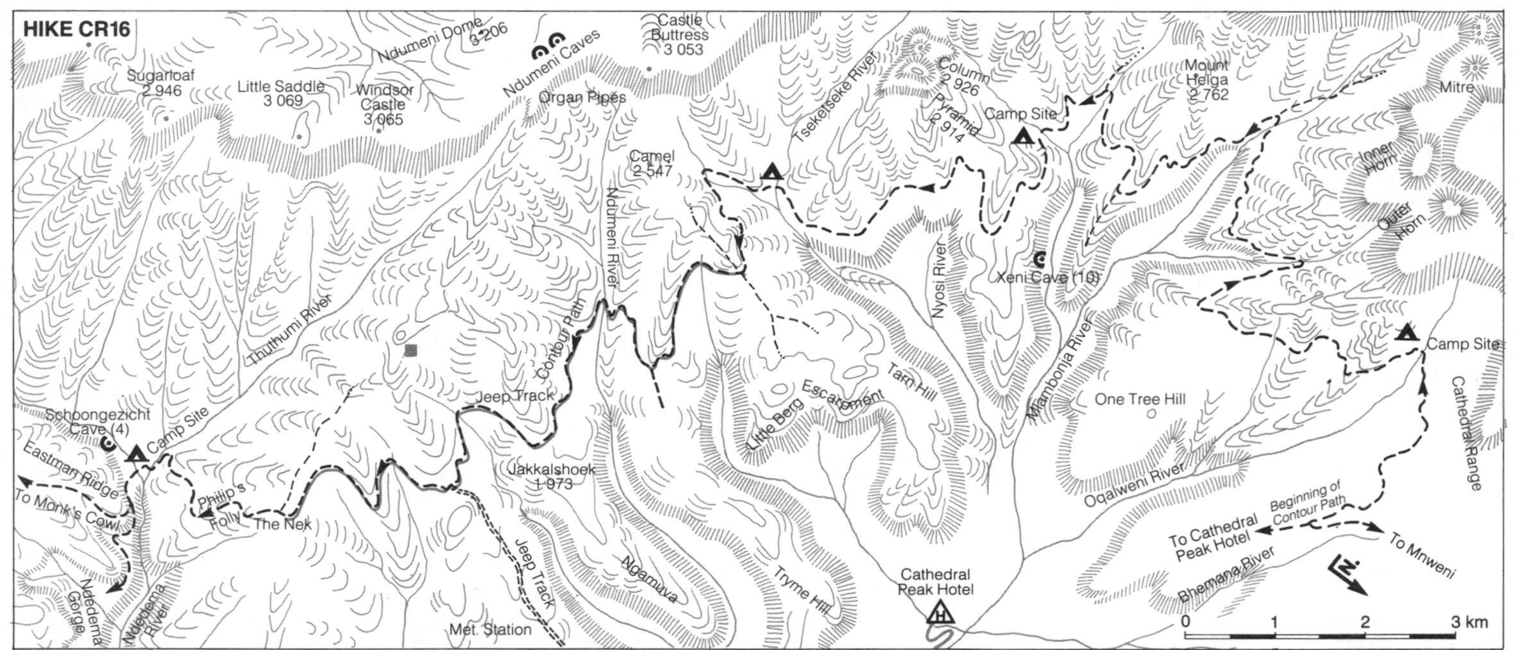

MDEDELELO

Mdedelelo, or 'the bully', is the Zulu name for Cathkin Peak, which thrusts its massive form out from the Escarpment, dominating the area. It is also the name of the Wilderness Area that stretches from the Giant's Castle boundary near the Old Woman Stream in the south to Ndedema Gorge in the north. The headland behind Cathkin finds its highest point at Champagne Castle (3 377 m), which is the second highest peak in South Africa. Its name derives supposedly from the first known ascent of the peak by Major Grantham in 1861: his batman is said to have broken the bottle of bubbly which had been earmarked for consumption on the summit. The ascent of Champagne Castle is via Gray's Pass and involves nothing more than a long slog except, of course, during severe winters. Cathkin Peak is another matter.

This peak is guarded on all sides by precipitous cliffs. The first attempt on the mountain was made in 1888 by the formidable Stocker brothers, who reached within 150 metres of the summit before being turned back by what looked like an unclimbable wall. Between then and 1912 many attempts were made on the peak from various angles, until the final approach was successfully negotiated up the South Gully in 1912 by George Amphlett, Father Kelly and four others. Since then, other, harder routes have been forged up taunting Mdedelelo, claiming a number of lives.

One of George Thomson's (he of Column fame) earliest climbs was up Cathkin Peak one Christmas Eve. Leading near the top, he found an old rope, which he foolishly began to climb. Needles to say, the rope and Thomson hurtled past his companions to land on a ledge 30 metres below. Concussion and a broken ankle weren't enough to deter this marvel of the mountains and he proceeded to finish the climb, only to be pelted by a furious thunderstorm. Eventually he asked his companions to go for help. The next morning a mounted party from Champagne Castle Hotel found him at the bottom of the peak, which he had descended alone during the night, crawling home on his hands and knees.

Between Cathkin Peak and the Escarpment looms Monk's Cowl, to many climbers, including myself, the most ominous of all the Drakensberg's peaks. The Zulus call it 'Nkosana' or chief, for that is just what it looks like, an animated bringer of divine justice to those who flaunt its precipitous walls. Monk's Cowl was first climbed in 1942 by J. Botha, E. Ruhle, A. Hooper and H. Wong, but the first attempt was made in 1938 by Colin Gebhardt and Dick Barry. Dubbed 'the Tiger' by his contemporaries, Barry was one of the finest climbers ever, although he was only 28 years old when he made this fateful climb. It was to be Barry's first and last trip to the Drakensberg, for he plummeted to his death from the Cowl after an ordeal made all the more tragic by his tenacity. Barry lies buried in a grove of trees near the Cathkin Park Hotel, from where the tip of Monk's Cowl is just visible.

Nkosana is also the name of the inexpensive and informal mountaineers' lodge in the area. The host, Ed Salomons, is an experienced mountaineer and his policy is always to have a soft bed and a warm meal available for tired hikers and climbers. Other accommodation offered in this popular area includes the Cathkin Park Hotel, the Nest, established in 1858 on the farm belonging to David Gray, El Mirador Hotel, two luxury caravan parks, well-appointed bungalows and, at the time of writing, Southern Suns was bulldozing ahead in the construction of a new hotel, despite objections from far and wide. Lawn tennis courts and a lush nine-hole golf course are situated in this area, which is also home to the Drakensberg Boys Choir, as well as that child of the Drakensberg, Reg Pearse, who lives at Emkhizweni, the 'place of misty rain' in the shade of Cathkin Peak. At Monk's Cowl Forest Station there is a grassed and terraced camp site with showers and toilets, but it tends to become a quagmire during the summer, especially when churned up by cars and caravans.

It should by now be clear that we are in the most popular holiday area of the Drakensberg. Access is by tarred road from Winterton, crossing the Bergville-Estcourt road midway. All hikes in the area begin either at Monk's Cowl Forest Station, where wilderness permits must be obtained, or from Cathkin Park Hotel. Apart from Slingsby's map, there is another, drawn up by Reg Pearse and J. Peck and available from Emkhizweni and Champagne Castle Hotel, and yet another available from the Dragon Peaks Caravan Park, drawn up by its proprietor. The Cathkin Park Hotel also sells a simple map and booklet covering some of the hikes in the area.

(Opposite.) Barry's Grave faces Monk's Cowl, where Dick Barry, who, during a climbing accident in January 1938, 'gave up his life to the mountains he loved'.

Fern Forest *Hike MD1*

Route: *Cathkin Park Hotel to Fern Forest*
Distance: *1 kilometre*
Duration: *30 minutes*
Grade: *Easy*
General: *This is a short, enchanting walk along a forested stream to a waterfall and a picnic spot surrounded by verdant coolness: ferns and brightly coloured fungi, tall yellowwood and massive, buttressed mountain hard pear trees and thick, twisted climbers. There is some confusion between Pearse's and Slingsby's maps regarding this hike, but I think that Slingsby's Forthlo Forest is actually Fern Forest, whereas Pearse's Fern Forest is really Kwa-Ndema Forest. (Precise directions can be obtained from the reception at the Cathkin Park Hotel.)*

▶ Starting from the hotel's tennis courts, pass between the stables and the servants' quarters and through a paddock gate into a black wattle (*Acacia mearnsii*) thicket (this tree is commercially important, but left unchecked it becomes a ruthless invader of our forests and riverine bush and its spread is now something of a national problem). At a fork in the thicket take the path marked 'Fern Forest' and then follow the stream bank to the waterfall, or from the hotel take a path more to the right, following a bridle path over a stream and then up a short but steep, protea-clad slope.

▶ Continue along a fence and descend into the Fern Forest through the trees along a short, unstable path. The waterfall, which is upstream, can be reached by ducking under fallen trees and occasionally using stepping stones in the river bed. Crossing when necessary, return along the river bank to the hotel.

Barry's Grave and the Grotto *Hike MD2*

Route: *Round trip from Cathkin Park Hotel via Barry's Grave and the Grotto*
Distance: *7 kilometres*
Duration: *2 hours and 30 minutes*
Grade: *Fair*
General: *A pleasant, diverse walk through grass, along wattle plantation and into forest. The forest will be of special interest to bird enthusiasts; robin and thrush, shrike and flycatcher, batis and the occasional chat – all seem uncharacteristically visible. Barry's Grave should be of interest to climbers, for he was 'the Tiger' among a hardy breed, and particularly to those who have climbed or are planning to climb the Cowl.*

▶ Pass the hotel's tennis courts and stables and enter the dense black wattle thicket. Here you can turn right to the grave or left to the Grotto. Take the right-hand path for 1,5 km, which leads out of the wattles and up a protea-covered spur towards Jacob's Ladder. Beware of the criss-crossing cattle paths, all of which are culs-de-sac. After 2 km, a path leads off to the left, through more wattle plantations and across grass and broken slopes. It crosses a stream shaded by indigenous bush and leads to Barry's Grave, which is surrounded by a low stone wall near a wattle grove.

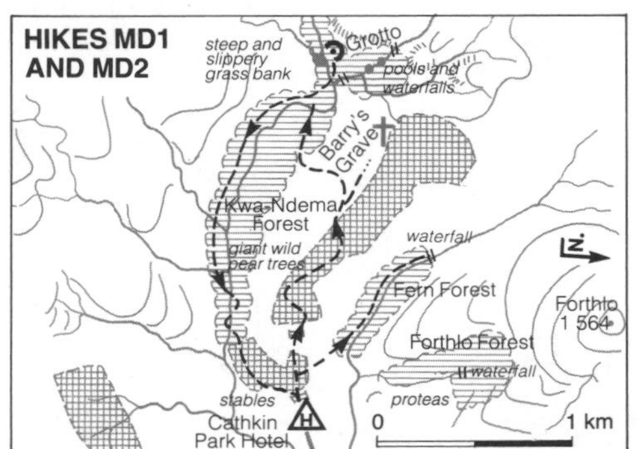

▶ From the grave, carry on diagonally into the Ndema Valley; approaching from the right, it is 1 km to the Grotto, an overhang next to a waterfall and pool, vaulted by tall forest trees. A little before reaching the Grotto one has to cross the river beneath another, higher waterfall. The stream above this waterfall can be explored by way of some ingenious route-finding but there are no paths and it becomes extremely dangerous in the rainy season – but you will be rewarded by some enchanting 'hanging' pools and cascades.

▶ From the Grotto it is 3 km back to the hotel, along the right-hand stream bank, past stout pear trees (*Olinia emarginata*) draped with heavy, twisted strands of monkey rope (*Secamone* sp.) and dense patches of ferns and large tree ferns (*Alsophila dregei*) festooned with silky spider webs, vivid lichens and fungal blooms on the damp, mossy tree trunks while butterfiles and small forest birds flit and sail in and out of laser-like columns of light. The path crosses the river and finally gives way to sterile wattle thicket just before the hotel is reached.

Stable Cave *Hike MD3*

Route: *Cathkin Park Hotel to Stable Cave*
Distance: *9,5 kilometres*
Duration: *3 hours and 30 minutes to 4 hours*
Grade: *Moderate*
General: *Although the route described here ascends the Steilberg to the top of the Little Berg, it is possible to go via Jacob's Ladder, beginning on the path past Barry's Grave (Hike MD2). The cave looks north from a narrow ridge of the Little Berg plateau towards the Valley of Pools.*

▶ The path up Steilberg begins 1 km before the hotel, on a bend before the Nkwakwa River. It leads uphill to the left (south-west), heading for a long spur where the path is clearly defined. After 5 km, the path steepens for about 1 km after which you will be more or less on the Little Berg plateau. At the skew junction turn back sharply to the left for 600 m, ignoring the side junction to the left 200 m on.

▶ At the next skew junction turn sharp right to traverse for 3 km along a thin, corridor-like ridge of the Little Berg and past Eagle Gorge, which drops off to the left. The path then zigzags down a short slope, at the bottom of which you must turn left. The path contours to Stable Cave 300 m away on the north-west slope of Verkykerskop (2 050 m), looking down into a valley and across to Vaalribbokkop (1 989 m). From here there are superb views down into the Mhlwazini and Nkosazana valleys to the west, with all the associated ridges and gorges.

▶ Jacob's Ladder ascends to a point just beyond the Stable Cave turn-off on the main ridge path. From the top of the Ladder, continue straight along the Little Berg ridge, going down and then up across a 2 km-long nek which looks like an isthmus connecting two Little Berg islands. The path leads straight to Hospital Spruit Cave, which is situated just below the top of the ridge, facing north-east. From here the more adventurous hikers can continue to the Valley of Pools, Crystal Beds and The Maze before reaching the lower Ndedema Gorge camp site at the point where the Ndedema River joins the Mhlwazini River.

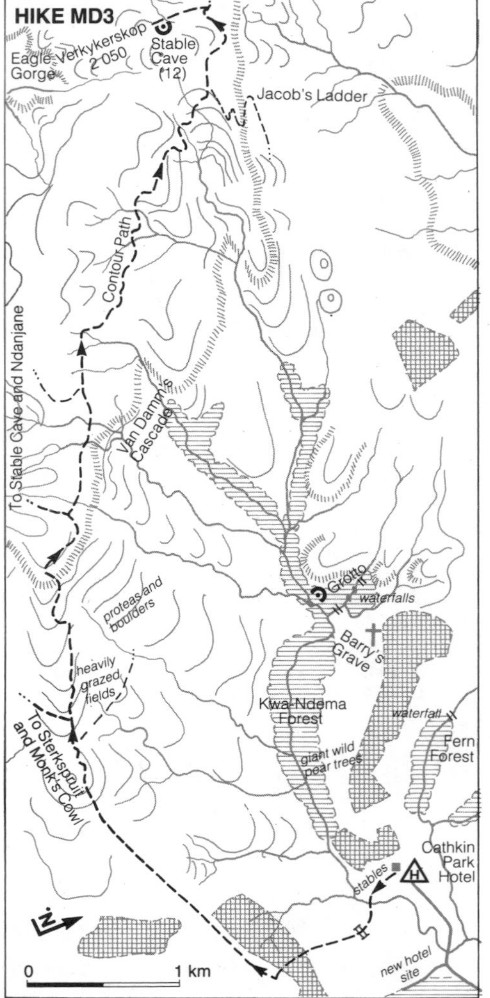

Jacob's Ladder and Van Damm's Cascade *Hike MD4*

Route: *Cathkin Park Hotel to Van Damm's Cascade*
Distance: *15 kilometres*
Duration: *6 hours*
Grade: *Moderate*
General: *This hike is something of a variation of the previous one to Stable Cave. I first 'discovered' the path to Van Damm's Cascade when floundering chest-high on bracken- and heath-covered slopes in search of an ever-elusive route between Fern Forest (Hike MD1) and the Grotto (Hike MD2). The moral of this scratchy tale is a basic tenet of 'Berg hiking: there is no such thing as a short cut. Any deviation from the established paths can be dangerous and ecologically harmful.*

▶ Take the Steilberg path starting on the left, 1 km before Cathkin Park Hotel (Hike MD3). The path climbs the long Steilberg ridge to the top of the Little Berg. At the 6- km mark, just below the top of the Little Berg level, there is a T-junction leading to the right. (The path to the left takes you to the top of the Little Berg ridge and on to Stable Cave). Take the right-hand path along an easy, slightly uphill traverse. The protea-studded traverse below the top of the ridge leads to a

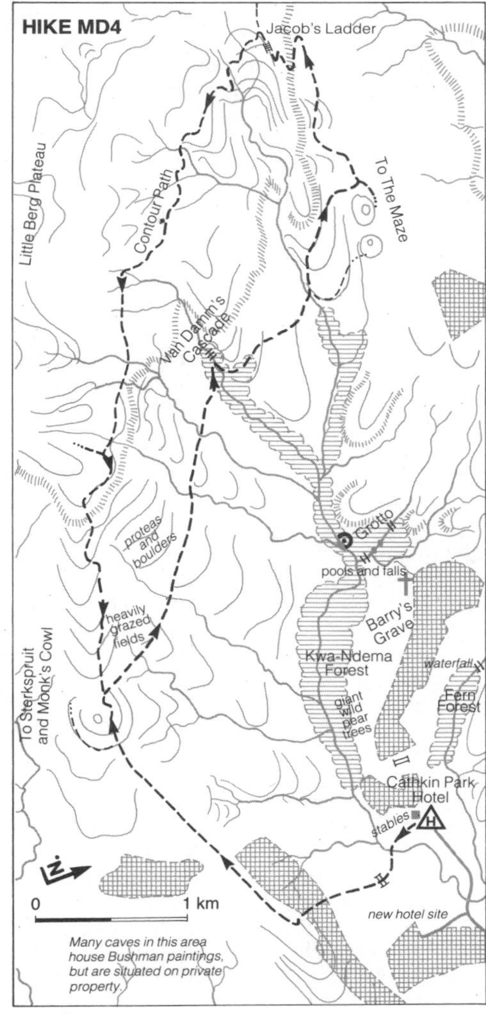

forest marking a deeply incised river course, on which you will find Van Damm's Cascade.

▶ Just before the forest a faint path (not shown on Slingsby's map) leads off down the slippery grass slope to the right to the Grotto (Hike MD2). Take this path, which leads to Van Damm's Stream and then leaves the forest, joining with the Jacob's Ladder path after 2 km. The junction is on the outer-most point of a tight, 1-km loop on the Ladder. This loop bypasses two breast-shaped koppies below the section of the path actually referred to as Jacob's Ladder. Proceed up the Ladder for 1 km to a junction, turn left and after 100 m bear right to Stable Cave on a cul-de-sac. If, however, you bear left at the Stable Cave intersection, you will pass Verkykerskop as you continue along an eroded section of the path and along the Little Berg ridge.

▶ After 3 km turn sharp left and then left again at the second side junction, 800 m past the previous turn-off. From here the path descends the Steilberg for 6 km from where you look down into the Kwa-Ndema Forest. Along this section it is almost impossible to lose the path, which eventually reaches the road to Cathkin Park just before the Nkwakwa River.

Crystal Falls and The Sphinx *Hike MD5*

Route: *Monk's Cowl Forest Station to The Sphinx*
Distance: *3 kilometres*
Duration: *1 hour 20 minutes*
Grade: *Fair*
General: *This hike is the beginning section of all the hikes radiating from the forest station. It is fairly steep but picturesque and varied, although one does not have views of the Escarpment until gaining a higher vantage point. The destination never fails to excite me, both for the majesty of the main peaks and for the romance associated with their heroic and tragic climbing histories.*

▶ From the guard hut at the gate of the forest station, where wilderness permits must be obtained and the mountain register completed, walk up the road towards the forester's office. A hiking sign some 500 m further on alerts one to the path branching off to the left to follow a stream uphill to a gate, where it becomes boggy in wet conditions. Go through the gate and along a fence (on private land) and then bear left through a kraal, where young 'nkosazazasana' will try to sell you carved knopkieries and walking sticks of varying quality – support local industry or spare the rod and soil your legs. Below you and to the left near two prominent koppies is a cave known as Maartens' Shelter, a favourite among mountaineers in days gone by.

▶ The path reaches a lower sandstone band and turns right to ascend this. The inclined path leads under a sandstone promontory, called The Sphinx for the way it projects its head-like overhang. Before the top of this formation is reached, the path turns off to the left and into a

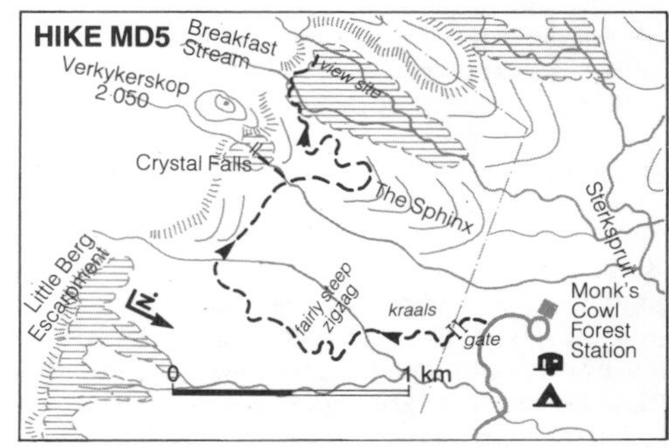

small wooded gorge. Once your eyes become accustomed to the gloom, a waterfall and pool can be seen deeper in the gorge. Crystal Falls is a welcome respite on a hot day for this hike carrys on ever upward.

▶ Continue up past the sandstone overhangs to the top of The Sphinx (not to be confused with the formation of the same name next to Ndedema Dome on the main Escarpment), where a community of silvery-leafed *Protea roupelliae* grows. From here one gains views of the KwaHlathikulu Forest and Sterkspruit Valley.

Sterkspruit Falls and Gorge *Hike MD6*

Route: *Monk's Cowl Forest Station to Sterkspruit Falls and Gorge*
Distance: *15 kilometres*
Duration: *6 hours*
Grade: *Moderate to Severe*
General: *This is an exciting full day's hike if rests, tea and lunch breaks are included. It is a rugged outing involving some rather tenuous paths, boulder hopping and river crossings much of the way. Few of the paths referred to here are shown on Slingsby's map, but they are known by the more avid local ramblers, so persevere.*

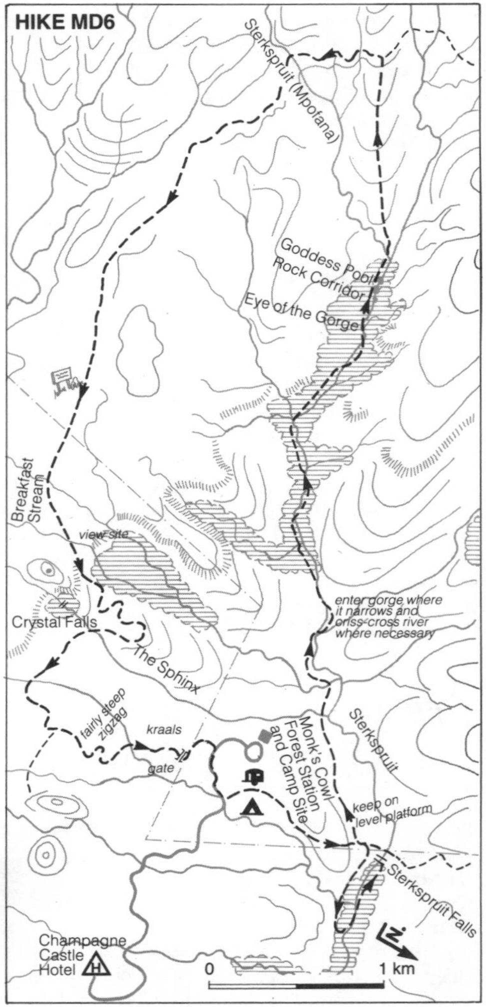

▶ From Monk's Cowl camp site follow a faint path parallel to and on the left-hand bank of the stream going down into Waterfall Bush, which straddles Sterkspruit. Half-way down to the valley the path joins the Forestry fence and follows it to the river, just above Sterkspruit Falls. Take care when entering the river near the lip of the falls as the rocks are slippery and dangerous.

In April 1969, a flash flood occurred here, with a 2 m-high wall of water washing tons of rock over the falls. The pool and forest below were obliterated, but the scars have now more or less healed. The pool, which is slowly reforming, can be reached by following the downstream left-hand bank for about 200 m, where a steep but obvious path leads down to the river below the falls.

▶ Avoid the falls by cutting across the valley on your left when you spot them. Skirt the hillside by finding a path on the first level platform below the steeper section, otherwise the going along here will be tough rather than enjoyable. Follow this path along the outer edge of the platform to where the gorge narrows and then go down to the river, criss-crossing and wading where necessary, but always keeping to the main, right-hand river course.

▶ You will pass through the Eye of the Gorge and along The Rock Corridor (neither of which is on Slingsby's map) until you reach Goddess Pool – a section as enchanting as Rainbow Gorge (Hike CR7) in the Cathedral area. The general inaccessibility of this hike, though, adds dimensions of seclusion and adventure not apparent in the other. A little way beyond Goddess Pool the gorge divides into two lesser ravines separated by a steep knoll. Climb this knoll until you reach the Contour Path at the base of the Amphlett (named after it's first ascender, one George Amphlett). Turn left to Blind Man's Corner (the first junction, after 1,25 km, is wrongly marked on Slingsby's original map). Take the side path to the left here, from where it is a clearly defined ramble along the Little Berg plateau with Cathkin Peak, 'the bully', leering at your back. The path crosses Breakfast Stream near Verkykerskop (again, not to be confused with its namesake above Jacob's Ladder), descends to The Sphinx and then loops down to the forest station.

View from Champagne Castle.

Champagne Castle via Gray's Pass *Hike MD7*

Route: *Monk's Cowl Forest Station to Champagne Castle*
Distance: *19 kilometres*
Duration: *9 hours*
Grade: *Extreme*
General: *The first officially recorded ascent of Champagne Castle was in 1888 by the Stocker brothers, who made impressive first ascents of many of the highest peaks between Giant's Castle and Mont-aux-Sources, thereby setting an astoundingly high standard of Alpinism in what was then a wild and unexplored range. They also made the first map of the range between these two points, in itself an astonishing feat of exploration and precision for those times. As has been said in the introduction to this chapter, no technical ability is needed for this long slog, which goes up the Mhlwazini Valley, between Champagne Castle and Dragon's Back on the right and Cathkin and Monk's Cowl on the left, with views so dramatic that if the path doesn't take your breath away, then the scenery certainly will.*

▶ From Monk's Cowl Forest Station follow the Bridle Path past The Sphinx (Hike MD5) and up past Verkykerskop, cross Breakfast Stream to reach the Little Berg plateau and then head straight towards the menacing Cathkin Peak, past the Mdedelelo Wilderness Area sign, to meet the Contour Path at Blind Man's Corner (marked as M3 2100 on Slingsby's map). Turn right along the Contour Path, which is an easy stroll winding in and out of river gullies, pass-

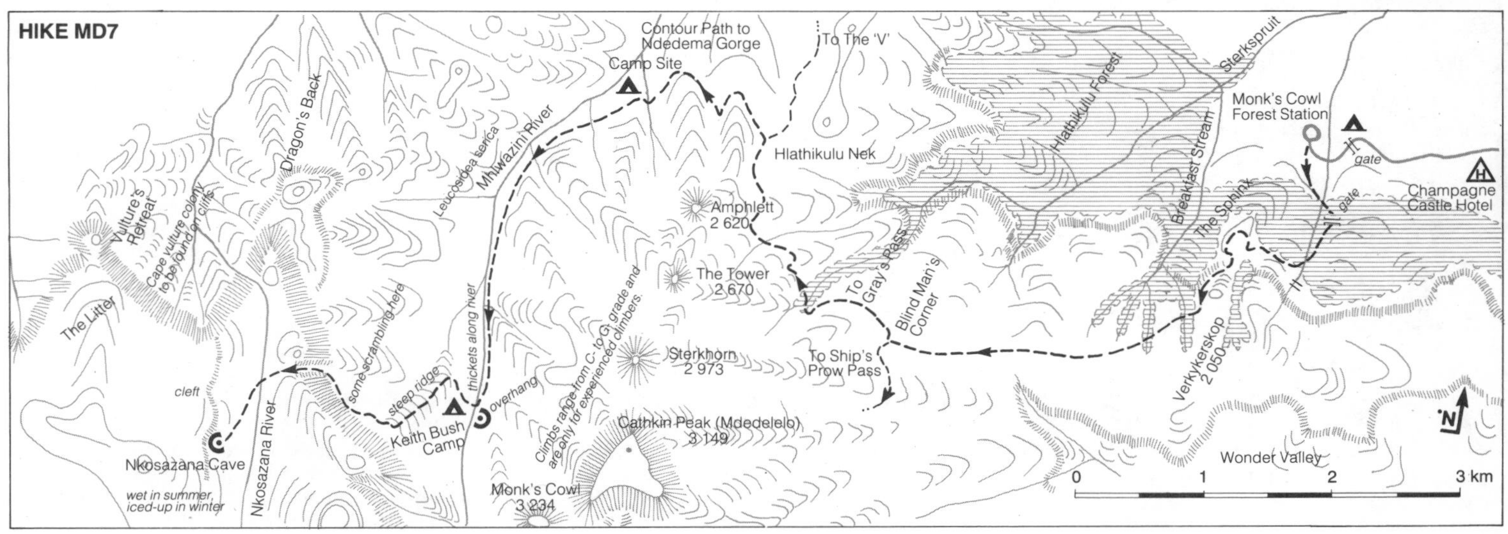

The waterfall at Vulture's Retreat plunges down the cutback between the Dragon's Back and The Litter. Hikers can reach this point via Gray's Pass (Hike MD7).

ing along the southern flank of Cathkin Peak, Sterkhorn, The Tower and the Amphlett to Hlathikulu Nek where you must turn left around the base of the Amphlett.

▶ One and a half kilometres from the nek, an eroded path descends into the Mhlwazini Valley. Here you must take the left fork, keeping the Amphlett on your left. This path heads slightly uphill along the left-hand bank of the river for 4 km, crossing the river below Keith Bush Camp on the northern base of Cathkin Peak. (There used to be a mountain hut here called Base Camp, but it has since been removed in keeping with the policy of keeping Wilderness Areas pristine. There is, however, a cave on the opposite side of the river, surrounded by boulders and ouhout trees, which serves as a convenient shelter for late arrivals.) The camp was named in memory of Keith Bush who died here on 20 September, 1955. That day Bush and two others made the first successful ascent of the North Face of Cathkin Peak, but while abseiling down the sheer upper cliff his anchoring sling broke and Bush plunged hundreds of metres to his death.

Standing on the level site of the old Base Camp hut is a grove of ouhout (*Leucosidea sericea*) bushes, which glow in autumn with the scarlet minarets of *Leonotis* flowers. This plant is also called wild dagga because its leaves are dried and smoked by the Zulus. In the late afternoon the sun casts its copper plating on the Monk's Cowl, giving this normally dark, cloud-shrouded peak a warmer countenance.

▶ Gray's Pass begins on the hill slightly upstream and to the right of the camp. It keeps to the crest of the ridge and does not follow a stream's gully as shown on the map. The slope is badly eroded, with the erosion barriers tenaciously hanging on, so take care not to damage them further, keeping to the path where possible.

▶ After about 1 km of steep climbing you will reach the lower reaches of the basalt cliffs. Here the path swings to the right and follows the cliff line for about 1,5 km of less strenuous climbing. Keep an eye out for the baboons often encountered around here. Finally, the path makes for the short but steep gully between the top of the Dragon's Back and the ramparts of Champagne Castle. This gully is very rocky and the path winds back and forth across its width. From the top of the pass it is a short walk across boggy ground across the upper Nkosazana River to view Vulture's Retreat and the waterfall which plunges in long trailing veils down the Escarpment, while in winter it ceases to flow, frozen solid in walls of ice and huge hanging icicles.

Looking from here across to The Litter you should see the large Cape vulture colony and you can watch these massive sailplanes gliding the updraughts for hours. The view to the north takes a line across the Cathedral Range to the Devil's Tooth and the Eastern Buttress of the Amphitheatre. Although it seems wasteful not to climb to the top of Champagne Castle while up here, I haven't found a better vantage point than the one at the top of Vulture's Retreat. The highest point of Champagne Castle is set about 2,5 km back from the Escarpment corner nearest to Monk's Cowl, but the best spot from which to see the Cowl, Cathkin Peak and the scaly back of Sterkhorn is from the prominent hill between Champagne Castle and the top of Gray's Pass.

▶ To reach Nkosazana ('little chief' or 'heir') Cave cross the stream and head a few hundred metres upstream, following the cairns. In summer the floor of the cave is a slushy bog while in winter it is more comfortably frozen solid. The long valley here is a favourite grazing area for the Basotho's herds in summer, so don't be surprised to find horses and cattle, as well as many ice rats, sharing your camp site.

Champagne Castle via Ship's Prow Pass *Hike MD8*

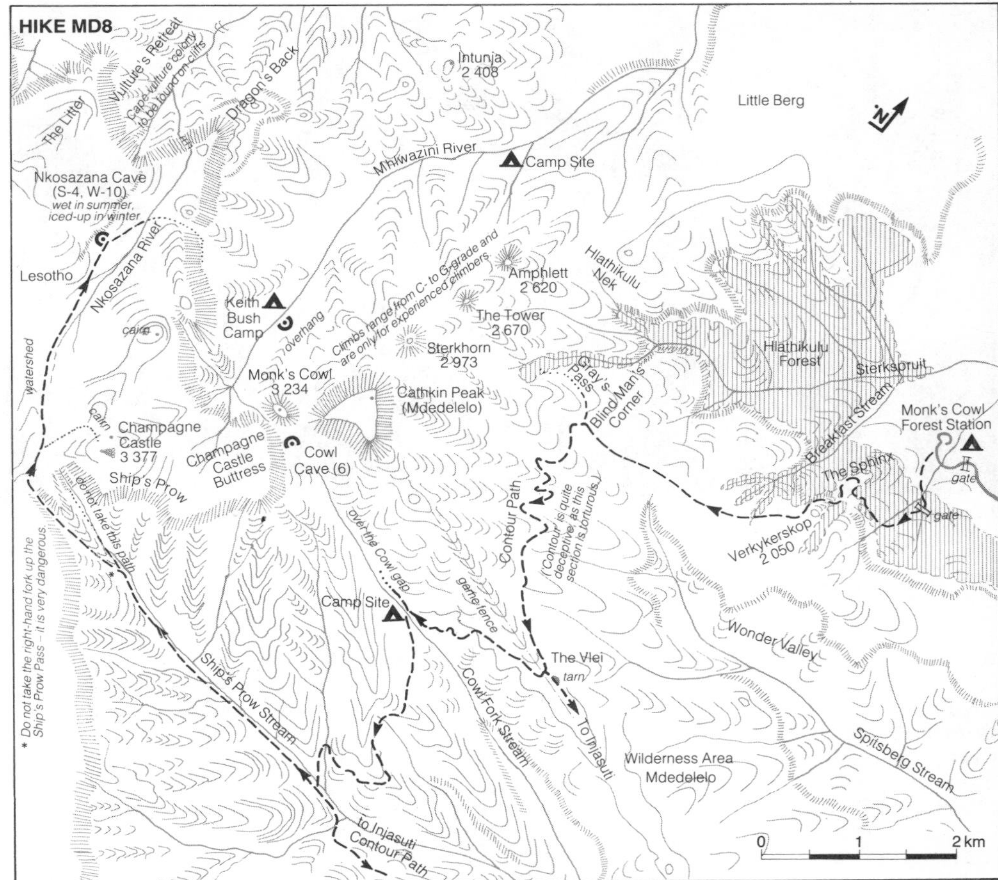

Route: *Monk's Cowl Forest Station to Champagne Castle*
Distance: *21 kilometres*
Duration: *10 to 11 hours*
Grade: *Most Extreme*
General: *This alternative route up Champagne Castle is, to me, the foulest in all the land and I fail to understand why anyone uses it – and yet they do. In the late 1970s, a group of young students died in the upper reaches of the pass, crushed by boulders loosed by one of the 'Berg's infamous cloudbursts.*

▶ Follow the Bridle Path from Monk's Cowl Forest Station to Blind Man's Corner (Hike MD7). Turn left here along the Contour Path for 4 km to what is wrongly marked on the map as Blind Man's Corner, but is in fact The Vlei, near a tarn. The first part of this Contour Path section climbs in and out of ravines and around spurs, gaining 100 m in altitude. From The Vlei the path cuts back towards Champagne Castle and descends for 2 km to a camp site below the Monk's Cowl Gully. Once again the path leads away from the Escarpment and up for a little over 2 km, back into a valley and then out along a sharp spur and once again back into a ravine where the stream coming down from between the Cowl and Champagne Castle meets the Ship's Prow Stream. The stretch from the forest station to this spot is in itself a strenuous hike for anyone carrying a fully laden pack.

▶ Follow the left-hand stream bank for 3 km to a fork at the base of the pass, at an altitude of 2 650 m. At the fork bear left *away* from the stream's course or you will place your life in jeopardy: parties have been discovered foundering up the right-hand fork days after departing from their base camp. This latter variation consists alternatively of treacherous scree and vertical rock. From the fork it is a 2,5 km-long arc, generally to the right, meeting the top of the pass at the head of the Nkosazana Valley, with Champagne Castle directly on your right and less than 1 km to the summit.

A blanket of mist envelops the view from Gray's Pass across to the valley of the Mhlawazini River.

HINTS TO HELP YOU ENJOY YOUR HIKING

The secret to enjoyable hiking is to take it easy and slow. You have to find your own pace and forget about walking in step with others. In fact, you shouldn't even consider hiking with people who won't accommodate your pace. In the rush to get to the top of a mountain, we often forget why we are there. Stop at your leisure to swim in rivers or drink tea, to study the birds, trees and flowers or just to dream.

The surest way to ruin any hike and invite disaster is to get blisters, yet they are easily prevented by wearing two pairs of socks. If your boots are new, rub dry soap on the heels of your outer socks and soften the heels of the boots with polish, water or by beating them into a pliable state. At the very first sign of a blister, whip off your boots and put on a large, thick plaster over the area – little ones are useless.

Finally, carry as light a pack as possible to minimize soil erosion and to make going uphill easier.

The Mhlwazini Valley *Hike MD9*

Route: *Monk's Cowl Forest Station to the lower Ndedema Gorge camp site*
Distance: *24 kilometres*
Duration: *9 hours*
Grade: *Moderate to Severe*
General: *The distance given here is from the Monk's Cowl Forest Station to the lower Ndedema Gorge camp site, but half of this is spent just getting from the forest station to the river valley. The scenery is, however, spectacular and the going pleasant: the 'severe' rating is for the distance if covered in one day. The Mhlwazini is one of the major headwaters of the Tugela catchment area, which is fed in turn by the Nkosazana and Ndedema rivers before reaching the Mlambonja River near Cathedral Peak Forest Station. The Mhlwazini rises on the slopes of Champagne Castle and drops into Eland Grove at the base of Monk's Cowl near Keith Bush Camp.*

▶ From the forest station proceed up the Bridle Path to Blind Man's Corner (Hike MD7) and turn right along the Contour Path along the southern flank of Cathkin Peak, Sterkhorn, The Tower and Amphlett, to Hlathikulu Nek. At the Nek bear right to The 'V' and not left around the base of the Amphlett. At 3 km from Hlathikulu Nek turn left down a spur into the Mhlwazini Valley, reaching a camp site where the path leads around a spur below Eagle Gorge and then cuts back to the river. If you are the type of hiker who spends a lot of time engrossed in the environment and as little as possible walking (like me), then this is a good place to camp for the night.

▶ Cross the river near the camp site to the left-hand bank and then contour along the bank, with the river dropping away on the right. About 2,5 km from the crossing the path zigzags down to the river and then crosses over to the right-hand bank. Once again the path contours away from the river and passes the Nkosazana River confluence before descending to rejoin the bank about 800 m downstream of the confluence. Follow the river, with one more crossing before reaching the camp site; here the valley opens out and Ndedema Gorge branches off, temptingly, to the right. Not only was this thought to be the last refuge of Bushmen in the Drakensberg, it was also one of the last real hunting grounds with the last-known leopard and python sightings in the Drakensberg.

The wilderness spirit still lingers in these remote valleys. In 1926, about 20 years after the last Bushman was shot in the mountains near Giant's Castle, a local farmer found a perfectly preserved bow and some arrows next to a carefully prepared sleeping place where fresh grass had been laid. The cave where this discovery was made is called Eland Cave for its remarkable paintings – over 1 000 in all, including a one metre-high polychrome of an eland. San hunters must have lived here for centuries or even millenia, practising their frugal lifestyle and perfecting their art which is now considered to be among the most sophisticated styles of painting ever practised. Yet it took only 100 years to eliminate every other sign of this harmonious culture. So explore at leisure, but take care not to damage any cave paintings and other treasures of the wilderness.

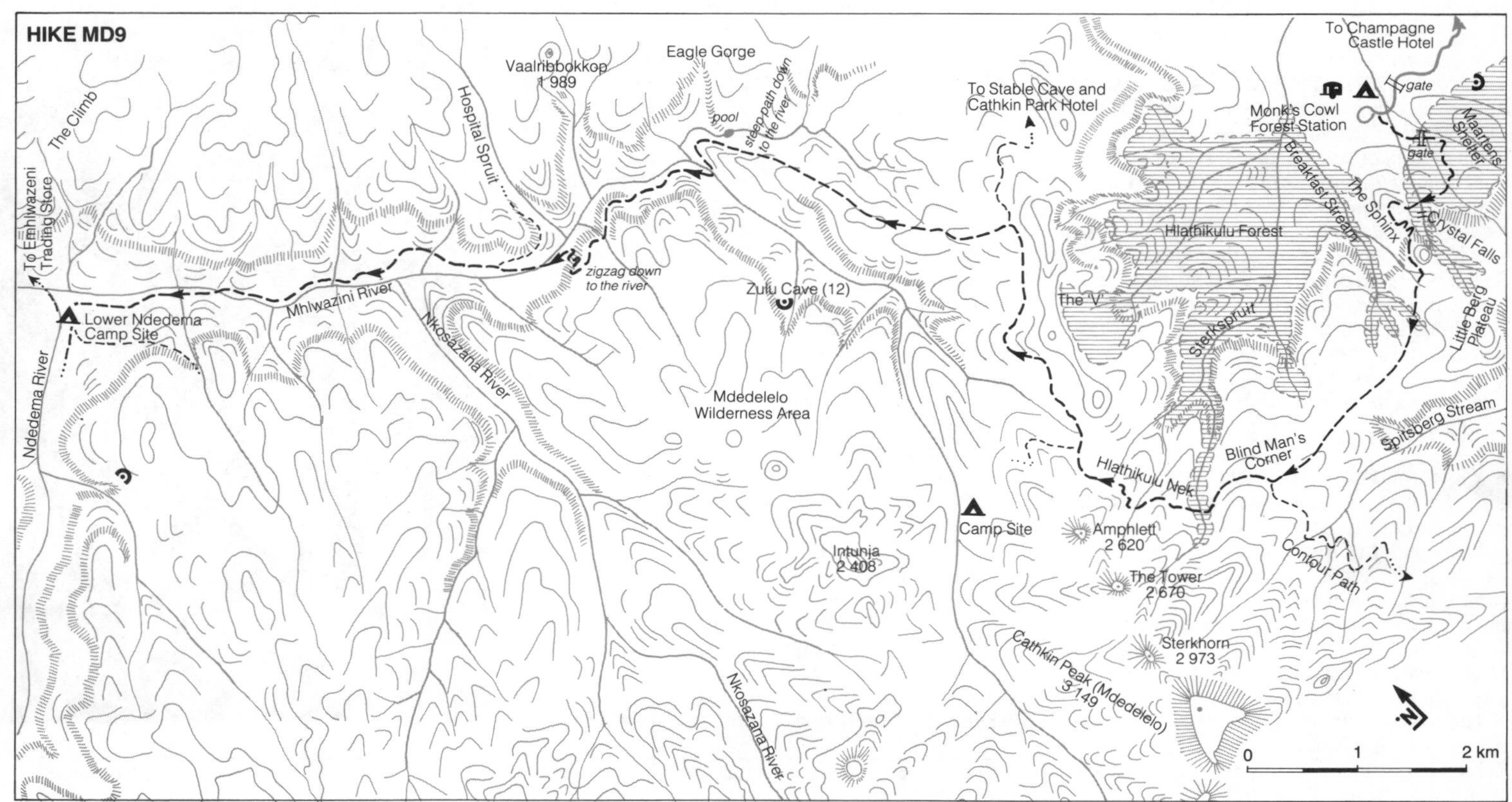

Contour Path – Ndedema to Monk's Cowl *Hike MD10*

Route: *Lower Ndedema Gorge camp site to Monk's Cowl Forest Station*
Distance: *27,5 kilometres*
Duration: *10 to 12 hours or 2 days*
Grade: *Moderate to Severe*
General: *This hike, to me the finest section of the Contour Path, would be a challenge for anyone to complete in one day. But to meet this challenge would be foolish as the finest landscape in southern Africa would be reduced to a sweat-blurred haze. To the north the Cathedral range guards your back, while in front of you Mdedelelo stands defiantly. The entire hike traverses the Mdedelelo Wilderness Area, so take your time, take photographs, take sketch pads, field guides, candles, red wine, paté and your favourite person with whom to share it. Spend two or three days in the unforgettable Ndedema Gorge, using Harold Pagar's classic* Ndedema *as your guide. Pagar was an anthropologist and author who spent two years living in the rock shelters of Ndedema, documenting and interpreting the thousands of Bushman paintings he found there.*

▶ You should now be ready for the wider vistas afforded by a trip along the Little Berg. From the camp site at the head of Ndedema Gorge, near Schoongezicht Cave, follow the right-hand side of the gorge for 500 m to a right-bearing side junction. This is the Contour Path which must be followed upwards and southwards along Eastman's Ridge. The ridge was named after H. A. 'Grandpa' Eastman who first climbed the peak via this ridge in 1935.

The first-known conquerors of the peak were a group of Bushman cattle raiders who were driven there last century by angry Zulus. The Bushmen escaped by loosing a shower of poisoned arrows at their pursuers and then slipping away over the Escarpment.

▶ After 4 km the path curves to the east for 1 km to a junction, where the Contour Path cuts back towards Eastman's Ridge and then winds in and out of a series of spurs and stream gullies to a camp site 6,5 km from the junction. From the camp site you can look up the Nkosazana Valley to Vulture's Retreat between the twin scaled ridges of The Litter and Dragon's Back. The camp site is situated behind a hill just beyond the main head of Nkosazana Gorge. Cross the twin forks of the gorge, then circle a koppie on the left, and follow a long and winding road around Intunja ('the Eye of the Needle'), down into the beautiful Mhlwazini Valley at the head of its gorge.

On the far bank of the river there is another camp site, 6,5 km from that at the Nkosazana River. From this site you can see the grandeur of the Cathkin ridge – the Amphlett, The Tower, Sterkhorn, Cathkin itself, and the brooding and secretive Monk's Cowl, all rising in Gothic spires, gargoyles and flying buttresses to secure the massive wall of Champagne Castle.

▶ From the Mhlwazini River, zigzag up to Hlathikulu Nek and then around the southern flank of Cathkin ridge for 2,5 km to Blind Man's Corner junction (M3 2100 on the map). Turn left here and proceed across the Little Berg plateau, away from Cathkin Peak, past the Mdedelelo Wilderness Area sign. The path then bypasses Verkykerskop where it slips over the Little Berg and zigzags down to The Sphinx, past Crystal Falls and finally down to the forest station.

*Thorny rope climber (*Dalbergia armata*) is found in densely wooded ravines. Here it climbs vigorously around a mountain hard pear tree (*Olinia emarginata*).*

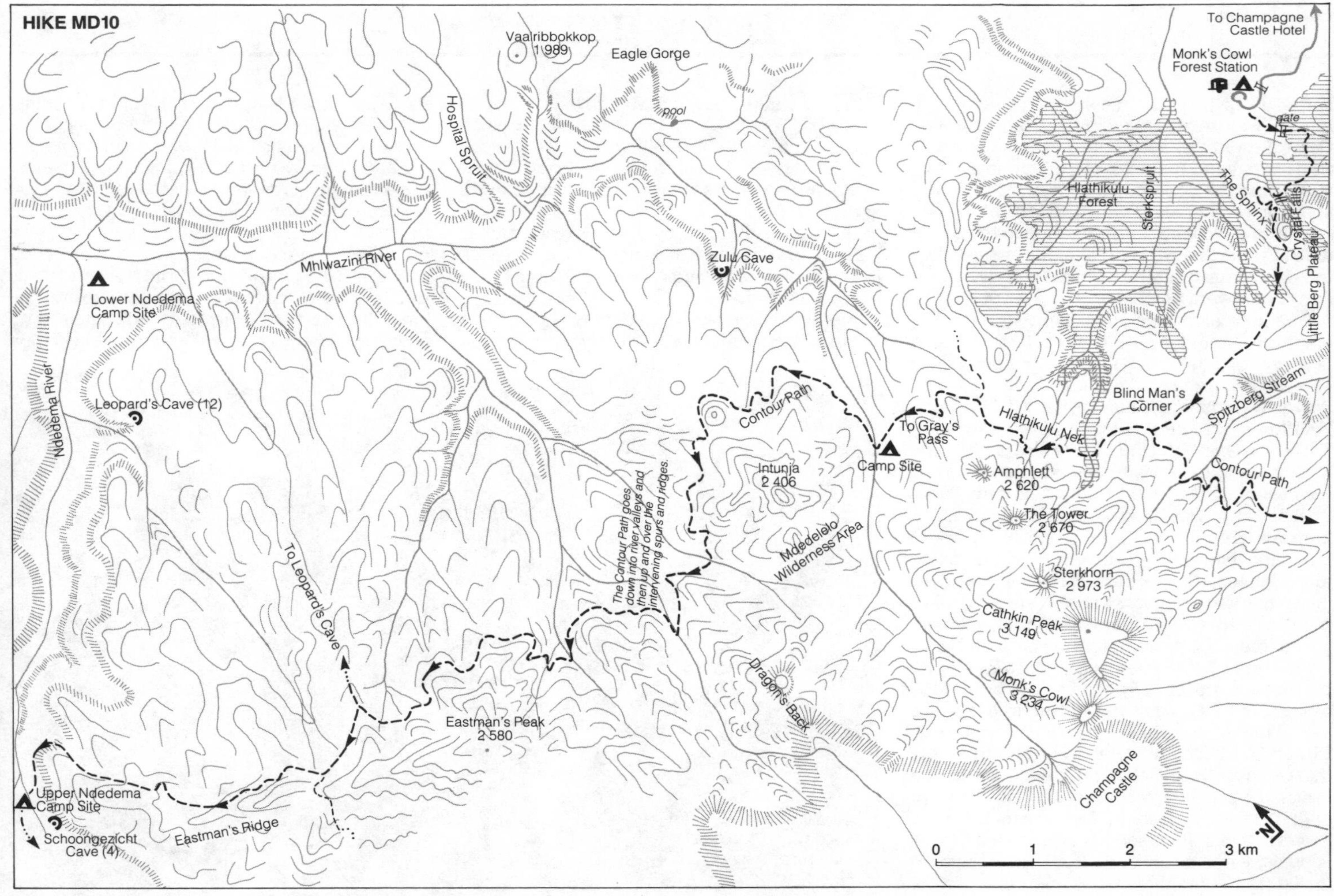
HIKE MD10
Vaalribbokkop
1 989
Eagle Gorge
pool
Hospital Spruit
To Champagne
Castle Hotel
Monk's Cowl
Forest Station
gate
Hlathikulu
Forest
Sterkspruit
The Sphinx
Crystal Falls
Little Berg Plateau
Mhlwazini River
Zulu Cave
Lower Ndedema
Camp Site
Ndedema River
Leopard's Cave (12)
Contour Path
To Gray's
Pass
Camp Site
Hlathikulu Nek
Blind Man's
Corner
Spitzberg Stream
Contour Path
Intunja
2 406
Amphlett
2 620
The Tower
2 670
Sterkhorn
2 973
Cathkin Peak
3 149
Monk's Cowl
3 234
Mdedelelo
Wilderness Area
The Contour Path goes
down into river valleys and
then up and over the
intervening spurs and ridges.
To Leopard's Cave
Dragon's Back
Eastman's Peak
2 580
Champagne
Castle
Upper Ndedema
Camp Site
Schoongezicht
Cave (4)
Eastman's Ridge
0
1
2
3 km
N

INJASUTI

Formerly a private resort called Solitude, Injasuti was incorporated into the Giant's Castle Game Reserve in 1980 and the name Solitude was changed to that of the main mountain formation in the area. Injasuti is the anglicized spelling of the Zulu name eNjesuthi, which means 'the well-fed dog', referring to the multitude of game that was found in this fertile valley by early Nguni hunters, whose dogs never went hungry for want of left-overs.

This area along the High 'Berg starts at the northern boundary of Giant's Castle Game Reserve on the slopes of KwaMfazo Gaya Mabele or The Old Woman Grinding Corn. Between the spectacular Trojan Wall and Red Wall tower are the three free-standing Injasuti Triplets. One of the first areas of the Drakensberg to be visited by whites, the lower reaches of the Injasuti valley around the Parks Board camp was also a long-time favourite hunting ground of Nguni tribesmen, while Bushmen had used it as a refuge for much, much longer. Like the other forests in the lower 'Berg, the large yellowwood forests here were plundered by woodcutters during the last century to meet the demand for this hard timber.

The upper Escarpment, however, was among the last areas of the Drakensberg to be tackled by climbers. Of course, the main prizes here are the Triplets, which are ranked along with Devil's Tooth, Mponjwane and Column as the most exposed and challenging climbs in the range. The Middle and Eastern Triplets were both first conquered in December 1950, the Eastern Triplet (G-grade) by a party led by Ted Scholes, while a few days later another party, including two of the best women climbers of that time, made it to the top of the Middle Triplet (F-grade). It was another year until anyone dared attempt the frightening prospect of scaling the sheer walls of the Western Triplet (G-grade), which was conquered by Bob Davies and David Bell.

There is a number of small forest patches around Injasuti camp, but the valley of the well-fed dog shelters the most southerly large forest in the Drakensberg: it was here that the pioneering game warden, Philip Barnes, built a hut to which he and his wife could escape from the hectic pace of life at Giant's Castle. In spring, this area, especially the paths that pass below and above the Cave Sandstone belt, is a myriad of contrasts: the dark green foliage is offset by the brilliant flame-red blooms of the Natal bottlebrush (*Greyia sutherlandii*). Directly in front of the Lower Injasuti Cave there is a number of these gnarled trees, with soot-coloured bark and round, bright green leaves with scalloped edges. During the autumn the long walls of the Escarpment and triple ramparts of Injasuti glow gold and crimson at day-

break and dusk. When you feel the need for solitude, this is the place to find it.

Accommodation at Injasuti camp consists of well-appointed bungalows as well as a caravan and camp site 200 m downstream of the main camp. In autumn, this aspect of Monk's Cowl is always in deep shadow, but the view is brightened by the orange *Leonotis* flowers that crowd the river banks. At the Parks Board office one can buy only permits and souvenirs; everything else must be brought in, except pets and firearms, of course.

One of the satellite camps of the Giant's Castle Game Reserve, Hillside tent and caravan camp site is intended as a base for horse-riding enthusiasts wishing to embark on one of the famous horse trails in the area, or for those who would rather go out on easy rides in the vicinity of the camp. Of course, staying at Hillside in no way obliges you to go for a ride, but that would mean missing a unique opportunity. The horse trails are conducted by the camp ranger and there are two-, three- and four-day trails, using caves for overnight accommodation. The trails cost (at time of writing) R35,00 a day and are very popular, so anyone wishing to go on one should find out when they are scheduled and book well in advance.

None of the caves in the area is available for hikers, so all the hikes described from the camp are of a day's duration or less. (The two caves used on the horse trails are Tom's and Tree Fern caves, as well as the iNtabamnyama Hut.) The hikes are confined to the exceptionally wide portion of the Little Berg, 20 km east of Leslie's Pass.

The Injasuti Triplets stand out from the top of the Escarpment wall like the ramparts of a castle.

Van Heyningen's Pass to View Point *Hike IN1*

Route: *Round trip from Injasuti Camp via Van Heyningen's Pass*
Distance: *8 kilometres*
Duration: *3 hours*
Grade: *Moderate*
General: *This medium-length, steep walk should be your first from Injasuti Camp to orientate yourself with the surrounding landscape and major peaks.*

▸ Follow the path from behind Chalet No. 4 and cross the wooden footbridge over the Delmhlwazini River. Turn left to follow the right-hand stream bank for 2 km up to the forest guard hut above the river. Just before the hut, turn sharply back to the right to follow the base of the Little Berg cliffs for 1,5 km into a forested ravine. Cross the stream and then turn left to climb the zigzag path, passing through a gate, to the top of the Little Berg; this section is called Van Heyningen's Pass. Once at the top of the pass, turn left and make your way back to View Point at the edge of the Escarpment to observe the dragon's lair, unless, of course, the mists of summer have descended below knee height.

▸ Make your way back along the edge of the cliff top to Van Heyningen's Pass, descend the pass and turn left at the junction. After 800 m you will come to another junction where the main path bears left along the base of the cliffs while our route goes to the right, downhill towards the Injasuti River. Various sections of this 2 km-long stretch are zigzagged and eroded, so take care. Cross the river and turn right along the road to return to the camp site.

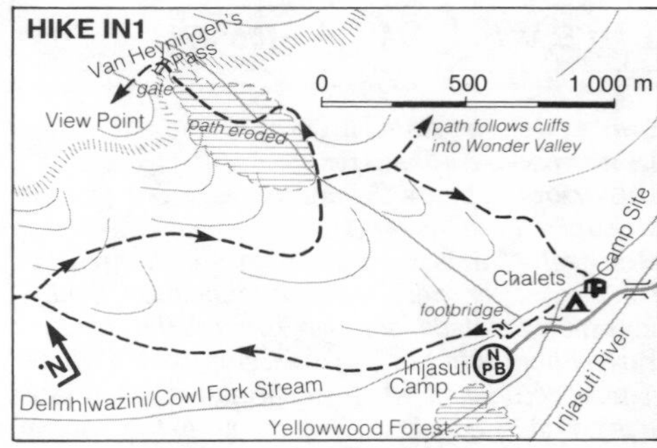

Junction Pool *Hike IN2*

Route: *Injasuti Camp to Junction Pool*
Distance: *2,5 kilometres*
Duration: *45 minutes*
Grade: *Easy*
General: *This is a short walk along the Injasuti River to a pleasant pool.*

▸ Take the road away from the camp but turn left at the track just before the main vehicle bridge near the camp site. Go left past the Mdedelelo Wilderness Area sign and follow the river to a junction with a side stream coming in from the north. The pool is situated at a large eroded rock on the left-hand side of the river.

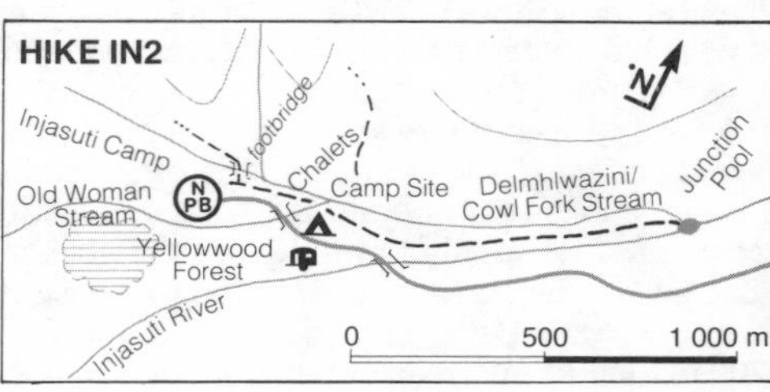

Fergy's Cave *Hike IN3*

Route: *Injasuti Camp to Fergy's Cave*
Distance: *6,5 kilometres*
Duration: *2 hours 15 minutes*
Grade: *Fair to Moderate*
General: *This is one of three caves in the area that can be used for overnight accommodation; bookings must be made, however, through the Natal Parks Board office at Injasuti Camp, with a R10,00 deposit refundable when you bring back your litter. It is possible to make a short detour to the historic Battle Cave, which is fenced off and can only be visited in the company of a game guard.*

▶ From Chalet No. 18, follow the road to the main vehicle bridge and then proceed up the embankment on the right-hand side of the road to follow a path up the right-hand river bank. After a kilometre the path enters the tip of a large patch of forest, which clings to the Injasuti River for a good 7 km. Proceed through the forest and cross the river with the help of stepping stones above Boundary Pool. Climb the ridge and continue up the left-hand bank above the river until you reach a T-junction on the level platform. To the left is Poacher's Stream with its small shaded pools. Take the path to the right through varied grasslands, with tree ferns and yellowwoods growing among rocky outcrops. (Take along a Parks Board booklet, as it provides a wealth of information on the natural history of each portion of the path.)

▶ The path contours above the river for 2 km, slowly edging its way towards the river, which is then skirted for another 500 m to a crossing on the eMbovaneni Stream. Cross the stream. The path to Battle Cave goes uphill to the right, while Fergy's Cave can be found to the left, 700 m further upstream, on the opposite bank.

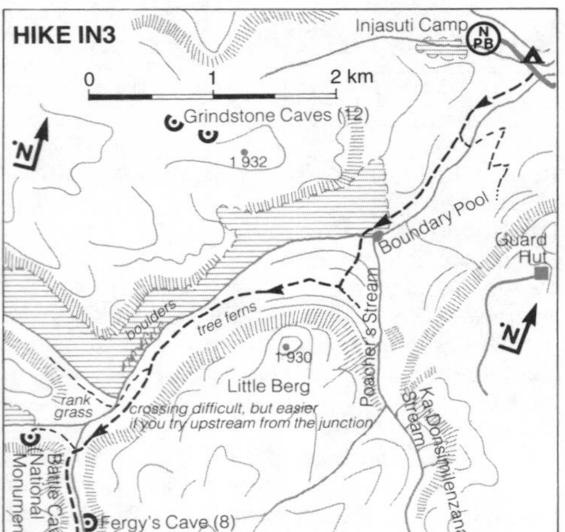

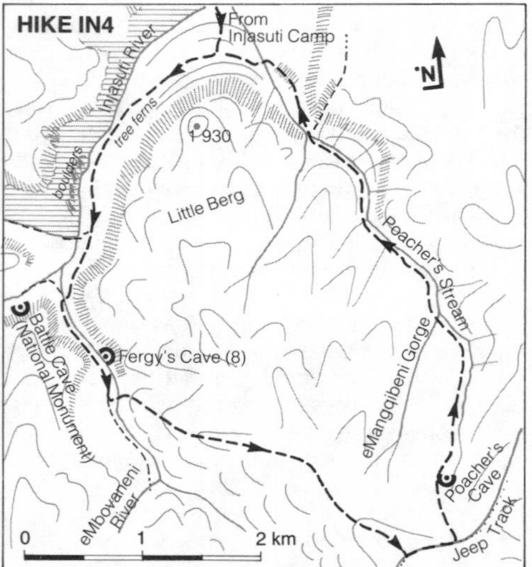

Fergy's Cave to Poacher's Cave *Hike IN4*

Route: *Round trip from Injasuti Camp to Poacher's Cave*
Distance: *17 kilometres*
Duration: *7 hours*
Grade: *Moderate*
General: *This hike and the previous one make a pleasant two-day outing among the foothills of Injasuti. The overnight spot is at Fergy's Cave, which must be booked at the Parks Board office, with a maximum of eight people allowed. Poacher's Cave is to be found near the source of Poacher's Stream, but it does not appear on Slingsby's map as it is out of bounds as a overnight stop.*

▶ Follow the route to Fergy's Cave (Hike IN3) and then continue for 400 m up the eMbovaneni Stream. At this point the path heads off up the spur on the left-hand side of the river; be careful, as it is eroded. Follow the path for 3 km up the steep spur to a flat area that is as close to the Little Berg plateau as can be found around here. At Cloudland Col turn left and, after 500 m down the eMangqibeni Gorge, turn left again along the left-hand bank of the stream. Poacher's Cave can be reached less than a kilometre down the Ka-Donsimilenzana (Poacher's) Stream. Follow the left-hand bank for another 3,3 km to a side stream crossing and a path going up the sandstone cliffs on the right, but continue down the right-hand stream bank for another kilometre.

▶ Cross the river again and head uphill to the level platform, which follows the Injasuti River upstream. Turn right 500 m up from the stream to cross the Injasuti River. Proceed through the corner of the forest back to camp, 2 km further on.

Poacher's Stream and Boundary Pool *Hike IN5*

Route: *Round trip from Injasuti Camp to Boundary Pool*
Distance: *6,5 kilometres*
Duration: *2 hours 15 minutes*
Grade: *Easy to Fair*
General: *Once again, you can choose a different combination of paths to lengthen or shorten the hike. The more one gets to know an area, the better one is able to choose the more satisfying hikes. Until then, I think exploration and boldness should be your motto.*

▶ Walk towards the vehicle bridge over the Injasuti River and take the path up the embankment to the right just before the bridge. Follow the path to the forest, getting your feet muddy before leaving the forest near the river (the map incorrectly shows the river crossing before the forest). Use a line of stepping stones to cross the river, where you will probably also get a chance to wash the mud off your boots (carrying a pair of running shoes in case of wet boots, or wearing gaiters is a good idea). You will now be just upstream of Boundary Pool.

It is well within acceptable bounds to swim here, in fact I think it is obligatory. After a dip in the chilly, fast-flowing water, dry off by lying prone in the long grass beside the river – it helps give one a perspective of the walking done and of that to follow.

▶ Continue along the path up a grassy hill to a level platform between the sandstone cliffs and the river. Once on the platform, turn left at the T-junction, cross Poacher's Stream and then turn immediately left again.

▶ Wend your way along the contour obliquely towards the cliffs now on your right, and parallel to the Injasuti River on your left. After 1,5 km, take the path to the left, zigzagging downhill towards the river. A path will be reached at a T-junction near the river and here you must turn right and make for the road, 800 m further on. Follow the road back to camp.

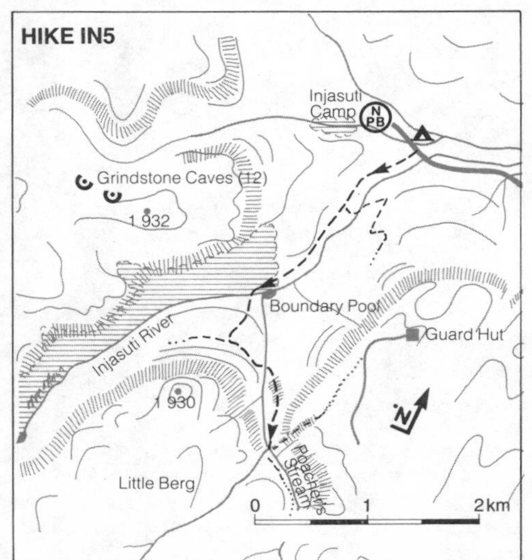

FISHING

Few hikers take advantage of the free meals and sport which fishing provides in the mountains. Get a permit and you can live on trout, if you manage to master the patient skill of fly fishing. It is illegal to fish for trout by any other means, but they would not taste as good if they were simply hauled out of the streams.

Poacher's Stream *Hike IN6*

Route: *Injasuti Camp to Poacher's Stream*
Distance: *6,5 kilometres*
Duration: *+ 3 hours*
Grade: *Fair*
General: *This route description takes you part of the way up Poacher's Stream, but stops where the river forks and the path follows the left-hand branch up to the Injasuti Track. From here two circular hikes are possible, but, in my opinion, only the longer one via Cloudland Col and Fergy's Cave is worth the effort. The length of this circular hike is 17 km – a good day's outing.*

▶ Walk to Boundary Pool (Hike IN5), cross the Injasuti River and climb the grassy hill opposite. Turn left along the level platform and cross Poacher's Stream. Instead of turning left, as in the previous hike, go to the right in an arc away from the river and return to it after 1 km. Cross the river here and then follow the right-hand bank of the stream for 2,5 km to the fork mentioned above. This is the end of the hike description, but quite an arbitrary one. The return trip is up to you.

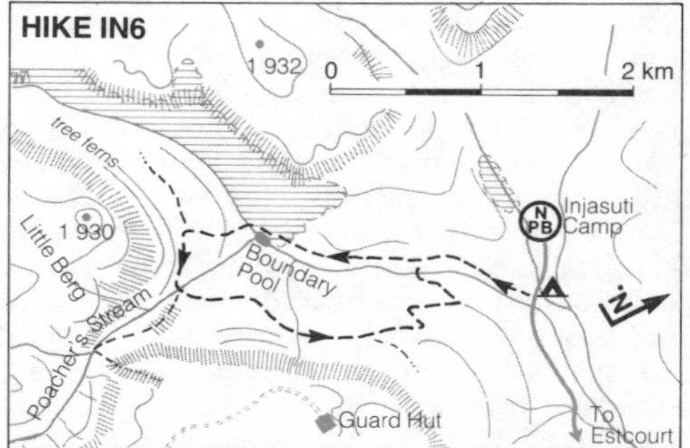

Battle Cave to Lower Injasuti Cave *Hike IN7*

Route: *Injasuti Camp to Lower Injasuti Cave*
Distance: *8,5 kilometres*
Duration: *3 hours*
Grade: *Moderate*
General: *Time your trip to coincide with the guided tour of the Battle Cave to see a pictorial display of Bushman life in this bountiful valley, complete with a taped guide to the paintings. The cave is named after a scene painted in red monochrome of a battle between two feuding Bushman groups. You can stay overnight at the Lower Injasuti Cave, but bookings must be made in advance for both this and the Battle Cave tour. The hike ends at the cave, some way short of the amphitheatre between Scaly Peak and the Injasuti Triplets, where the Injasuti River rises. This, however, is no reason not to continue up the river to the base of the Escarpment wall.*

▶ Proceed to the eMbovaneni Stream crossing *en route* to Battle Cave (Hike IN3). Cross the stream and turn right, going uphill to Battle Cave rock art museum. Once you have satiated yourself with Stone Age history, continue along the fence through the rank grass down to the river. Shortly after you have passed a forest patch on the opposite bank, cross the river. The river is defined on the left by a low sandstone embankment and on the right by bush which affords numerous places for a quiet snack and a snooze. Follow the stream for 3 km, crossing back and forth where necessary. The path leads up to the left, where the river cuts through the sandstone. After a while it is possible to look down from the rocky lip into the gurgling waters of the gorge.

▶ The path heads downhill again to the river where a side tributary must be crossed. Here the gushing stream has scoured out a series of circular pools which make great jacuzzis. After a short tricky section over sloping rocks, a path leads uphill to the left for 3 km to the Giant's Castle Contour Path. Do not take this path unless you want a close-up view of the Trojan Wall; continue along the left-hand bank of the Injasuti River through bottlebrush and ouhout thicket to the cave. This is a comfortable overhang, which looks down to the river below and is shielded by a leafy screen. Through a gap at the end of the overhang you can just see the Injasuti Triplets. These secretive freestanding towers are seldom seen by hikers; the one closest to the Escarpment was only 'discovered' by climbers attempting to scale the outer two. All three present high-grade challenges to rock climbers.

Standing on the watershed behind the Triplets is Mafadi Peak, at 3 446,1 metres the highest point in South Africa. On the eastern slope of Injasuti Dome, the prominent point just south of Mafadi Peak, the Injasuti Summit Cave looks out across the Injasuti Valley. Like the Mponjwane Cave in the Mnweni area, this cave is a favourite mountaineer's hideaway.

FOOTWEAR

For long hikes in the 'Berg you need boots. Keep the following in mind and you should cover many kilometres free from the agony of blisters:

- The best hiking boots are made of light-weight nylon and gortex, with rubber soles. They give support, but are light and very comfortable.
- All boots need time to wear in and take the shape of your feet, so don't buy a pair on Friday and rush up the mountains on Saturday.
- Running shoes are useful when you have finished the day's hike and your feet are tired or when your boots get wet.
- Slippers can be worn at camp sites and take up very little space in a pack.
- Waterproof gaiters keep boots dry and socks free of burrs and grass seeds.

The red monochrome paintings of a battle of feuding clans has given Battle Cave its name. This cave also houses one of the few pictures of a lion to be found in the 'Berg. Many of the rock paintings have been defaced by thoughtless visitors who have thereby destroyed some of the last reminders of what life for these hunter-gatherers was like in this area during the latter half the Stone Age.

Junction Cave and Marble Baths *Hike IN8*

Route: *Injasuti Camp to Marble Baths*
Distance: *8,5 kilometres*
Duration: *3 hours*
Grade: *Moderate*
General: *This hike is only one of a network of paths which criss-cross the area. Marble Baths, for instance, can be reached via a path which cuts back to the right from Lower Injasuti Cave over a series of spurs that lead up to Scaly Peak. From the baths you can get to Leslie's Pass by continuing up the Buttress Fork Stream for another 5 km, ascending the Escarpment to the left of The Molar. Junction Cave is the third cave where overnighting is allowed in the Injasuti area, again with a maximum of eight people.*

▶ Follow the route to Fergy's Cave (Hike IN3), but 500 m before the eMbovaneni Stream turn right, down to the Injasuti River. This path is often overgrown and indistinct. Cross the river, using the irregular stepping stones, just above the confluence of the Injasuti River and the Buttress Fork Stream.

▶ Proceed up the rank left-hand bank of the Buttress Fork Stream and down to a boggy area alongside the stream after 1,5 km. Cross the river here, but at a fork in the river, 1 km further on, cross back over to Junction Cave, which is set just above the river in the cliffs on the left. The path goes directly under the cave overhang and becomes indistinct. Try to follow the intermittent cairns which mark the route, or just thread your way upriver. One kilometre from the cave, you will reach the unmistakable Marble Baths, where the river has polished the sandstone to a shiny white as it flows down through a series of narrow pools. Above the slope to the left loom the Injasuti Triplets.

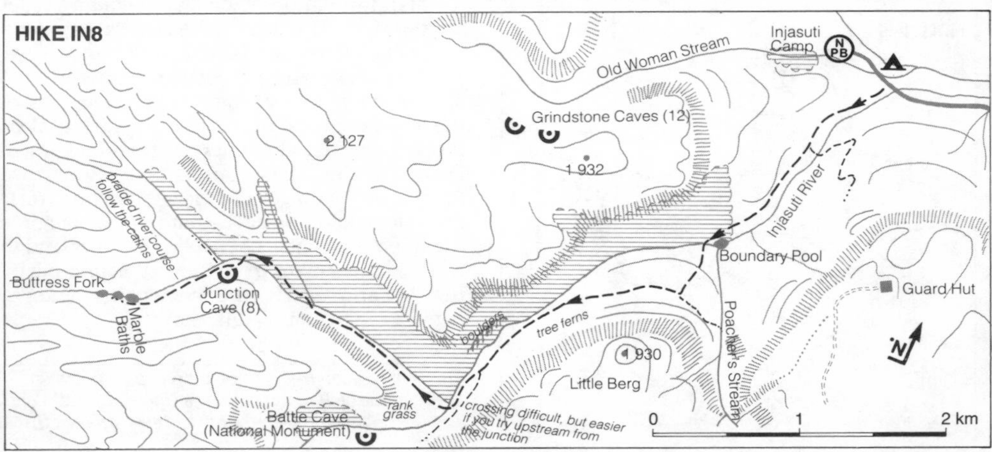

Grindstone Caves and Cataract Valley *Hike IN9*

Route: *Round trip from Injasuti Camp via Cataract Valley*
Distance: *13 kilometres*
Duration: *+ 4 hours*
Grade: *Moderate*
General: *This hike begins at Injasuti Camp but most of it lies in the Mdedelelo Wilderness Area. Your permit into Injasuti Camp will, however, be accepted as your ticket into the Wilderness Area. The route described here is only one of a number of possible routes connecting the two main points mentioned. Use Slingsby's map if you wish to compile an alternative circuit.*

▶ Begin behind Chalet No. 18, cross the stream at the bridge and head off to the right, following the Old Woman Stream to a second bridge, which must also be crossed. Then turn left to enter a forest about 1,2 km from the camp. After crossing a third bridge in the forest, leave the forest to climb the steep hill up to the left, towards the sandstone cliffs. The path proceeds uphill for another 1 km, but less steeply now, to the two Grindstone Caves; between the two caves there is a path going uphill to the left to the Contour Path 3 km away.

▶ From here the path contours above the Old Woman Stream for another kilometre before turning a corner to the left to cross the stream above a gorge where the stream plunges over the lip. The path leading down to the river is badly eroded, so tread carefully. After crossing the stream and passing a small waterfall on a side stream, climb the easy grassy slope to Cataract Valley. At the crest above the valley, the path turns to the left and comes to a scissor-like junction 1 km down the slope. Turn sharply back to the right here and follow the path through three more wide zigzags before reaching the river. The path is the easiest way down, so don't be tempted to take a short cut.

▶ Two more river crossings follow in quick succession before the path heads steeply down the left-hand bank of the river for 1,2 km. Cross the stream just above its confluence with the Delmhlwazini River, but then contour away from the river and under the sandstone cliffs for just over a kilometre. The path drifts out across the open grass plain between the cliffs and the river. About 2,5 km from the last river crossing, turn left and head for the river again to enter the camp 1 km from this junction.

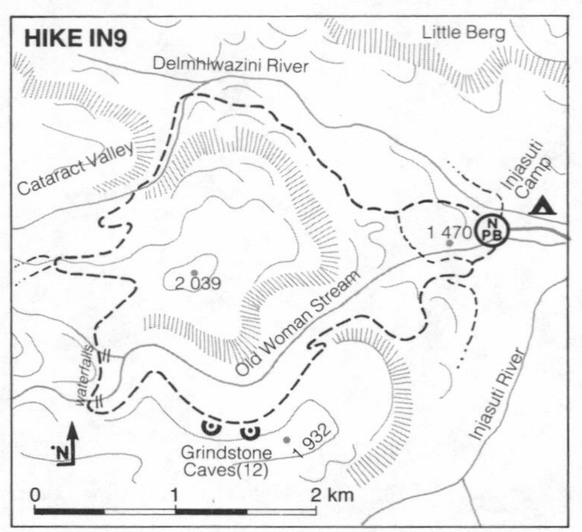

This yellowwood tree (Podocarpus sp.) has grown between the cleft of a rock in the Upper Injasuti Valley. The tree is thus protected from the ever-present threat of fire.

PACKS AND BAGS

There are many makes of back pack and your pocket will dictate your choice. For hiking, I prefer an external H-frame pack as it is flexible and adjustable and doesn't make you sweat as much as an internal frame pack which hugs the body; it also easy to attach tents and mats to a H-frame.

A sleeping bag is vital and it must be warm enough for below freezing conditions. Down bags are most common for mountaineering, with prices varying according to the amount of super-fine down used. Down traps body heat but totally loses its insulating capacity when wet. New synthetic fibre bags overcome this problem to some extent, but good ones are very expensive. I use a super-down bag, a thin inner sheet for warmth and hygiene, a waterproof 'bivvy bag' or groundsheet and a close-cell foam 'gaper' mat for warmth. If comfort is important, take along a soft foam mat, which you can carry rolled up on the outside of your pack.

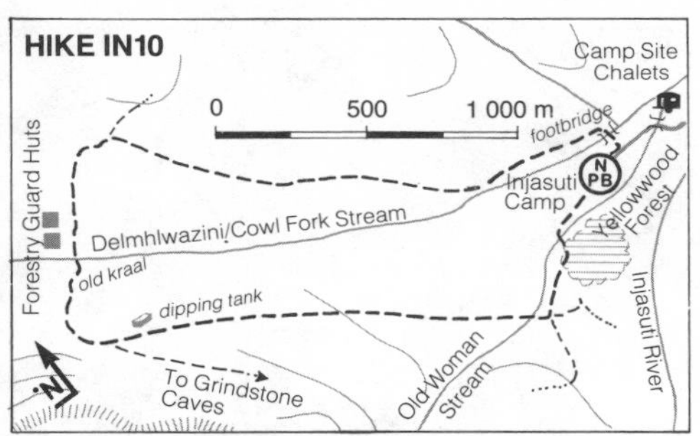

Looking up the Injasuti River towards the Injasuti Triplets and the Trojan Wall. This area was a long-time favourite hunting ground of Nguni tribesmen.

Old Kraal and Yellowwood Forest *Hike IN10*

Route: *Round trip from Injasuti Camp via Yellowwood Forest*
Distance: *2,5 kilometres*
Duration: *50 minutes*
Grade: *Easy*
General: *This is an interesting short stroll in the vicinity of the camp.*

▶ Take the Cowl Fork Stream (Delmhlwazini) path between the Parks Board office and the chalets, facing west to Monk's Cowl Peak, which looms over the camp. Walk up the left-hand side of the river, going uphill a little way. At the top of the incline turn left and pass a coppice of trees surrounded by the stone walls of the Old Kraal. Just past the kraal turn sharply left again, pass a dipping tank and continue downhill towards the Old Woman Stream.

▶ Cross the river and then turn left to cross the river again at a bridge, before entering the Yellowwood Forest due west of the camp. Just follow the path through the forest and it will lead back to whichever of the two main paths you choose.

Guard Huts and Yellowwood Forest *Hike IN11*

Route: *Round trip from Injasuti Camp to Yellowwood Forest*
Distance: *6 kilometres*
Duration: *2 hours*
Grade: *Easy*
General: *This hike is longer than the previous one (Hike IN10), but also expends little energy. Although the outbound route takes a different course to the Old Kraal path, the return trip is through the same small forest.*

▶ Proceed from the wooden footbridge behind Chalet No. 4 and up the right-hand bank of the Cowl Fork Stream (Delmhlwazini) for 2 km. Turn left away from the sandstone cliffs on the right and go past a ruin to cross the river near the guard huts, from where smoke drifts out and clings to the tall blue gum trees. About 1 km from the junction on the other side of the river, turn left again and proceed under the band of cliffs to the same dipping tank which was encountered on the previous hike.

▶ Proceed down to and cross the Old Woman Stream, turn left and proceed to the left to cross the river again at a footbridge. Enter the Yellowwood Forest and just follow the most obvious path back to camp – you can't get lost as both main paths head back to the camp, which is only a few hundred metres away.

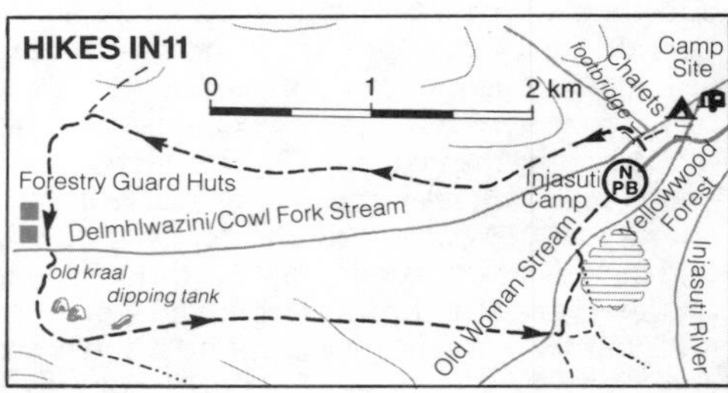

Contour Path – Monk's Cowl to Injasuti Hike IN12

Route: *Monk's Cowl Forest Station to Injasuti Camp*
Distance: *21 kilometres*
Duration: *9 hours*
Grade: *Severe*
General: *This hike is neither the shortest nor the best route, in fact it is the longest, hardest and least-used of three possible routes between the forest station and Injasuti camp. The aim of these Contour Path descriptions is, however, to describe a continuous route from one end of the range to the other, along what might one day be a continuous trail. It is possible to do a circular route from Monk's Cowl to Injasuti by going up Van Heyningen's Pass and Shada Ridge, in and out the gates in the game fence and to The Vlei (marked incorrectly as Blind Man's Corner) on the Contour Path. Where the path crosses over and heads down the right-hand side of Cataract Valley, continue to the left to zigzag down to the river and follow that path all the way back to camp.*

▶ Starting at Blind Man's Corner, turn left where the Bridle Path from Monk's Cowl Forest Station meets the Contour Path (junction M3 2100). Round the spur, which comes down from Sterkhorn to a camp site 1 km from the start, and then wind in and out of the folds below Cathkin Peak for about 2 km. After this the path straightens out and levels off to The Vlei near a tarn. From here one path goes obtusely to the left, out along the plateau, along the fence, down Shada Ridge and to Van Heyningen's Pass. Turn sharply to the right here and proceed slowly and then more steeply downhill to the camp site on Cowl Fork Stream, 2 km from The Vlei.

▶ Now it's 4 km up, up again, down and down again around the base of Monk's Cowl to a stream descending from the corner of Champagne Castle. There is something about this section of the Contour Path that makes me wonder if the name isn't a private joke among the foresters who made it – for contour it does not. After tackling this nasty little section of the Contour Path, there are still those people who want to climb the even nastier Ship's Prow Pass.

▶ This pass begins on the far bank of Ship's Prow Stream, which is crossed 800 m past its right-hand tributary, going sharply to the right up the gully to the extreme left of Champagne Castle. The Contour Path now turns away from the Escarpment for 4 km with KwaMfazo Gaya Mabele (Old Woman Griding Corn) on your right. Once again the path pays scant respect for its name, going up-down, up-down, up-down to finally enter Cataract Valley. From the river the path first follows the right-hand bank and then turns slowly away from the river. Continue uphill for 1,5 km to a four-way junction which looks down into the wooded part of Cataract Valley to its confluence with the Delmhlwazini River. For those of you who have had enough of all this 'contouring', take the branch on the far left, back down into the Cataract Valley, following the path and then the Delmhlwazini River to Injasuti camp.

▶ Die-hards should take the path acutely to the right up the grassy bank and then down the other side in more or less a straight line to an intermittent stream. Cross the stream at the point where a path turns at right angles to the left along the contour. Only foolish hikers would think that this was the route, for sure enough the Contour Path proceeds directly ahead, up the hill to the ridge of the major spur which descends from the Old Woman Grinding Corn and continues on a straight course, but not too

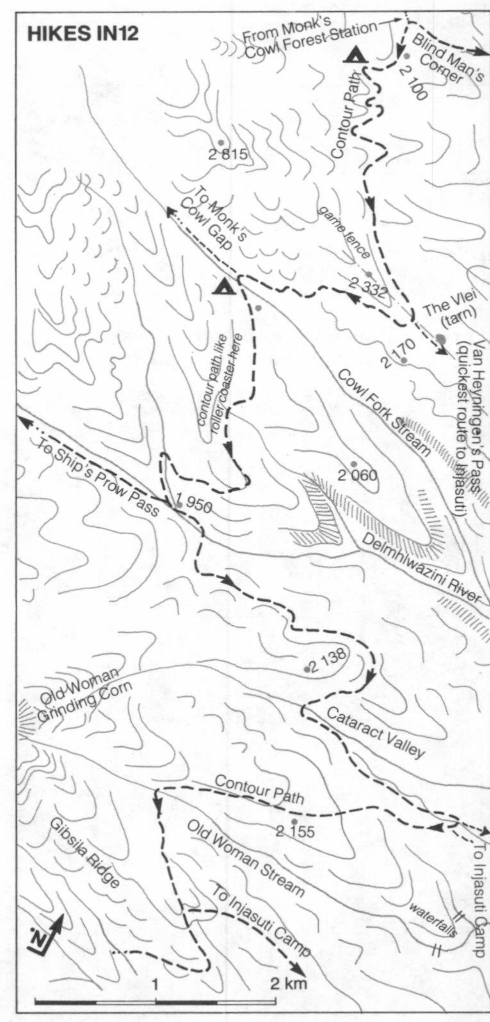

steeply, down into the Old Woman Stream valley.

▶ Cross the river, climb diagonally up the Gibisila Ridge for 1,5 km, pass a side junction on the left and descend the ridge along an eland fence. One kilometre down the ridge the path turns sharply to the right, passes through a gate in the fence and enters an unnamed river valley. At this point the Contour Path ends. The quickest way back to Injasuti camp from here is down the stream to Junction Cave and then keep left all the way to the camp 9 km away. On the other hand, it is possible to join up with the Giant's Castle Contour Path below Injasuti Dome and the Upper Injasuti Cave: head for the Injasuti River (below Junction Cave) and then turning up towards Lower Injasuti Cave and from there ascend the ridge on the left for 3 km.

MOUNTAIN HYGIENE

In Colorado's Grand Canyon, river rafters have to carry their own faeces to prevent degradation of the river ecology. You don't have to go to these lengths in the Drakensberg, but there are very definite routines that you should follow.

• Carry a trowel with which to dig a small hole. After defecating, cover the hole with soil and place a stone on top to prevent erosion and unsightly encounters. Once you get used to the practicalities of 'bush patrols', you can begin to explore spots with good views or comfortable back rests, but keep away from paths, camp sites and steep slopes.

• Never use soap, shampoo or washing detergents in streams or pools, for they kill the organisms that live there. Carry water from a river or tarn to a suitable spot (where it won't just run straight back) and do all washing there. Some pharmacies sell special detergents and highly bio-degradable soaps and shampoos, which are a little more expensive than ordinary ones, but less damaging to the environment.

Never forget the most important code of the wilderness, to leave as little trace as possible that you were there.

Viewed from the south-east, Champagne Castle and Cathkin Peak loom in the distance.

Forest Walk *Hike IN13*

Route: *Round trip from Hillside Camp Site via the Forest*
Distance: *4,5 kilometres*
Duration: *1 hour and 30 minutes*
Grade: *Easy*
General: *This outing takes place close to the camp site and can be arranged to coincide with a guided tour given by one of the game rangers. A brochure is available from the NPB office, describing the most interesting aspects of the environment. Don't go without it.*

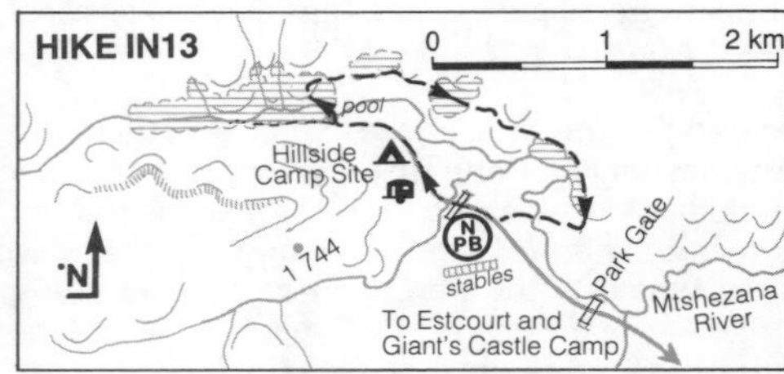

▶ Walk to the river at the end of the camp site, bear left upstream and cross the first footbridge you reach. Once on the opposite bank, continue upstream over two more footbridges; from here you can carry on upstream to an attractive pool, or you can turn right uphill and pass through four forest patches alternating with bracken-laced grass slopes. From the river the path ascends for a short distance and then contours above the camp site for about 2 km. After passing the fourth forest patch, the path descends to the river and goes past the ranger's house, following the road back to camp. On hot days it is not uncommon for this hike to take all morning or all afternoon, with hikers deciding that the pool mentioned is worthy of deep analysis.

Zulu homes are threatened by a wide, darkening sky in the Injasuti Valley near Hillside Camp.

iNtondolo Forest and Flats

Hike IN14

Route: *Round trip from Hillside Camp Site via iNtondolo Flats*
Distance: *8 kilometres*
Duration: *2 hours and 45 minutes*
Grade: *Fair*
General: *This hike explores a wide plain and a forest, and can be tackled from either direction without affecting the grade. The forest can be chosen to begin or end the outing.*

▶ Walk to the end of the camp site near the Mtshezana River and turn left to follow the left-hand bank upstream. On the opposite bank is a forest and about 1 km upstream you come to a pool which is the unofficial camp swimming hole. At the far end of the forest the path turns left to ascend to the iNtondolo Flats, which are reached after 1,2 km. On reaching the flats, the path turns 90° to the left and proceeds to a four-way junction at iNtondolo, at the base of the eMsathanini Ridge. Turn left here across the flats and then go down to the Mtshezana River. Cross the river and walk diagonally away from the river at this level for nearly 2 km. Just short of the camp the path turns sharply to the right and back to the river, which is recrossed. From the crossing it is a few hundred metres to the road and then left along the road back to camp.

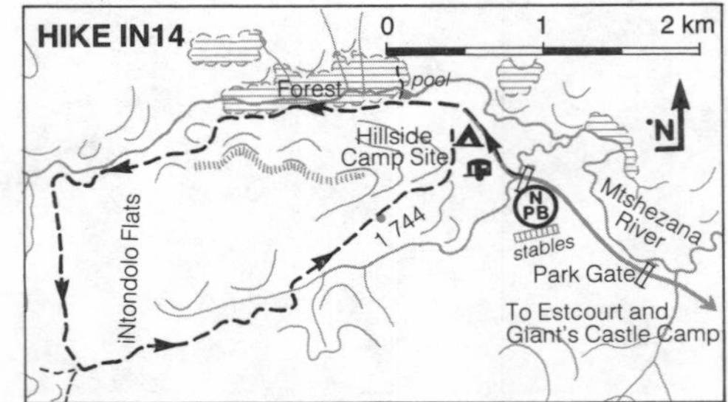

Tom's Cave *Hike IN15*

Route: *Round trip from Hillside Camp Site via Tom's Cave*
Distance: *17 kilometres*
Duration: *6 hours*
Grade: *Moderate*
General: *This hike makes a figure '8' with a common middle section of 500 m. Hikers may not stay overnight in the cave, which is reserved for horse riders.*

▶ From the camp site follow the iNtondolo Flats path to a four-way junction after 4 km (Hike IN14) and turn left there. Bear left again after 500 m and then, at a fork a little further on, bear to the right around a guard hut, past a tarn on your left, and down the Little Berg escarpment to the Shayaka Stream. Cross the river and head to a junction 1 km from the river where the route takes the path to the right. Continue along

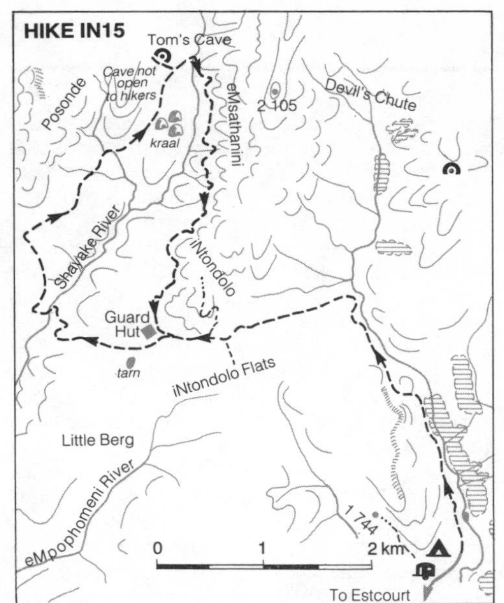

an easy gradient for 2 km to the cave, which is set off the path to the left.

▸ Carry on to cross the river where the path turns back down the opposite bank, weaving in and out of the scalloped cliff line for 3 km, at the edge of a level platform above the river. This brings you back to the junction at the guard hut, where you must turn left and continue for 500 m to a four-way intersection at the edge of the iNtondolo Flats. Carry straight on over the intersection across the flats, towards the Mtshezana River. On reaching the river, 1 km from the intersection, the path curves around to the right and follows the river's left-hand bank all the way back to camp, passing the forest upstream from Hillside.

Tree Fern Cave *Hike IN16*

Route: *Hillside Camp Site to Tree Fern Cave*
Distance: *12 kilometres*
Duration: *4 hours*
Grade: *Moderate*
General: *You will have to return to the camp site after your visit to Tree Fern Cave, as the cave is reserved for horse riders and camping out is not permitted in the game reserve.*

▸ From the camp site take the path up the left-hand bank of the Mtshezana River and then across the iNtondolo Flats (Hike IN14) to a four-way intersection. Turn right here and then sharp left and sharp right again to ascend the iNtondolo spur above the river. The path now follows the crest of the eMsathanini Ridge, going to the left on the contour where the ridge rises to a higher level.

▸ The next section is exciting: the path clings precariously between the steep slope on the right and the cliffs on the left, above the Shayaka Stream. The path curves slowly around the head of the Shayaka River gorge and gently uphill to a junction 6 km from the four-way intersection at iNtondolo. Bear to the left here, going first gently downhill for about 1,2 km and then more steeply down a 200-m slope to a T-junction, with the cave situated in front of and below you, looking out over a forest in the valley ahead and into the Injasuti Valley, which in turn leads into the Little Tugela (Thukelana) Valley.

The cave is named after the plant *Alsophila dregei*, the tree fern which grows in partly shaded, seepage areas in the Little Berg. These plants, like the cycads, can be considered living fossils, as they are little changed from the earliest trees on earth, before flowering plants evolved.

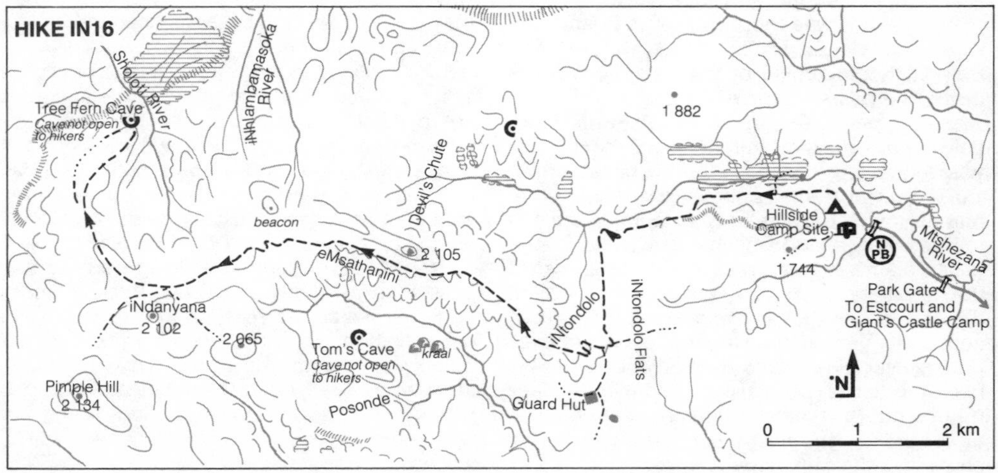

GIANT'S CASTLE

The wide grassy plateau between Injasuti and the Lotheni rivers accentuates the massive form of Giant's Castle, which is really a prominent peak and a ridge, four kilometres long. The main peak is, at 3 314 metres, the fifth highest in the Drakensberg. In 1903 the area was declared a game reserve to protect the dwindling herds of eland that migrated seasonally between high slopes of the 'Berg and the sweeter grasses of the Thornveld plains of Natal. Before this, however, little was known of the area immediately to the north of the Giant's Castle ridge, although it had seen a short but controversial military skirmish, which left an indelible mark on these mountains.

In 1873, trouble brewed between Langalibalele, a local Zulu chief, and the British colonial government of Natal. Langalibalele fled with his tribe up what was then known as Bushman's Pass, and a fight broke out on the summit, leaving five members of the Natal Carbineers dead. The pass is now named after the chief, while the peaks Erskine, Bond, Potterill, Kambule and Katana have immortalized the soldiers who fell during 'the smoke on the pass'. Mount Durnford was named after the regiment's commander, with Carbineer Point completing the military ensemble of peaks. At the top of the pass a stainless steel cross marks the graves of the Carbineers, while the ruins of a rock wall in the lower pass is a remnant of the British authorities' attempts to stop cattle thieves fleeing over the mountains. Many of the passes here and to the south are littered with boulder fragments which are the remains of attempts to block the passes during the last century by blasting in the rock ramparts.

The last Bushman was seen – and duly shot for the tribe had been officially classified as vermin – in the Giant's Castle area just a few years before the game reserve was proclaimed. The little man in question was of special interest, because around his waist he carried a belt of antelope horns, containing all the powdered colours used in Bushman rock art. This death was tragic beyond belief, for this last lonely survivor of an essentially peaceful and graceful culture which had been destroyed by greed and intolerance, was probably one of the world's great anonymous artists. What a chance was missed here, for had he and his fellow hunters survived just a few more years they would certainly have found refuge in the new reserve, and continued their old ways, sharing with us their wisdom of nature. With their passing the spiritual giants of the Drakensberg disappeared into the realm of legends.

Accommodation at Giant's Castle is offered at a rustic bungalow camp: most of the buildings are made of stone and the roofs of some of the huts have been camouflaged by the planting of indigenous grass. No camping facilities exist, but hikers may book the two mountain huts which lie neatly at either end of the area, level with the Contour Path. (The huts are situated near the bases of Giant's Castle and Bannerman passes respectively, and bear those names.) Camping inside the reserve, and especially in the once-popular caves, is now prohibited, but hikers can ascend the passes and then camp anywhere on the summit. Bannerman's Cave is usually used as an overnight spot there, but remember to carry your passport as you will be in Lesotho. Be sensible about where you find your drinking water when sharing the upper valleys of the Jarateng River with the herds that graze there. There is a third, smaller hikers' shelter, called Meander Hut, on the edge of the Little Berg above Meander Stream.

The main river in the reserve is the Bushman's, which rises at the head of Langalibalele Pass. It is stocked with trout, and fishing is a favourite pastime here. My only complaint about the reserve is its seeming disdain for hikers in the 'civilized' areas of the reserve, which has long been the haunt of mountaineers. Perhaps it is official policy to provide only toilets at a picnic spot, with access to all other facilities being restricted to bungalow guests. Because of this, no hot meal or shower, no drink or fireside chat awaits the weary hiker on his or her return from the Giant's stronghold.

Game is what Giant's Castle is really all about. Hikers will see baboon, eland and grey rhebuck, blesbok and the shy oribi if they are lucky, while bushbuck, klipspringer and reedbuck are common but seldom seen. There are about 20 red hartebeest in the reserve as well as duiker, which, although shy, are often seen around camps and cultivated areas. It is the birds, however, that make this game reserve special, for the giants of the mountains are now the lammergeiers – half-eagle, half-vulture – which rely on mountains and pastoral societies for their survival. These great birds were once found from the Western Cape, up eastern Africa and through the Middle East to China and the Himalayas. Today, in southern Africa, only Lesotho offers the conditions essential for the endangered lammergeiers' survival. A hide has been established at Giant's Castle where the birds are fed during the winter and from where bird enthusiasts can watch them along with black eagles, jackal buzzards, rock kestrels, lanner falcons, Cape vultures, crows and ravens, all taking their place in pecking order around the carcasses.

Unless stated otherwise, the distances given for all hikes in the Giant's Castle area are from the main camp or from the picnic area, which are only 500 metres apart. Hikers who are not staying in the bungalows must park their cars at the picnic area and begin their hike from there.

The Contour Path route (Hike GC14) across the Giant's Castle Game Reserve passes the peak after which the park was named. The easiest way from Giant's Castle Main Camp to Giant's Hut (seen here) is to follow the Oribi Ridge path described in Hike GC9.

Main Caves *Hike GC1*

Route: *Giant's Castle Main Camp to Main Caves*
Distance: *2 kilometres*
Duration: *40 minutes*
Grade: *Easy*
General: *This picturesque hike leads from the camp, along the river near the edge of a forest, up to the large caves, which are important archaeological sites and have been turned into a museum showing the Bushman's way of life. The Main Cave paintings can be found to the right of the museum cave. Tours are conducted throughout the year at set times in the company of a game guard; an entrance fee must be paid at the NPB office. This is the appropriate place to begin you acquaintance with Giant's Castle.*

▶ Starting from the Parks Board office, continue through the camp and along the concrete path above Two Dassie Stream, which is a tributary of the Bushman's River, to the caves. You shouldn't get lost as the path is signposted. It is also possible to approach the caves from the picnic site, going down to the river and following the River Walk for 1,5 km upstream to the junction below the caves. The path then winds downstream to a group of large boulders where

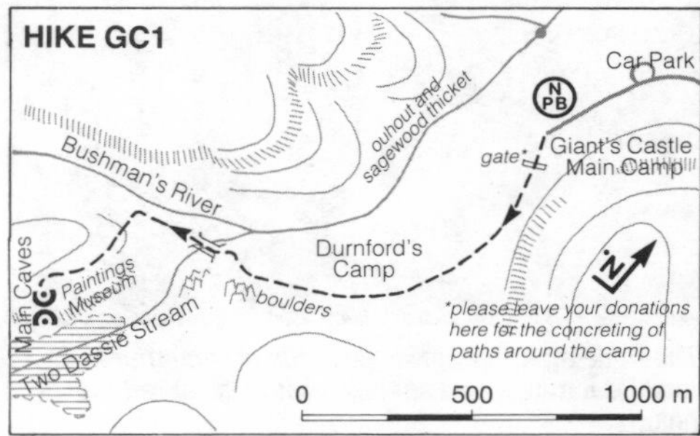

you will find '75' carved into one of the rocks: this was, no doubt, inscribed by one of the 75th Regiment during attempts in 1874 to block the escape routes of cattle raiders by blowing up strategic points in the passes. Cross Two Dassie Stream and the path, once again concreted, goes up to the Caves.

The river bank is overgrown with the ubiquitous ouhout and sagewood. The drooping leaves of the sagewood are a favourite winter food for the eland, which can no longer reach the sweeter grass of the Thornveld when the sour grasses of the Drakensberg withdraw their nutrients into their roots. It is not uncommon at this time of the year to approach within 100 m of the eland as they browse along the river bank, or to round a corner and virtually bump into these largest of all antelope.

The male mountain pride butterfly is sometimes mistaken for a small sunbird as it feeds at red-hot pokers.

Forest Walk Hike GC2

Route: *Giant's Castle Main Camp to the Forest*
Distance: *2,2 kilometres*
Duration: *1 hour and 45 minutes*
Grade: *Easy*
General: *This is a delightful walk: the blurr of water rushing over pebbles and gnarled roots, the gold and chocolate-brown hues of forest litter and the variety of fern fronds and moss-coated tree trunks combine in the colours and textures of a rich tapestry.*

▶ Take the path leading to Main Caves (Hike GC1), as far as the junction on the left-hand bank of the stream. From here you can follow either bank through the forest: the left-hand bank (going upstream) travels above the river while the right-hand path hugs the river, with three crossings over wooden foot-bridges. Ideally, you should follow one and then the other bank by way of backtracking, as the two paths do not meet. The path on the right-hand bank is a cul-de-sac, whereas the left-hand one leaves the gorge just before it narrows, and then follows the Two Dassie Stream up to Giant's Hut. Either way, several excellent, enticing pools are to be found along the river.

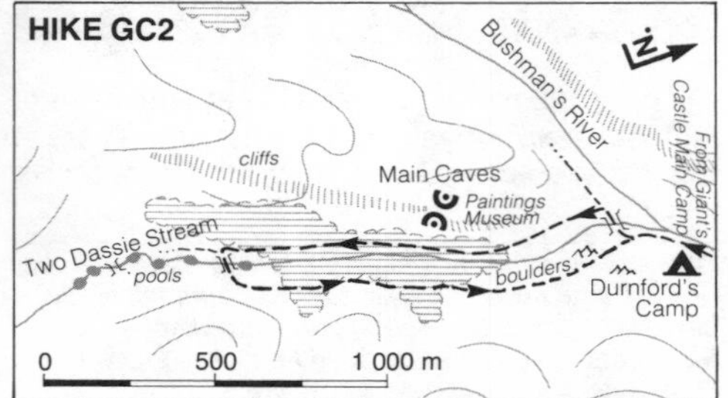

Grysbok Bush Hike GC3

Route: *Giant's Castle Main Camp to Grysbok Bush*
Distance: *4 kilometres*
Duration: *2 hours and 30 minutes*
Grade: *Fair*
General: *This hike takes you up the Bushman's River to the largest forest in the Giant's Castle area (the largest forests in the reserve are to be found along the Injasuti River to the north). This is the place to sit quietly in the hope of seeing a bushbuck. This most beautiful of all antelope is easily recognized by the white spots on the rump and dark stripes across the saddle, and its sharp bark. They eat mainly wild fruits, shoots and roots in the forest.*

▶ Follow the path to Main Caves (Hike GC1) and cross Two Dassie Stream just above its confluence with the Bushman's River. Climb towards the caves, but keep to the right-hand path, along the left-hand bank of the Bushman's River, while the path to the left goes uphill to the caves. About 500 m past the turn-off to the caves, another path branches off to the left, up the Giant's Ridge. Continue straight along the river, however, towards Middle Ridge, where a path goes up to the left after 1 km.

▶ Follow the river bank for another 500 m to a footbridge across the river, where a path goes across the bridge and up the ridge on the left towards the Contour Path and Langalibalele Pass. Do not cross the bridge, but take the more left-hand path marked Grysbok Bush. The path is concreted along a stretch of ground that tends to be boggy in summer.

▶ Cross a footbridge as you enter the forest. After another 15 to 20 minutes of walking, you will arrive at a series of pools and cascades, which become torrents and whirlpools when the river is in flood.

Eland browsing in the Giant's Game Reserve. In 1903 this area was proclaimed a reserve to protect the dwindling herds of eland that migrate seasonally between the high slopes of the 'Berg and the sweeter grasses of the Thornveld plains of Natal.

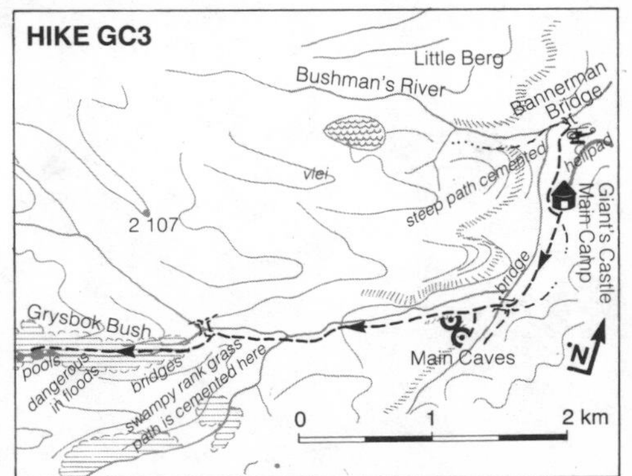

River Walk Hike GC4

Route: *Giant's Castle Main Camp to Bushman's River*
Distance: *1,5 kilometres*
Duration: *30 minutes*
Grade: *Easy*
General: *This pleasant stroll, which was mentioned in Hike GC1, has no specific destination and can join the Forest Walk (Hike GC2) for a most enjoyable, varied ramble of about 3 km.*

▶ Starting at the picnic site, take the concrete path down to the river, where you can swim among the trout in the large pool. Do not cross Bannerman's Bridge but find the path leading up the left-hand bank of the river, as it winds in and out of the tangled bush – it is quite easy but hardly serious to lose the path here from time to time. Eland like to browse on the sagewood bushes during the winter (Hike GC1).

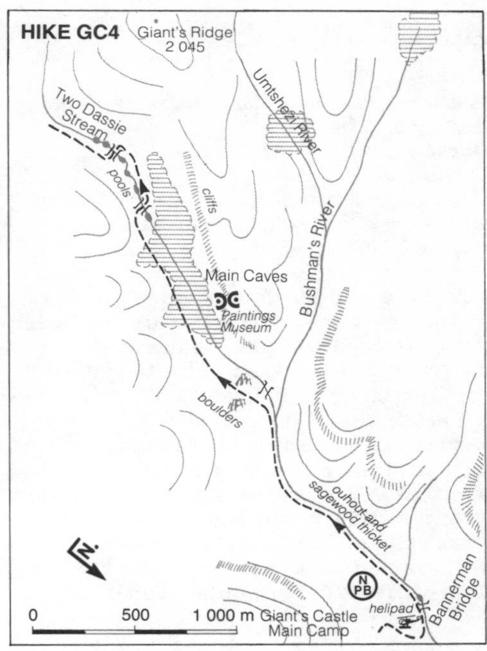

▶ After 1 km a path comes down from the hutted camp on the left and continues past the boulders where you will find the carved figure '75' marking the spot where the 75th Regiment camped during its attempts to thwart cattle raiders in 1873. Further on, you will come to a junction in the path next to a footbridge where you can do one of four things: cross the bridge up to the main caves, continue straight on into the forest (which you can also reach from the opposite bank – see Hike GC2), turn back, or sit down and have a rest.

Berg View Hike GC5

Route: *Giant's Castle Main Camp to Berg View*
Distance: *5 kilometres*
Duration: *1 hours and 40 minutes*
Grade: *Fair*
General: *This hike along the Little Berg plateau affords one of the best views of the Escarpment, ranging from Giant's Castle to Cathkin Peak.*

▸ Begin behind the game warden's residence and turn left away from the hutted camp, up the hill to the south-east, passing an iron shed. The path is marked 'Berg View Walk – Meander Hut'. At the top of the hill bear left for 500 m and then left again, away from Meander Hut. The path winds along for 2 km, parallel to and above the main road of the park. Turn right at a four-way intersection. The path goes gently downhill to a stream and then up to a fork. Bear left here, going uphill and passing to the right of the koppie before dropping a little way to a level platform where a side junction leads off to the left.

▸ You should be treated to some magnificent views along this path. After 1,5 km, the path does a 2-km loop around a series of tarns called The Lakes. If you are here at dawn or dusk, sitting quietly and camouflaged in the grass, you are likely to see yellowbilled and black ducks, as well as grey rhebuck and other small antelope.

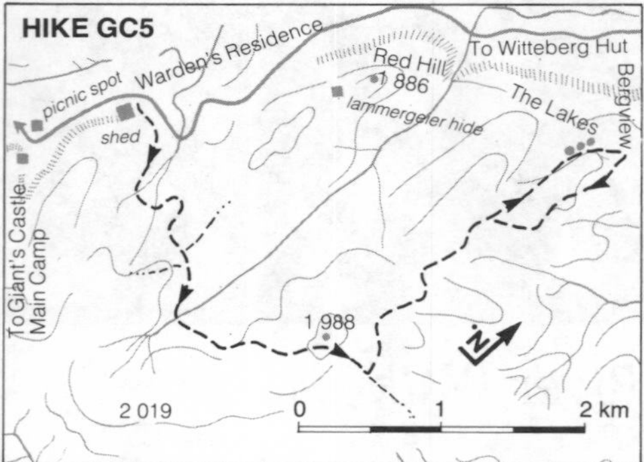

Meander Hut Hike GC6

Route: *Giant's Castle picnic area to Meander Hut*
Distance: *5,5 kilometres*
Duration: *2 hours*
Grade: *Fair*
General: *There are two ways to get to this hut, which overlooks the Meander Stream from its perch on top of the cliffs of the Little Berg. The first route is a 5,5 km trip starting on the path behind the warden's residence, while the second is the 4-km variation going up a path 1 km beyond the warden's residence towards the Park gate. A circular trip would make a very enjoyable 9,5 km hike. The hut accommodates four people and it must be booked. I will describe the slightly longer but more commonly used route starting from behind the warden's residence and perhaps you can make your own way back along the other path. Of course, this 'slightly shorter' route is longer if you include the walk along the tarred road back to your starting point.*

▸ Park at the picnic spot and walk 200 m up to the game warden's residence where you must take the path to the right, above and past an iron shed. If you plan to stay overnight at Meander Hut, then sign the register at the game warden's office. After 1 km the path reaches a level section and branches off to the right, back to the hutted camp. Continue straight ahead for 500 m to another side path, which leads to the right this time, towards Berg View. Once again, carry on straight and slightly downhill for another 500 m to a T-junction which overlooks Meander Stream.

▸ Turn left here and follow the line of cliffs above the river for 3 km. About 1,5 km from the T-junction the path ascends and passes to the right of a prominence marked by a beacon at 2 019 m. From here the path goes gently downhill for another 1,5 km to a junction near the hut. This section of the hike is most attractive. Bear right for a few hundred metres and you will reach the hut situated above the gorge. If you haven't booked into the hut, you will now wish you had.

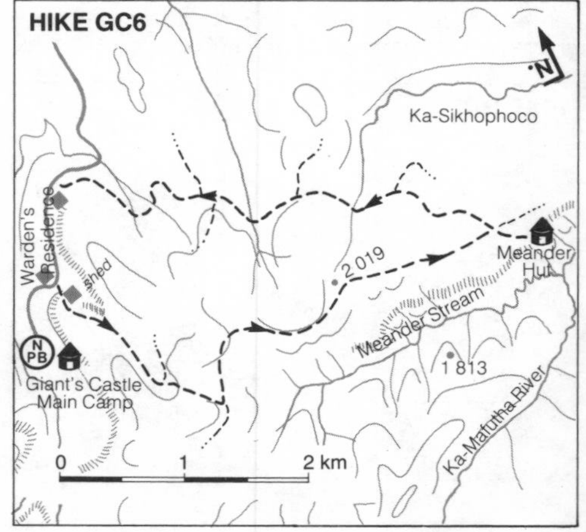

(Far left.) Easily one of the most impressive birds of the Drakensberg, the lammergeier or bearded vulture (Gypaetus barbatos) *sometimes flies up with a bone and then drops it on a rock to smash and expose the marrow. The lammergeier seen here is feeding at the hide in the Giant's Castle area.*

(Left) Secretary birds (Sagittarius serpentarius) *are found in the tall grasses of the 'Berg, where they attack and kill snakes by means of blows of the feet.*

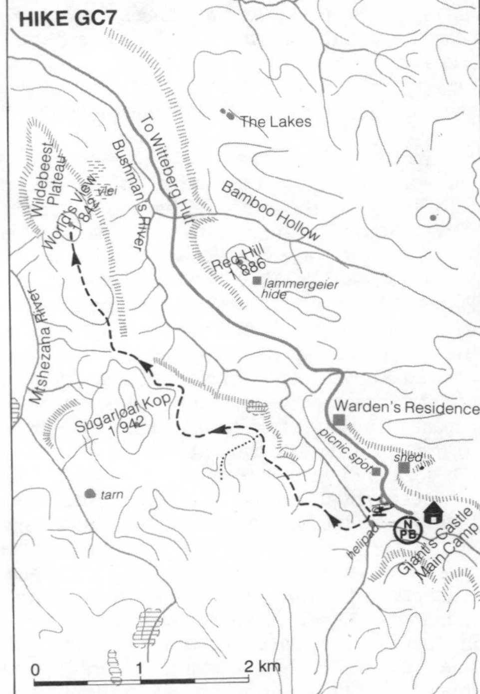

World's View Hike GC7

Route: *Giant's Castle picnic area to World's View*
Distance: *7 kilometres*
Duration: *2 hours and 30 minutes*
Grade: *Fair to Moderate*
General: *From World's View, the highest point on the Wildebeest Plateau above the Bushman's River, the views of the Drakensberg are even better than those from Berg View.*

▶ From the picnic area take the concrete path down to and across Bannerman Bridge. Go left up the right-hand river bank for about 100 m and then take the path that heads steeply up to the right for the first 200 m. Although the gradient eases off, the path climbs for another 1,8 km to a fork. At this fork bear right along a path, which contours for most of the way across a potentially swampy area. After 1 km you will pass Sugarloaf Kop on the left and a little further on, at the base of the kop, the path descends through a stream bed simply called 'Col'. The path then climbs gently for a short way to stop at an altitude of 1 777 m. A few hundred metres further on is the actual spot called World's View, which can easily be climbed. From here the high peaks of the Drakensberg describe a massive arc in front of you, accentuated by the prominent arms of Giant's Castle and Cathkin Peak at either end and by Popple Peak (3 325 m).

Wildebeest Plateau *Hike GC8*

Route: *Round trip from Giant's Castle picnic area via Wildebeest Plateau*
Distance: *18 kilometres*
Duration: *6 hours*
Grade: *Moderate*
General: *Although the hike to World's View ends at a point on the Wildebeest Plateau, the two paths diverge, with the path described not actually gaining the Little Berg plateau here, but circumnavigating the area and then climbing along a stream's course to the Little Berg much further along the hike and nearer to the Escarpment. This hike is perfect for a day's outing with opportunities to relax and swim, and to observe the surroundings at leisure.*

▶ Starting from the Giant's Castle picnic area, cross Bannerman Bridge and then turn sharp right to follow the left-hand bank of the river downstream. For the first 3 km, the path keeps fairly close to the river below the ridge, which leads to World's View and the Wildebeest Plateau. Many small streams will be crossed along this section. After 6 km the path reaches the point midway between the river and the plateau. Above the confluence of the Bushman's and Mtshezana rivers, from where you look across to the gate of the reserve, the path curves to the left to follow the left-hand bank of the Mtshezana River upstream.

Of ecological interest is the way the trees have re-established themselves on the grassy slopes above the rivers. The most prominent tree here is the mountain cedar (*Widdringtonia nodiflora*), which is common in Fynbos mountain areas. The ongoing controversy of the management of grasslands by fire is pertinent in this area: would the grasslands naturally tend toward forest if left unburned – and should they be allowed to. During the autumn months rangers all over the Drakensberg will be seen busily preparing fire breaks for the burning of large grassland areas during the winter.

▶ The path contours for about 3,5 km along the Mtshezana River and then, at the base of Sugarloaf Kop, it turns perpendicularly to the left and begins a long climb up a side gully to the top of the Little Berg, another 3,5 km away. At

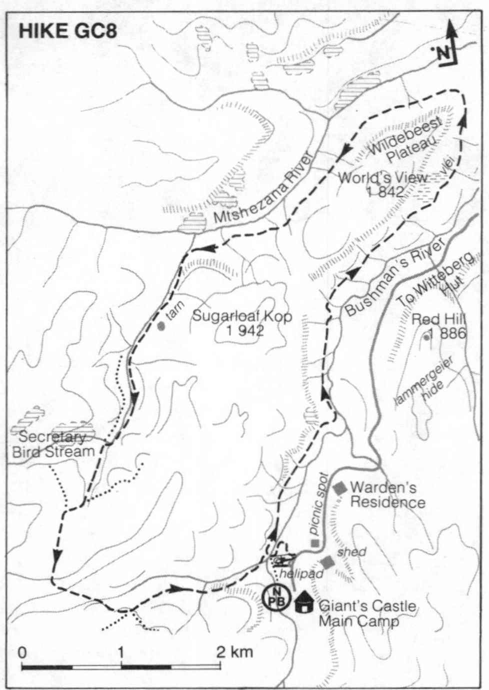

first the path runs parallel to a path on the opposite of the gully which is a stone's throw away. They meet finally after 2,5 km and carry on as a single path, past one side junction to the left, one to the right and then a second to the left before reaching the 2 000 m contour. The path then descends immediately to cross a stream and joins a main path, which leads from Bannerman Bridge to the Contour Path.

▶ Turn left here towards the bridge and, in warm weather, you can enjoy a well-deserved swim in the Bushman's River. A concrete path takes you back to the picnic area.

Giant's Hut via Oribi Ridge *Hike GC9*

Route: *Giant's Castle Main Camp to Giant's Hut*
Distance: *10,5 kilometres*
Duration: *4 hours*
Grade: *Severe*
General: *This is probably the easiest way to reach the hut, but it is not the shortest. The path up Two Dassie Stream is a little shorter, starting off fairly level but becoming very steep. On the other hand, the Oribi Ridge path climbs steadily, without becoming very steep, all the way to the Contour Path near the hut. It is also possible to reach the hut via Giant's Ridge, but it is then a 2-km walk along the Contour Path to the hut. Ultimately, you gain the same height whichever path you choose, so take either of the two up and the other down for the best hike. The hut sleeps eight and is equipped with gas cooker, pots, bunks, a toilet, running water and candles, but you must have booked to stay there.*

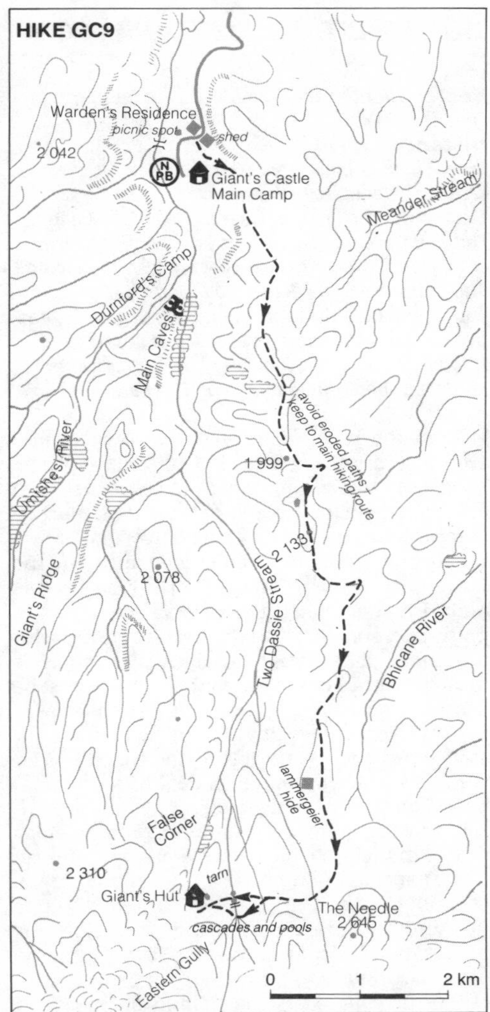

You should carry water on this hike as there is none until you reach the hut. It is always best to drink as much as you can before starting a long hike, even if you are not thirsty, for you will perspire and lose a lot of body fluid. Dehydration is not always apparent, but it turns a pleasant hike into a misery. It is better to carry water than to suffer from dehydration.

▶ Follow the path from behind the game warden's residence marked 'Giant's Hut' (and 'Meander Hut'). Climb the hill, bearing right where the Meander Hut path branches off. Keep to this path, climbing past four prominent points on the ridge and past the disused lammergeier hide. The Contour Path is met 1,5 km from the hide and from here you can see the hut to your right. Turn right and follow the path as it descends into a stream gully where deep pools and a water chute are to be found downhill from the crossing.

▶ Continue along the deeply eroded path to where the path dips and then climbs up out of one more gully before reaching the hut. In front of the hut is a tarn where, in the early morning, game is often seen drifting silently and alert through the mist around the water's edge, while in the evening ducks come to roost. This is an exceptionally peaceful and grand setting under the imposing tower of Giant's Castle. Return down Two Dassie Stream, which turns off down a ridge from a lower variation of the Contour Path leading from the hut. A route description is not really needed for this, other than to say the grass along the path is often rank and the path tends to be obscured from time to time. But fear not – just follow the river all the way back to the camp. Watch out for spitting cobras on the Oribi Ridge path: they are deadly accurate at a short distance, so if you meet an angry one, keep still and don't stare as they aim for the eyes of any adversary.

Giant's Castle Pass

Hike GC10

Route: *Giant's Hut to Giant's Castle Pass*
Distance: *6 kilometres (from Giant's Hut)*
Duration: *3 hours and 30 minutes*
Grade: *Extreme*
General: *This is one of the most difficult passes to negotiate as the gully is littered with rubble which regularly threatens to avalanche. Keep to the left-hand side of the gully when crossing the long scree bed two thirds of the way up the pass. The top of the pass and all of Giant's Ridge are actually in the*

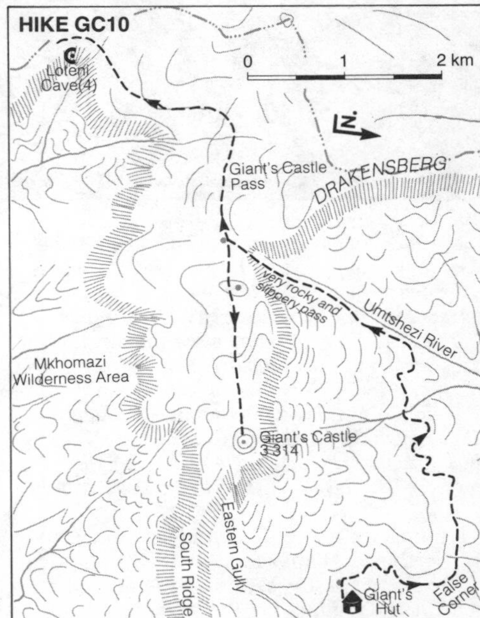

Mkhomazi Wilderness Area and not in the game reserve, so camping is permitted here. No permit is needed to enter the Wilderness Area as your entrance into the game reserve will cover this. Giant's Castle was first climbed via the pass in 1864 (an A-grade route), but the first real rock climb was negotiated by Ted Scholes and his party in 1950. On a drizzly day, Ted forged a route up a slanting, slippery chimney of the North Face directly below the highest point on the ridge; this is still regarded as one of the finest rock lines in the Drakensberg.

▸ From Giant's Hut follow the Contour Path to the north past Giant's Ridge, which goes downhill to the right. Cross four streams and then head up the mountain, 4 km from the hut, along the Umtshezi River's left-hand bank, making for the main break in the cliffs between the Escarpment and Giant's Castle range. The first kilometre is steep, but the second is far worse. On reaching the cliff bands, do not be afraid, but do be wary of trying any of the fancy variations that traverse along to the left – just keep going up.

▸ The top of the pass is marked by a cairn situated in a nek between the Escarpment and Giant's Castle. To reach the top of the Castle (3 314 m), walk for about 1 km on the contour as if to carry on straight over the ridge, but then turn left up the easiest part of the spur and just make for the highest point 2,5 km along to the east: if, however, you can't see the top of the Castle then you shouldn't be climbing it.

Bannerman Hut *Hike GC11*

Route: *Giant's Castle picnic area to Bannerman Hut*
Distance: *11 kilometres*
Duration: *4 hours and 30 minutes*
Grade: *Moderate to Severe*
General: *The hut itself is a replica of the Giant's Hut and the same conditions apply here. With an early start it is easy to make the hut by mid-morning and Bannerman Cave in time for lunch. The later you start a hike the longer you have to hike in the heat of the day – unless, of course, it is snowing, raining, hailing or just cloudy (these conditions apply for about nine months of the year).*

▸ From the picnic site proceed down to and cross Bannerman Bridge. Continue upriver, bearing to the left, for 200 m to cross a stream and then head up the well-defined path marked 'Bannerman Hut' (concreted on the steeper sections), past a lone tree at a stream and up to the Little Berg plateau. When first hiking up this path, I contemplated the relative steepness of paths and concluded that it is an equation with a number of essential variables: first, there is the actual gradient of the path, but this must be assessed according to its length; then there is the weather, the weight of your pack and your state of fitness, not forgetting the second-order variables such as state of health, amount of body fluid and, of course, degree of enthusiasm.

I know people who rush up and down steps all day in their job, but then tremble with fear at the prospect of hiking a few easy kilometres in the mountains. The moral of this anecdote is that unless pursued by angry wild animals, never rush. The most important factor in enjoying a long hike is to find your own pace, and let others in your party lag behind or speed off

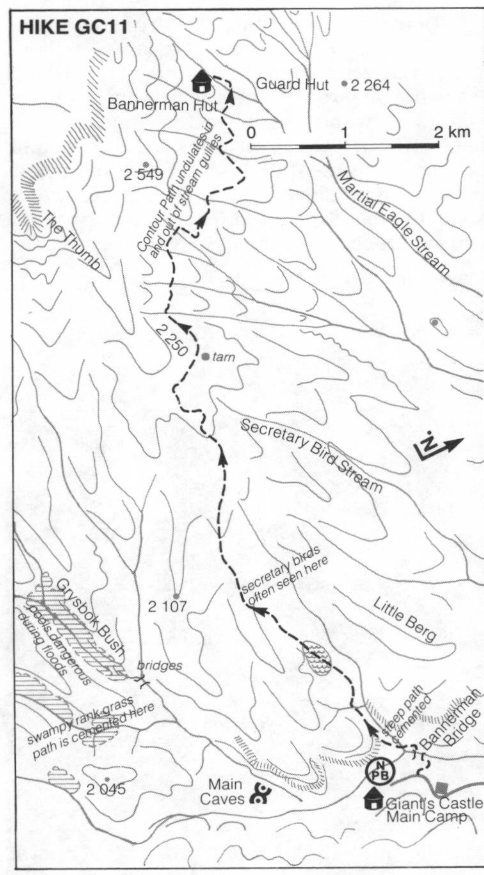

(Opposite.) Bannerman Hut is approximately 11 kilometres from Giant's Castle Main Camp at the foot of Bannerman Pass which can be seen in the background.

ahead. Stop as often as you like to rest and to admire the high peaks and the shapes of the clouds that caress them.

▶ On reaching the Little Berg it is an easy 4-km hike to the Contour Path, where you are likely to see the tall, magnificent secretary birds (*Sagittarius serpentarius*) strutting on long legs in search of lizards, snakes and rodents. Turn right along the Contour Path (northwards) to traverse under The Thumb and Bannerman Face for 4,5 km, crossing several streams *en route* to the turn-off up Bannerman Pass. The hut is situated a little way up a ridge between Bannerman Face and Gypaetus (lammergeier) Point. The last section up to Bannerman Hut always seems to be the hardest part of the hike and a mean trick to play on tired hikers. (I have not been able to establish the origin of the name 'Bannerman', and so would welcome any information in this regard.)

Bannerman Pass to Bannerman Cave *Hike GC12*

Route: *Bannerman Hut to Bannerman Cave*
Distance: *5 kilometres*
Duration: *3 hours*
Grade: *Extreme*
General: *The route description begins at Bannerman Hut (Hike GC11). Relatively speaking, this is one of the easiest passes up the Drakensberg. It is possible to do a round trip of 18 km from Bannerman Hut (or from the hutted camp), using Bannerman Cave as a midway point and returning down Langalibalele Pass – another 'easy' one. Remember to take your passport into Lesotho.*

▶ From Bannerman Hut continue on the path that goes uphill behind the hut, all the way up the pass to the cairn at the top. The top half of the pass goes up a boulder-strewn gully but small cairns mark the way through the maze. Half-way up the pass you will find Spare Rib Cave tucked away to the left in the first basalt band that is reached. There are actually two caves here: the first is shallow but the second is large and deep. Whether the origin of the name is culinary, cannibalistic or feministic I wasn't able to discover, for the Parks Board does not allow camping in the cave.

▶ From the top of the pass head around the chasm to the left and take the easiest line up the slope to the lowest point on the skyline to the south. Don't be tempted to descend into the valley from here; rather contour to the left around the bowl-shaped side, dropping only 60 m in altitude from the ridge now behind you (not the 120 m as indicated on the map). The cave will be found set in a low band of rock on the eastern slope (your left) of the valley. An indistinct path does go that way and is marked irregularly by stone cairns, the largest of which is at the cave entrance. The cave, which faces west across Lesotho, is small, so don't expect luxury accommodation.

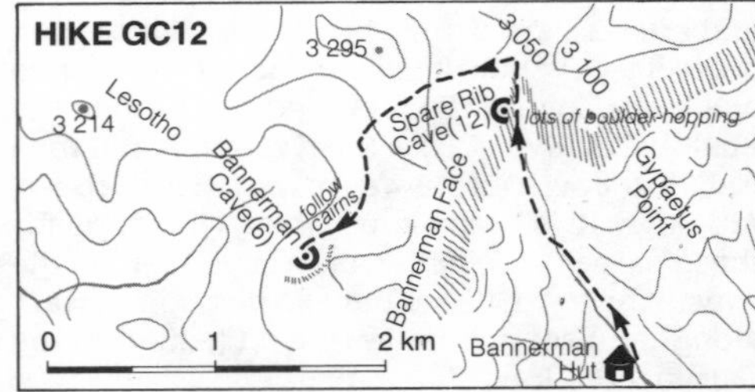

Langalibalele Pass

Hike GC13

Route: *Giant's Castle picnic area to Bannerman Cave via Langalibalele Pass*
Distance: *6,5 kilometres*
Duration: *3 hours and 30 minutes*
Grade: *Severe to Extreme*
General: *As I mentioned in the introduction to this chapter, this pass was used by the rebellious Langalibalele in his conflict with the British authorities in Natal in 1873; prior to this it had been known as the Bushman's Pass, where the river of the same name rises. This is the easiest pass by which to attain the summit of the mountains in the northern part of the range (that is, from Giant's Castle northwards). From Bannerman Hut, Langalibalele and Bannerman passes could make a hard but interesting one-day (17,5 km) Escarpment traverse. From the hutted camp you could combine the passes into a two- or three-day hike, sleeping first at the head of the pass and then on to Bannerman Hut (or the hutted camp) on the second day. The distance given for the hike is measured from the point on the Contour Path where it meets the path from the hutted camp, approximately half-way between the two passes.*

▶ Turn left along the Contour Path (Hike GC11) and after 2,5 km you will pass the path coming up from Grysbok Bush on the left. Continue along the Contour Path for another 1 km to the Bushman's River. Cross the river and then turn right to follow it all the way to the top of the pass. Although it is 3 km long (about standard for these passes), the path gains only 870 m on the way to the top. Once at the top of the pass, walk along the Escarpment to the left (south) to the Carbineers' Grave.

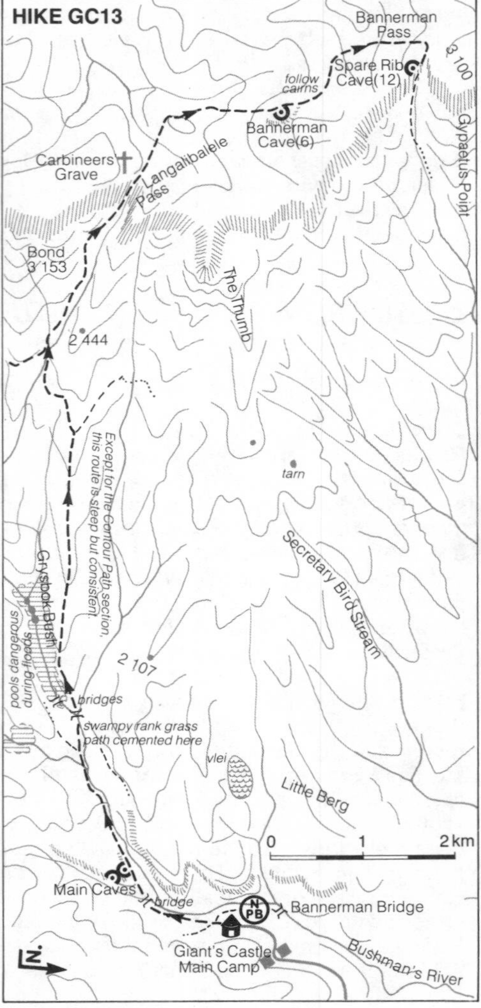

▶ To reach Bannerman Cave from the top of pass, follow the stream into Lesotho for about 1 km and then turn right up a tributary which leads northwards. Follow this stream uphill for about 1,5 km and the cave will be found in a rock band on your right directly below the high point on the Escarpment to the right and just below the level of the ridge directly ahead. The cave is small but quite sheltered from all but the western approach.

Hikers in the reserve are likely to come across game, such as this herd of eland below Giant's Castle peak.

Contour Path – Giant's Hut to Injasuti *Hike GC14*

Route: *Giant's Castle Main Camp to Lower Injasuti Cave*
Distance: *31,5 kilometres*
Duration: *2 days*
Grade: *Severe*
General: *While the Contour Path at Injasuti ends at no specific destination below the Trojan Wall, it is an easy hike from there down to the Lower Injasuti Cave. Both this cave and Bannerman Hut, the first night's stop, must be booked as camping out is not permitted. I would highly recommend this walk to anyone making the necessary arrangements, as it passes some of the most impressive scenery of the range. To the south the character of the Drakensberg changes, with the high peaks not quite as spectacular as those from Giant's Castle northwards, and the lower reaches of the mountains consist of homogenous grassland – it is more picturesque than dramatic.*

▸ **Day 1** (18 km): Begin by climbing to Giant's Hut (Hike GC9) and sleeping there if you wish, for it is certainly worth the stay, and the walk from here to Bannerman Hut is a full day's work. (Don't forget to book in advance if you plan to stay at Giant's Hut.) This 18-km section is easy to follow: just keep the Escarpment on your left and your feet on the well-defined path. The first 2-km stretch is flat but for one short climb, while the next 5,5 km go down to each stream and up the other side; with a heavy pack this is exhausting work indeed. Nine and a half kilometres from the hut the base of Langalibalele Pass is reached. Along the Escarpment you pass, in order, The Gable and South Ridge (with two holes through it), Giant's Castle and Long Wall, Katana, Carbineer Point, Kambule, Mount Durnford, Potterill, Bond and Erskine.

▸ From the bottom of Langalibalele Pass you will see why The Thumb was so named, standing as it does away from the main cliffs. Another 3,5 km brings you to the path which leads off to the right to the hutted camp. Five hundred metres further on is a tarn wedged between the Contour Path and the Secretary Bird Stream path. After four more kilometres of up and down, Bannerman Hut is a welcome sight.

▸ **Day 2** (13,5 km): On the second day the first kilometre past Gypaetus Point is easy, but thereafter the path climbs up for about 2 km before levelling off towards The Judge. While The Judge is the most obvious feature here, Popple Peak (3 325 m), set a little behind the Escarpment, is the fourth highest peak in South Africa.

▸ Judge Pass, between Popple Peak and The Judge, involves some serious rock climbing, so we will avoid that and carry on to The Corner, where the path becomes less well defined than before. The Corner Pass also involves rock climbing, so on we go around what is indeed a corner, for here we have to do a 2-km turn around its stubborn bulk. From the eMbovaneni Stream, which rises between The Corner's northern corner with the Escarpment, it is only 2 km along the base of the impregnable Trojan Wall to the path leading down a long, grassy spur to the Lower Injasuti Cave, which lies on the Injasuti River below the Triplets.

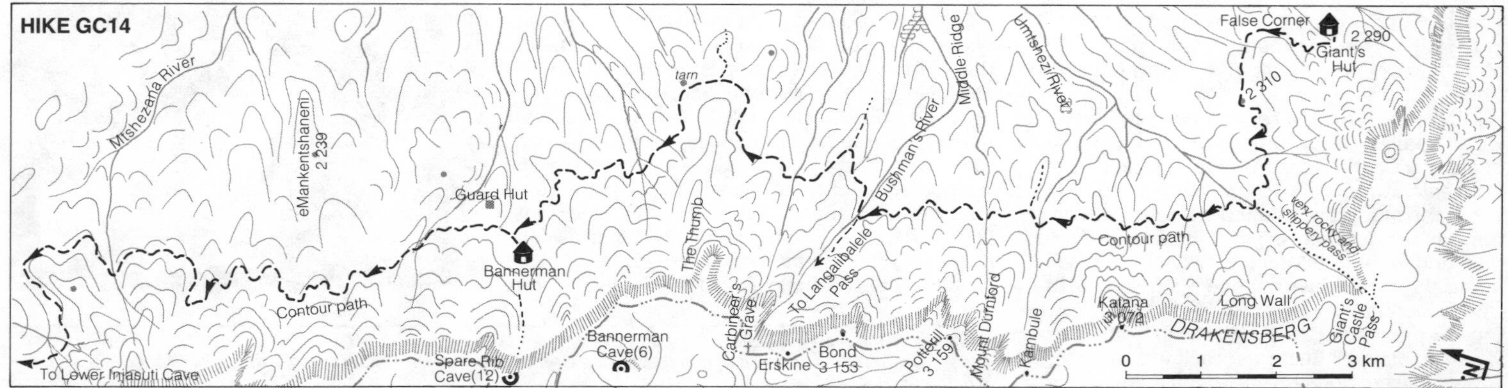

MKHOMAZI

The vast Mkhomazi Wilderness Area stretches from Giant's Castle in the north to Sani Pass in the south and includes the Loteni, Vergelegen and Mzimkhulwana nature reserves. While the foothills are well known to hikers and trout fishermen alike, the summit is probably the part of the High 'Berg least known to mountaineers. This is due to the long distances between departure points and the passes, the ridges of the Little Berg, which the mountaineer has to negotiate before reaching the passes, and the tortuous nature of the Contour Path, which is developed only over short stretches.

Highmoor Forestry Station stands north of the Giant's Castle ridge but beyond the limits of the game reserve, so few hikers use it as a base; it does, however, have camping facilities which Giant's Castle lacks. The main forestry station in the area is Mkhomazi, but there are no public facilities there and it is a long distance to hike from here to the Escarpment. The Mkhomazi Trail hut (under construction at the time of writing) is the only mountaineering facility near Mkhomazi, but it is situated well within the confines of the Little Berg.

Kamberg Nature Reserve, one of three Natal Parks Board reserves in this area, lies due east of Giant's Castle ridge and has a hutted camp. The main attraction of the reserve is trout fishing in the Mooi River, which rises at the base of the Castle's ramparts. There is also a unique, one and a half kilometre 'wheelchair walk' along the river. Just outside Kamberg, in the tiny Impofana Nature Reserve, is Game's Pass Cave (or Shelter Cave), which has one of the finest displays of Bushman rock art anywhere: rows of large, polychrome eland seem to walk right across the cave wall, superimposed on stylized Bantu figures, while Bushmen hunters leap above. Fossilized dinosaur footprints can be seen in the sandstone nearby.

Although the Loteni Nature Reserve is used mainly by keen trout anglers, it is also the most convenient base from which mountaineers can operate. There is a hutted camp as well as a caravan and camp site, only 10 kilometres from the prominent peaks of The Tent, The Hawk and Redi. When viewed from the camp site, Eagle Rock resembles the head of a raptor. This is the beginning of the route up the best pass in the Mkhomazi area and nine kilometres of Contour Path proper. At Vergelegen, another NPB trout fishing reserve, there are two cottages that may be booked through the NPB's central reservations office, and access up a number of passes is possible from here. To get to the Thaba Ntlenyana (3 482 m), the highest peak in southern Africa, one ascends the Nhlangeni Pass.

There are no really impressive free-standing peaks along this section of the Escarpment, but the relative height is as impressive as anywhere else, with a rugged summit plateau. Because the area is so seldom climbed, there is even a number of unnamed prominences of over 3 000 m. The main features of the Escarpment wall include some of the highest points on the subcontinent, such as, from the north, The Tent (3 130 m), The Hawk (3 077 m), Redi Peak (3 314 m – less than 1 m lower than Giant's Castle), Duart Castle (2 910 m), Mlahlangubo

(Opposite.) In January 1951, a survey party made up of Lorna Pierson (far left), Gillian Earle (centre), Joan Watkins (right), Des Watkins (below left) and Barry Anderson determined the highest peak in Southern Africa – Thabana Ntlenyana at 3 482 metres.

(3 071 m), Ngaqamadolo (3 006 m), ka-Ntuba (at 3 355 m this is the third highest peak in South Africa but is not often acknowledged as such) and the Twelve Apostles which terminate at Sani Pass.

At the bottom of Sani Pass is the luxury hotel of the same name, one that appeals more to the conference trade than the mountain spirit. The pass is a traditional trading route used by mountain tribesmen to ferry wool, mohair and skins to Himeville. The route was merely a bridle path until 1955 when David Alexander built a pass by which a transport company connected Himeville to Mokhotlong, which was once an outpost of the British Empire known as 'the loneliest settlement in Africa'. Today, the Mokhotlong Mountain Transport Company runs a daily service up the pass, starting at Giant's Cup Motors near the hotel and ending at the Mountaineers' Chalet in Lesotho – the highest, licensed resort in southern Africa and a place where mountaineers can feel at home. Only four-wheel drive vehicles are allowed up the pass, but it is possible to hike up from the NHW car park where the Giant's Cup Trail begins.

Giant's Castle forms a pivot in the Drakensberg where the range curves from a NW-SE axis to a NE-SW one. The vegetation here is Alpine veld (*Themeda festuca*) and is similar to the rest of the Drakensberg, but there are only tiny patches of relic Afro-montane forest along some rivers, such as that at Yellowwood Cave on the Ka-Masihlenga River. The main attraction to hikers in this area is the many caves of the Little Berg and so hike descriptions concentrate on these; most summit caves are now used by the Basotho as kraals. Mkhomazi Forestry Station is the main control point for the area and permits can be obtained from there or the three NPB reserves mentioned.

Contour Path – Giant's Castle to Sani Pass *Hike MK1*

Route: *Giant's Hut to Sani Pass*
Distance: *81,5 kilometres*
Duration: *5 to 6 days*
Grade: *Extreme*
General: *The Contour Path is not continuous across the Mkhomazi Wilderness Area; to complete the full distance involves descending to below the Little Berg in places, and ascending the Escarpment for a 3-km stretch. For the intrepid mountaineer, however, this is a superb but strenuous experience. Check permits, access and bookings before departure and remember to carry a passport. Many shorter variations of this hike can be undertaken.*

▶ **Day 1** (19 km): From Giant's Hut (in the Giant's Castle Game Reserve) the Contour Path follows the Giant's Castle/Ka-Mbevula ridge and descends to Loteni Nature Reserve. Five kilometres from the hut the path meets the Loteni Track at a T-junction where the route goes off to the right. The first 12 km are fairly flat and easy. The path then traverses across the western (right-hand) base of Sheba's Breasts, descends a long spur, crosses the Loteni River and a tributary and then veers right to the Loteni camp site.

▶ **Day 2** (14 km): From Loteni camp site head

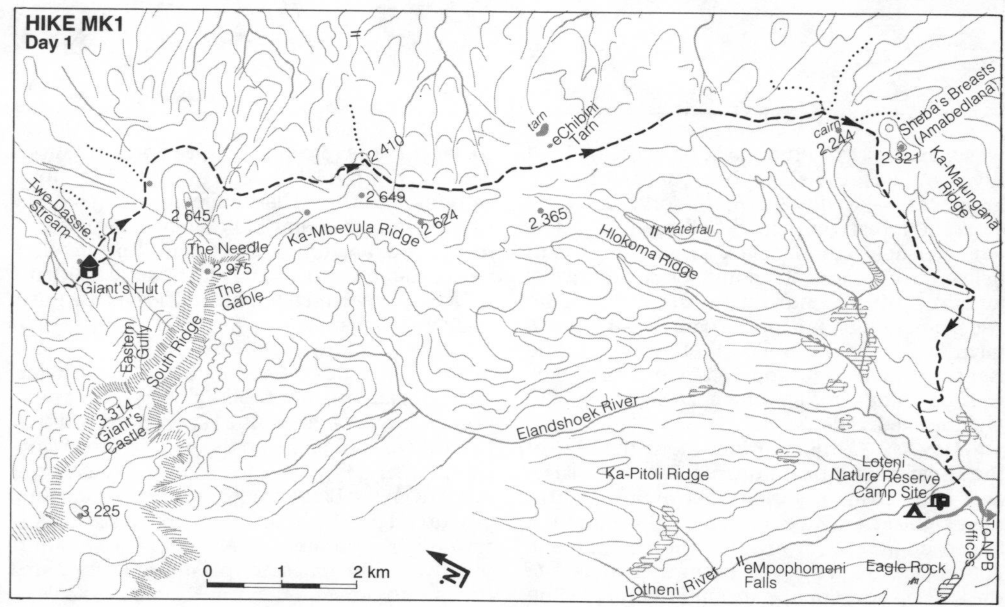

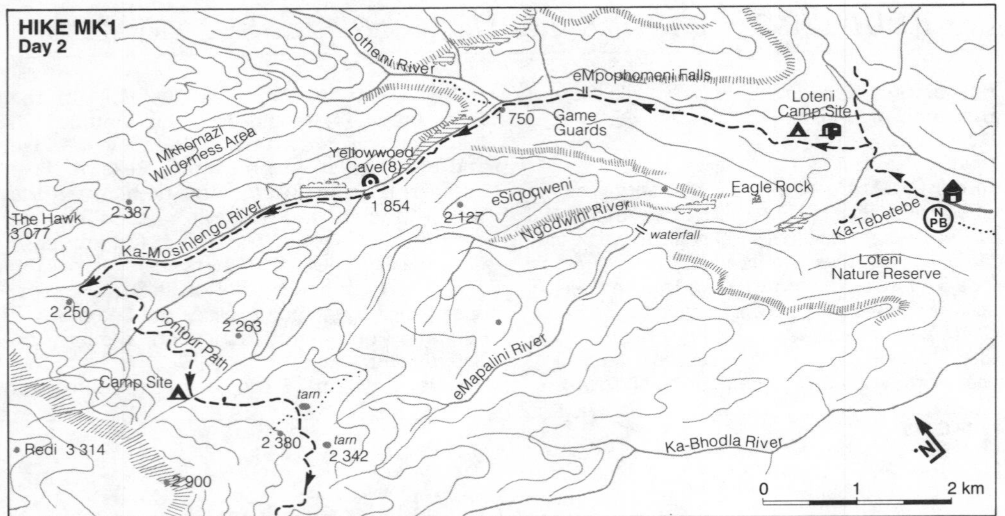

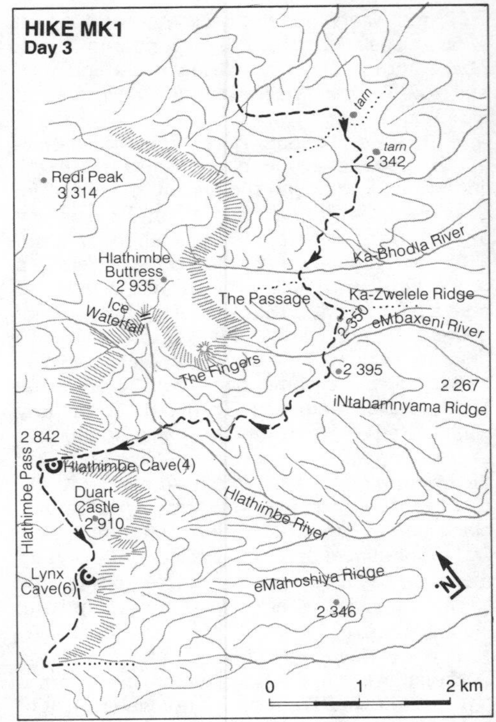

westwards up the left-hand bank of the Lotheni River and past the eMpophomeni Falls. After a kilometre take the left-hand fork, continue along a forest and pass Yellowwood Cave, which sleeps eight people. Cross a side stream below the cave and, 3 km further on , there is a junction; turn left to follow the base of the Escarpment for 4 km, past a camp site next to a tarn, to a four-way junction. Above you to the right are Redi Peak and Pass which involves rock climbing. This should make a good spot to end the second day's hiking.

▶ **Day 3** (9,5 km): Continue along the base of the Escarpment, past Buttress Pass (The Passage) after 2 km, and then after another 500 m turn right at a T-junction, curving around the folded spurs and in towards the Escarpment. For the next 3 km the path keeps more or less to the 2 360 m contour line, around Hlathimbe Buttress and the prominent Fingers formation. Once across the Hlathimbe River, the 'Contour Path' ascends the Hlathimbe Pass, where the cave of the same name is situated on the Escarpment lip, at an altitude of 2 842 m. Turn left and pass around the back of Duart Castle (2 910 m) to Lynx Cave, which should suffice as the third night's stopover.

▶ **Day 4** (19 km): Between Hlathimbe and Mlahlangubo passes the path crosses a wide valley head on the Lesotho side. The route descends the Mlahlangubo Pass, 1,5 km south of Lynx Cave, and picks up the true Contour Path 2 km down the path. Turn right here and veer away from the Escarpment, proceeding diagonally up a spur for 1 km. Turn sharp right back towards Mlahlangubo Peak (3 071 m), wending your way in and out of the pleated folds for 2 km. Cross a stream and the first Ngaqamadola Pass heads up the Escarpment to your right. Zigzag out and in and cross a stream. Pass the second Ngaqamadola Pass and Rock Arch on your right and for 4 km cross innumerable streams below The Saddle (not to be confused with the formation of the same name near Cathedral Peak).

▶ At a junction at Rock Bridge a path goes down a spur, but keep contouring for a few hundred metres over two streams, and then go steeply downhill for 2 km to the Mkhomazi River, where the Mkhomazi Pass heads up-

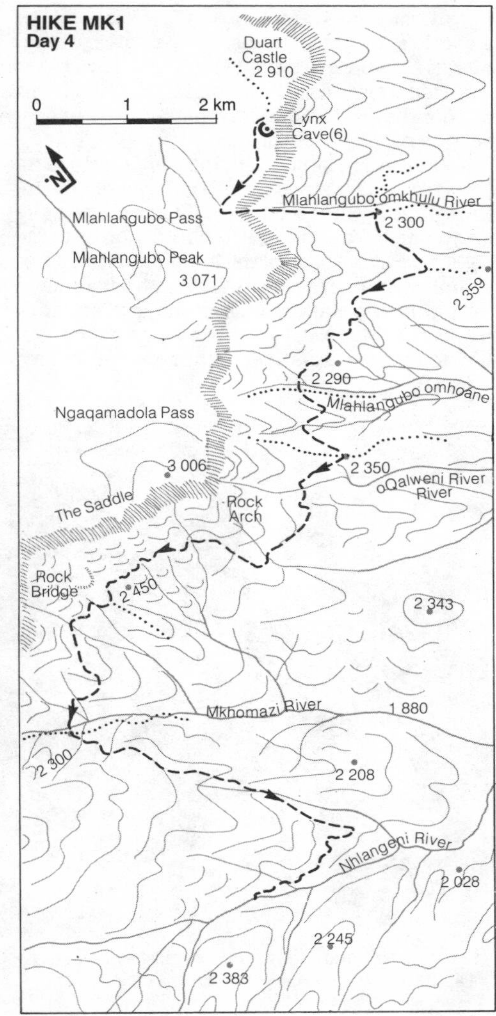

stream. Cross the river and veer diagonally away and down from the summit for 4 km (do not take the path down the Mkhomazi River), and then cut sharply back for 1 km into the Nhlangeni River valley. This 19-km stretch should be as far as your legs can carry you on the fourth day. Alternatively, camp near the Mkhomazi River 5 km further back (so I hope you read this before you set out).

▶ **Day 5** (20 km): If you wish to tackle the hike in 5 days, the final section from the Nhlangeni River to Sani Pass is a hard 20 km. Contour for 2 km and you come to a sulphur spring where you can bathe your bruised and aching body. Continue on to and cross the ka-Ntuba River and then head uphill to a junction 1,5 km from the river. Here the Mangaun Pass continues up the spur, diagonally away from the ka-Ntuba River. Bear left and after 1 km go uphill and to the right at a T-junction. Descend the slope to cross the Ntshintshini River, climb up and over a spur, cross a side stream and circle around another spur, arriving at a junction just across the next stream. One path goes down the river for 1 km to the large Kaula Cave overhang; carry on, however, along the contour for another kilometre to where a path comes up the Burnera Ridge. Here you head uphill to the right for 1 km to the Mqatsheni River, where a path leads up to the summit.

▶ Turn left here and continue for 4 km and 13 small stream crossings, passing The Pillars, to the beginning of the Twelve Apostles, 6 km from Sani Pass. Follow the base of the Apostles, meandering in and out of the spurs, across 18 streams to a gate on the Mkhomazana River; cross the river and you'll be standing on the Sani Pass road. The S.A. Police Post is about 4 km down the road, while the Mountaineers' Chalet, which is about 6 km up the twisting pass, is a good place to celebrate the end of your hike.

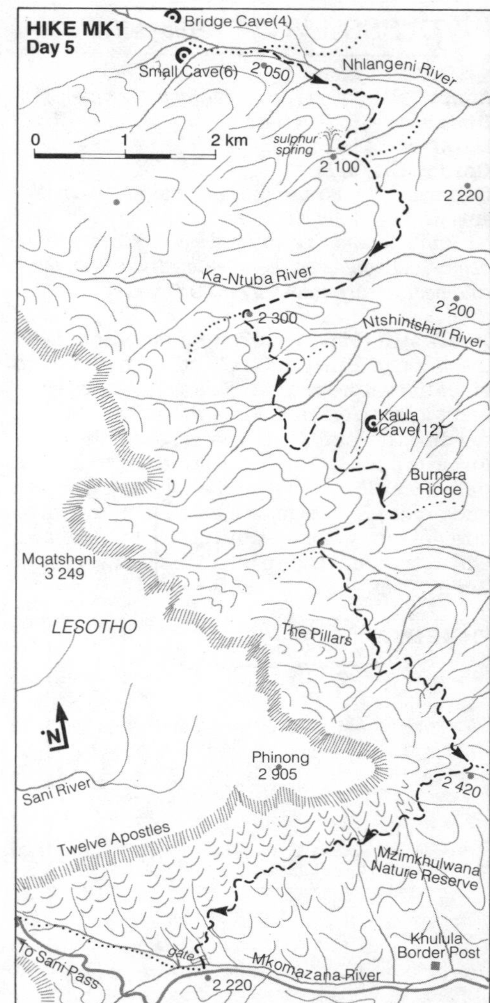

Cypress Cave *Hike MK2*

Route: *Mkhomazi Forest Station to Cypress Cave*
Distance: *4,5 kilometres*
Duration: *1 hour 30 minutes*
Grade: *Easy to Fair*
General: *This is one of the few short hikes in the area where a small party can use the cave, which has running water nearby and sleeps six to eight people, depending on the weather. There is an old ruin nearby surrounded by exotic trees.*

▶ Park at the Mkhomazi Forest Station (opposite the iNzinga Falls) and collect your permit to enter the nature reserve. Follow the only prominent path from the forestry office, starting northwards and then swinging to the west towards a river crossing. For the next 3 km the path does a loop and two wide zigzags up a ridge and across a plateau to a side junction. Carry straight on, going gently uphill to the cave, which is on the near bank of the iNzinga River. Return back along the same route.

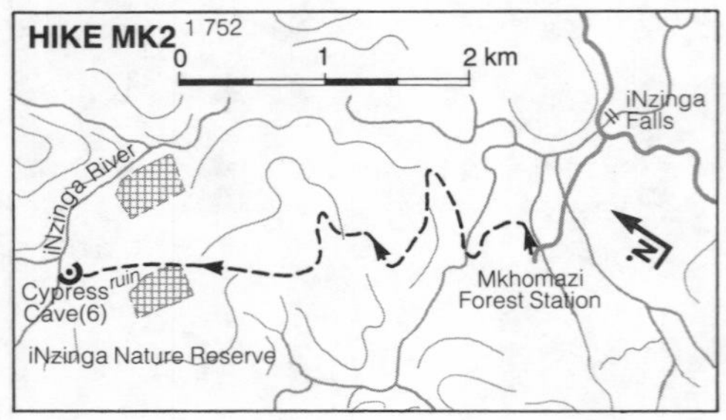

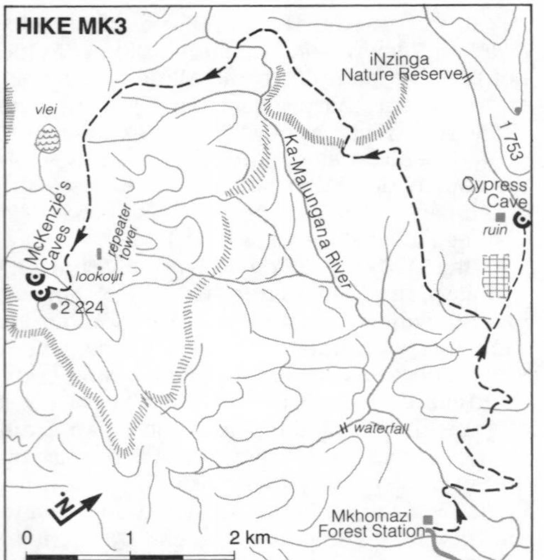

McKenzie's Caves *Hike MK3*

Route: *Mkhomazi Forest Station to McKenzie's Caves*
Distance: *11 kilometres*
Duration: *3 hours 30 minutes to 4 hours*
Grade: *Moderate*
General: *The two large caves sleep about 24 people altogether. Water is available along the path shortly before reaching the caves.*

▶ Begin along the Cypress Cave path (Hike MK2) and, after 3 km, turn left at the side junction. For the next 3 km the path ascends two spurs and then cuts diagonally left up a steep slope and then turns to the right to go very steeply up a short section. Where the gradient levels off, turn left along the top of the Little Berg. Cross the Ka-Malungana River and follow a gentle spur uphill for 2 km to a higher plateau of the Little Berg, from where you will be able to see a lookout and repeater mast. A large vlei can be found to the right of the path on the widest section of the plateau.

▶ Continue past the lookout and mast towards a prominent koppie straight ahead. Cross a river at the base of the koppie and the caves can be found a few hundred metres to the right, one at the base of the koppie and the other a short distance away to the west, both situated on top of the Ka-Malungana Ridge. The crags below the ridge are used for roosting by raptors, including the magnificent lammergeier. Return along the same route.

A gravel road winds down through rural settlements past the Mkhomazi Forest Station to the Loteni and Vergelegen reserves.

Sinclair's Shelter *Hike MK4*

Route: *Mkhomazi Forest Station to Sinclair's Shelter*
Distance: *11 kilometres*
Duration: *3 hours 30 minutes to 4 hours*
Grade: *Moderate*
General: *The cave sleeps six people. Although the route is of moderate grade, the final section ascends a steep ridge to the lip of the Escarpment.*

▶ Take the path to Cypress Cave (Hike MK2) and continue over the iNzinga River. Proceed up a tributary along the base of a ridge to a ruin, and then go diagonally left up a spur. The gradient of the path then slacks off but keeps ascending diagonally across the ridge to a T-junction, 3 km past the ruin. Turn obliquely to the right here and head towards a gully. Once above a stream head, ascend the steep incline and then take the path behind a prominent headland in the sandstone cliffs to the cave on the summit of the Ka-Nontshivovo Ridge. A stream rises on the plateau north of the cave, and on the northern edge of the plateau there is a tarn and a vlei.

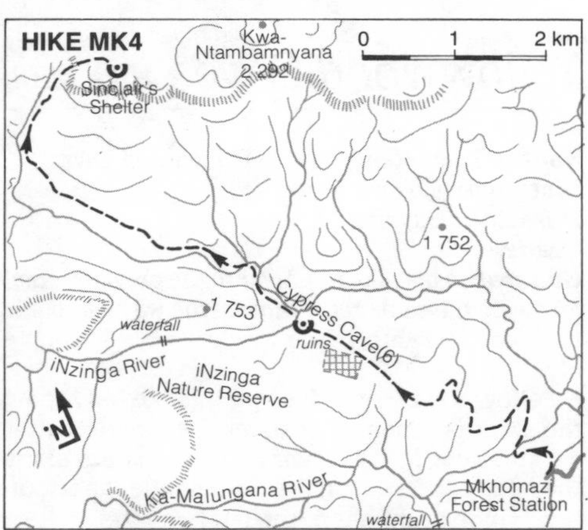

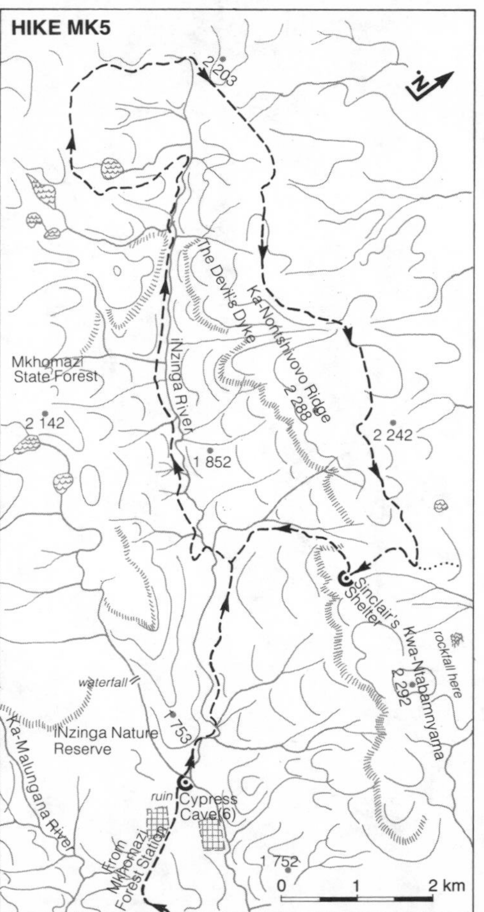

The Devil's Dyke *Hike MK5*

Route: *Round trip from Mkhomazi Forest Station via The Devil's Dyke*
Distance: *35 kilometres*
Duration: *2 days or 13 hours*
Grade: *Moderate to Severe*
General: *This is a long hike with ample water on the first section but little on the second, especially in the dry season. There are no caves on this hike, so a tent is essential.*

▶ Begin on the Cypress Cave path (Hike MK2) and continue up the iNzinga River valley. At the point where the Sinclair's Shelter path (Hike MK4) branches off to the right this route carries straight on, up the main valley with three river crossings *en route*. About 8,5 km from the Sinclair's Shelter junction the path narrows and veers sharp left up a spur and past a large vlei. The path curves to the right across the plateau, leading to a junction on the edge of the Ka-Malungana Ridge. As you are now over half-way, this is a good spot to look for a camp site.

▶ From this junction the route takes the right-hand path to the north. One kilometre further on, a path goes off at right-angles to the left, but carry on straight downhill towards a koppie. For the next 10 km the path follows the general line of The Devil's Dyke or Ka-Nontshivovo. This brings you to a T-junction where you must turn right to reach Sinclair's Shelter on the edge of the precipice. Proceed steeply down the gully to the right and then follow a stream down to the base of the Little Berg. Turn left here parallel to the iNzinga River. After 3 km you will cross the river next to a ruin and 1 km further on you will reach Cypress Cave across a stream near its confluence with the iNzinga River. The Forest Station is 4 km further on.

Mkhomazi Trail *Hike MK6*

Route: *Surprise Camp Site to Kerry or Bundoran*
Distance: *Approximately 25 kilometres*
Duration: *2 days or 9 hours 30 minutes*
Grade: *Moderate*
General: *At the time of writing this trail was under construction and so the information given here is subject to change. Overnight shelter will be provided either at Kerry or at Bundoran and possibly at both. For most of the way the trail traverses the base of the Ka-Malungana Ridge.*

▶ The trail begins at the Surprise camp site and heads up towards the ridge, passing through exotic trees and by the ruins of an old farm. (There are plans to turn the farm into an overnight hut.) The path follows a stream and then turns left along the base of the cliffs all the way to the iNhlambamasoka River and on to the hut. At this stage plans are afoot to take the return route back along the same path, although a more southerly return trip would be preferable.

Each year a few lucky hikers are able to see the lammergeiers that use the niches in the Ka-Malungana Ridge as a roosting site.

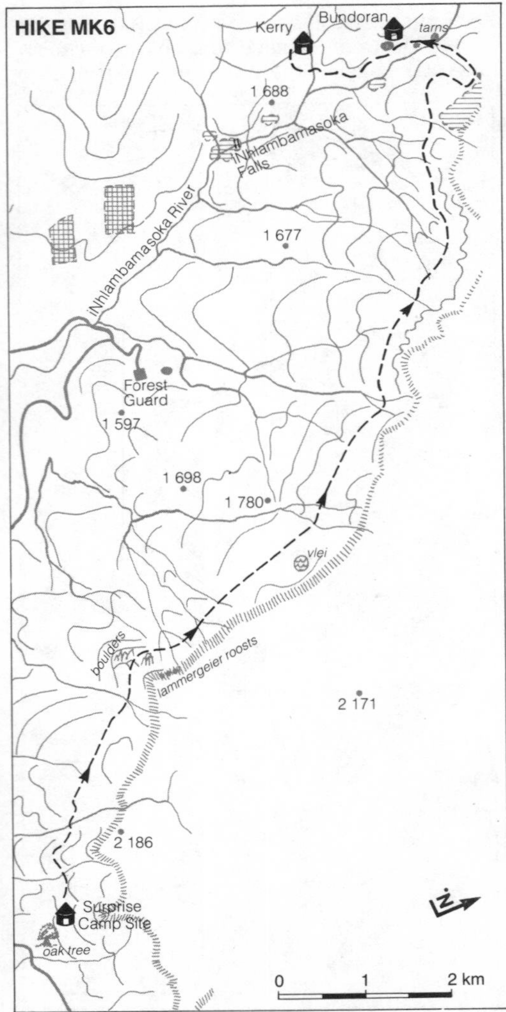

Ash Cave *Hike MK7*

Route: *Loteni Camp Site to Ash Cave*
Distance: *7,5 kilometres*
Duration: *3 hours*
Grade: *Fair*
General: *This pleasant, short hike allows a party of up to six people to leave the Loteni camp site for a wilderness experience, without the normal slog of a 'Berg hike. Remember to get a wilderness permit from the Forest Station or NPB offices.*

▶ Starting from the Loteni camp site, follow the main path up the left-hand bank of the Loteni River, past the eMpophomeni Falls to a fork 4,5 km from the start. Take the right-hand path and continue up the Lotheni River for another 3 km, crossing a tributary to reach the cave set in a narrow section of the gorge, with high cliffs on either side. It is possible to explore the small patches of forest further up the river, or any of the side gorges that excite your interest.

Yellowwood Cave *Hike MK8*

Route: *Loteni Camp Site to Yellowwood Cave*
Distance: *6,5 kilometres*
Duration: *3 hours*
Grade: *Fair*
General: *This hike is similar to the previous one, following the same route most of the way, although the going is slightly easier.*

▶ Follow the Loteni River path (Hike MK7) past the eMpophomeni Falls to meet a junction after 4,5 km. Keep left, following the main path along the edge of a forest on the Ka-Masihlenga tributary, which branches to the left from the Lotheni

River. The cave is situated on the right-hand bank of the stream, just short of a river crossing where the forest curves back behind a rock outcrop. It is slightly larger than Ash Cave, sleeping eight people. To ascend the Ka-Mashihlenga Pass, continue up this path for another 5,5 km.

The diamond-shaped tail of the lammergeier (left) and the orb-web spider (right).

Yellowwood Cave, Tarn and Waterfall *Hike MK9*

Route: *Round trip from Loteni Camp Site via Yellowwood Waterfall*
Distance: *22,5 kilometres*
Duration: *2 days or 8 to 9 hours*
Grade: *Moderate to Severe*
General: *This hike can be tackled as a strenuous one-day outing, or a more relaxed two-day walk. The cave is situated a third of the way along the route, and so a tent will be needed if the walk is to be divided into two stages.*

▸ Follow the Loteni and Ka-Masihlenga paths past Yellowwood Cave (Hike MK8) and another 3 km up to the Contour Path. Turn left at the base of the Ka-Masihlenga Pass and walk along the Contour Path for 3 km to a camp site on the bank of the second main stream bank. This marks the half-way spot, with Redi looming above. A kilometre further on you will come to a four-way intersection and a tarn. Take the left-hand path out along a prominent spur and ascend a steep crest of the ridge. After 1 km of steep climbing the gradient levels off for about 2 km and then descends steeply again to the Ngodwini River.

▸ The path does not cross the river, but veers to the right around a high point on the ridge and crosses the eMapalini tributary above a waterfall. The path then returns to the Ngodwini River and follows the right-hand bank back to the main Loteni camp. The camp site is reached 2 km to the left of the main camp.

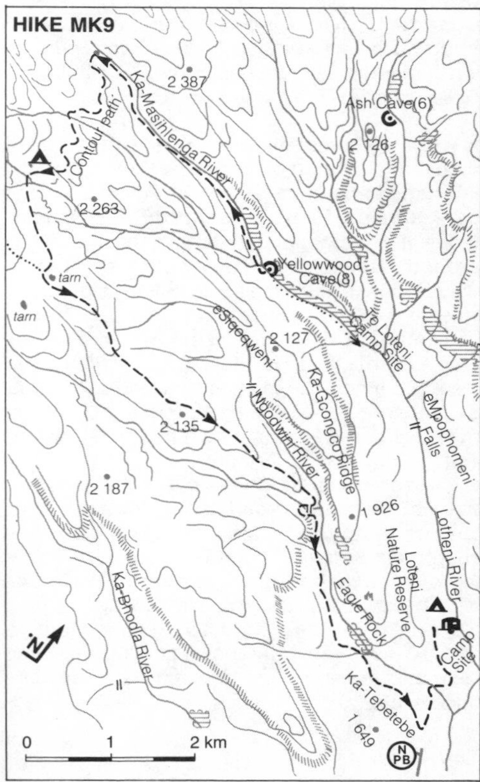

Redi Peak via The Passage (Buttress Pass) Hike MK10

Route: *Loteni Camp Site to Redi Peak*
Distance: *13 kilometres*
Duration: *6 to 7 hours*
Grade: *Extreme*
General: *This peak is not often acknowledged to be the sixth highest in South Africa, but it is. The direct route, up Redi Pass, involves rock climbing, so Buttress Pass is a close alternative.*

▶ From the Loteni main camp, take the first left turn out of the camp and follow the path up the left-hand bank of the Ngodwini River. The path passes below Eagle Rock on the Ka-Gcongco Ridge. At the eMapatini tributary the path loops around to the left and crosses a stream above a waterfall before looping back towards the main river and carrying on around to the far side of a spur. Ascend the steep right-hand side of the spur towards the crest of the ridge. After 2 km of steep climbing the gradient eases for another 2 km before the very steep climb for 1,5 km up the crest of the spur to a tarn near the Contour Path.

▶ Turn left along the Contour Path for two easy kilometres to the base of Buttress Pass. Turn right up the 1,5-km passage to the top of Hlathimbe Buttress. From here the route to the top of Redi Peak is obvious; head north (to the right) for 1 km and then turn left up the slopes of the main peak itself. About 60 m below the summit (3 314 m) you will cross a stock path. From here the views over Lesotho and Natal are quite spectacular.

The less dramatic, nevertheless relatively high section of the Escarpment near Redi, which, at 3 314 metres, is one of the highest peaks in South Africa.

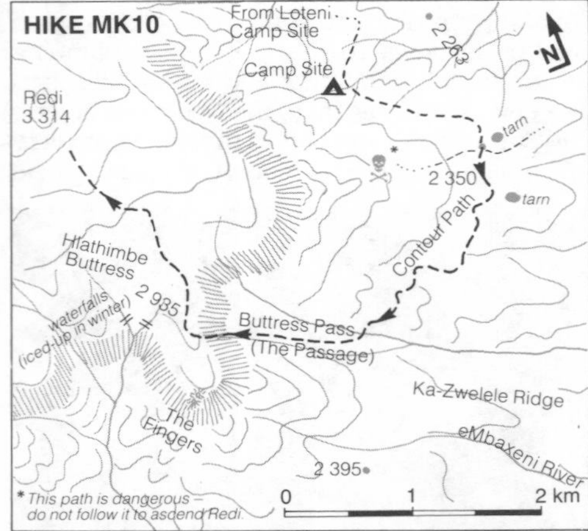

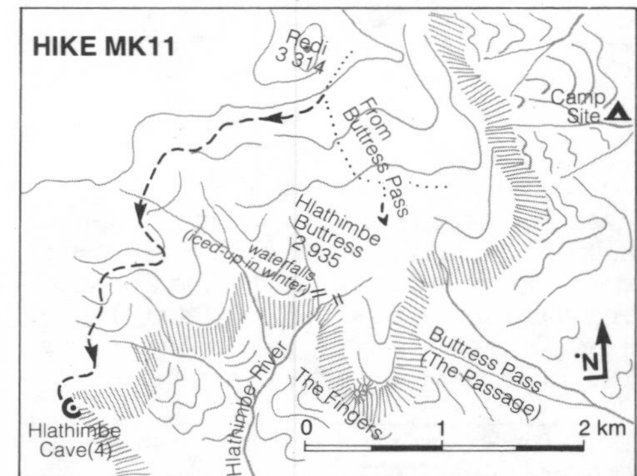

Hlathimbe Pass and Cave

Hike MK11

Route: *Loteni Camp Site to Hlathimbe Cave*
Distance: *16 kilometres*
Duration: *6 to 7 hours*
Grade: *Extreme*
General: *This relatively easy ascent of the Drakensberg follows one of the escape routes used by Bushman cattle raiders who plundered the Loteni valley during the last century. The cave is situated very near to the top of the pass, looking out towards The Fingers and Hlathimbe Buttress; it sleeps four people.*

▶ From Loteni hutted camp, follow the Ngodwini River path (bear left at the first path outside the camp). Follow the left-hand bank of the river (Hikes MK9 and MK10), pass the waterfall on the eMapalini tributary and then ascend the spur diagonally away from the river all the way to the Contour Path, 9 km from the start. Turn left here and continue for 2,5 km, passing below Hlathimbe Buttress and Buttress Pass. Five hundred metres further on veer right along the contour, where a path branches off to the left down the Ka-Zwelele Ridge. This path crosses the eMbaxeni River and reaches the Hlathimbe River 2,5 km further on. Cross the river and head straight up the gully on the opposite side, where you will reach the cave which is situated just below the head of the pass, on the left bank of a stream. From here one can head northwards (inland from this point) up Redi Peak and return either via the same route, or past Redi Peak and down Buttress Pass (Hike MK10) for a round trip. Lynx Cave can be found 1 km south of Hlathimbe Cave on the edge of the Escarpment, bypassing Duart Castle.

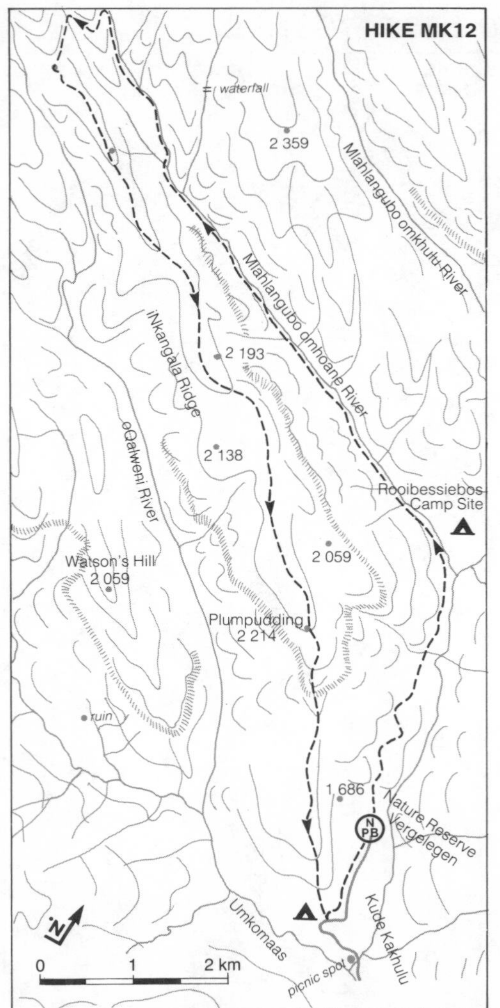

Mlahlangubo to iNkangala

Hike MK12

Route: *Vergelegen Nature Reserve to iNkangala Ridge*
Distance: *23 kilometres*
Duration: *8 to 9 hours*
Grade: *Severe*
General: *Starting at sunrise this is a full day's outing, hiking up the valley of the Mlahlangubo omhoane River to the Contour Path level and down a ridge above the same river. There are in fact five alternative routes to choose from, which gives you the opportunity to link up with the paths described in the previous hike.*

▶ From the Vergelegen NPB office proceed straight ahead for 3,5 km, up a slope and then parallel to a line of cliffs. Enter the Mlahlangubo omhoane River valley and continue up the left-hand bank of the river for 7 km, crossing 21 intermittent tributaries. This valley is exciting to explore, with waterfalls to be found on many of the larger streams coming in from the north (the opposite side of the river to that which you should be on). On reaching the Contour Path below the first Ngaqamadola Pass, turn left. Contour round a spur back into a gully and diagonally up the side of another spur to a junction at the base of the second Ngaqamadola Pass.

▶ Turn left here, passing a tarn after 200 m. Proceed to the lip of this promontory and follow the iNkangala Ridge for 8 km down to a low escarpment overlooking Vergelegen. Descend the sandstone formation known as the Plumpudding, but take care as this steep section is quite degraded. Continue onwards, down into the Mkhomazi Valley.

Lynx Cave via Mlahlangubo Pass *Hike MK13*

Route: *Vergelegen Nature Reserve to Lynx Cave*
Distance: *14 kilometres*
Duration: *5 hours 30 minutes to 6 hours*
Grade: *Extreme*
General: *Taking a somewhat contrived route, this hike follows the Mlahlangubo omkhulu River for much of the way. It is the shortest of three possible routes to the base of the pass (the others going up ridges on either side of the river valley) and is also the shorter route to the summit than the main pass in the area, that is Hlathimbe Pass, which begins at Loteni (Hike MK11).*

▸ From the Parks Board office at Vergelegen, where a permit must be obtained to enter the Cobham State Forest and the Mkhomazi Wilderness Area, the path leads off to the north-west and meets a skew junction on the left after 2 km. Continue for another 2 km to the Mlahlangubo omhoane River. An alternative path turns left up the river, but our route continues across the river to a camp site in a wooded grove which would make a pleasant base for a hiking holiday in this area. From the camp site three routes are negotiable, the best being to follow the middle one up the left-hand bank of the Mlahlangubo omkhulu River. This is a delightful valley walk with two river crossings and many large pools passed on the way. This is a suitable spot to relax before tackling the pass.

▸ The path comes to a four-way junction where the two ridge paths meet, forming a short contour section. Carry on straight up the Mlahlangubo Pass for 2 km to the watershed, which is just past the head of the pass. Turn right and follow the watershed for just over 1 km to Lynx Cave, which faces north-east from the same side of a small headland.

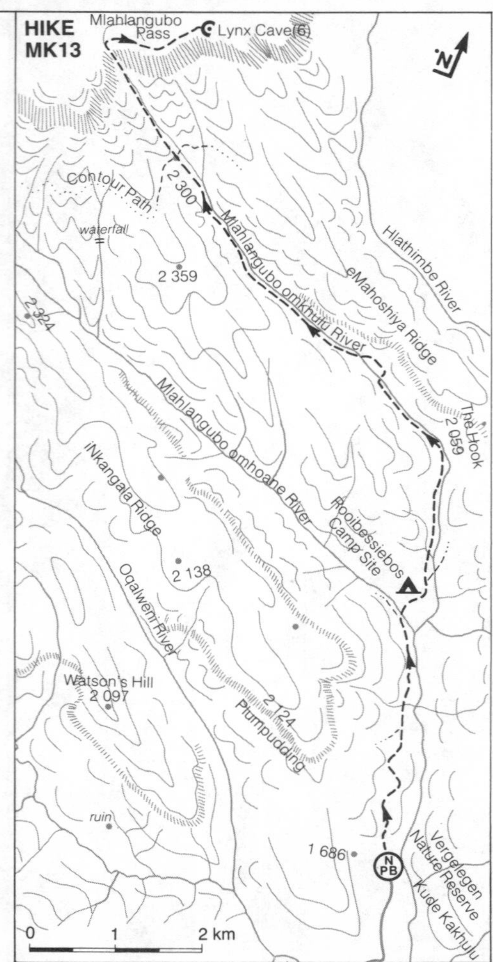

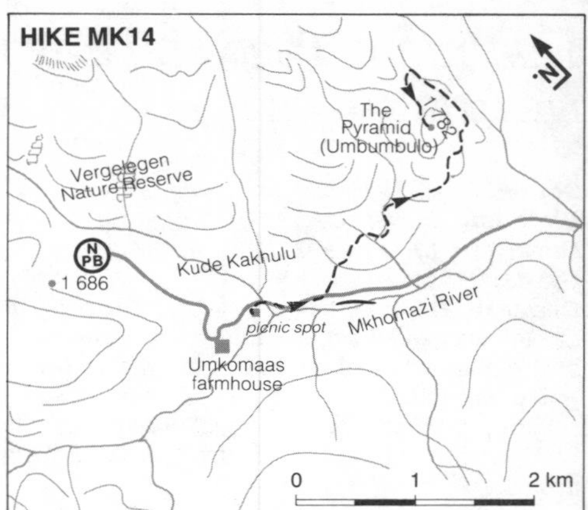

The Pyramid *Hike MK14*

Route: *Vergelegen Nature Reserve to The Pyramid*
Distance: *3 kilometres*
Duration: *1 hour 30 minutes*
Grade: *Fair*
General: *This is a short hike in the vicinity of the Vergelegen picnic site, with good views of the surrounding countryside.*

▸ About 500 m east of the Vergelegen picnic area the path goes off to the right towards the Escarpment. Follow the path uphill, crossing one stream and shortly thereafter following another for about 250 m. The path then curves slowly around the east slope of The Pyramid. It then turns sharply around at the northern end of the slope on an inward spiralling path to the summit of the hill. The Pyramid (Umbumbulo) is 1 782 m high and a good place from which to appreciate the surrounding countryside without having to go on a strenuous hike.

Mkhomazi Pass *Hike MK15*

Route: *Vergelegen Nature Reserve to Mkhomazi Pass*
Distance: *17 kilometres*
Duration: *7 to 8 hours*
Grade: *Extreme*
General: *This is another long but rewarding hike, following the Mkhomazi River to its source among the high ramparts of the Drakensberg. To reach the summit in one day it will be necessary to make an early start and keep up a good pace. There are no caves in the area of the summit, so a tent is essential. The valleys on top of the 'Berg can become real quagmires in the summer, so plan your route and choose a camping spot carefully.*

▶ About 500 m past the Vergelegen picnic site the road does a 90-degree, right-hand turn towards the NPB office. Take the path here to the left, keeping parallel to the river. Cross a tributary after 2 km and continue parallel to the river for another 1,5 km. The path then veers to the right and ascends the right-hand bank for 100 m before levelling off and swinging to the left above the river. About 1 km along this high bank the path descends to the river and crosses it, 5 km from the start.

▶ The path splits around either side of the ka-Ntuba Ridge. Take the main, right-hand fork, which follows the left-hand bank of the Mkhomazi River as it meanders in and out of the broken landscape. After 4 km the path follows a tributary of the Mkhomazi, as it bears to the left, past a branch of the tributary that also bears to the left. Cross two side streams and the tributary, and pass through the Ngcingweni Forest before heading up over a ridge and back into the main valley. From here the path runs along the left-hand bank of the river for 2 km before once again curving off to the left to follow a tributary; it may be difficult at this stage to tell which is the main channel.

▶ Follow this tributary steeply uphill for 200 m and bypass a fork in the river another 200 m further on. Cross this tributary and the

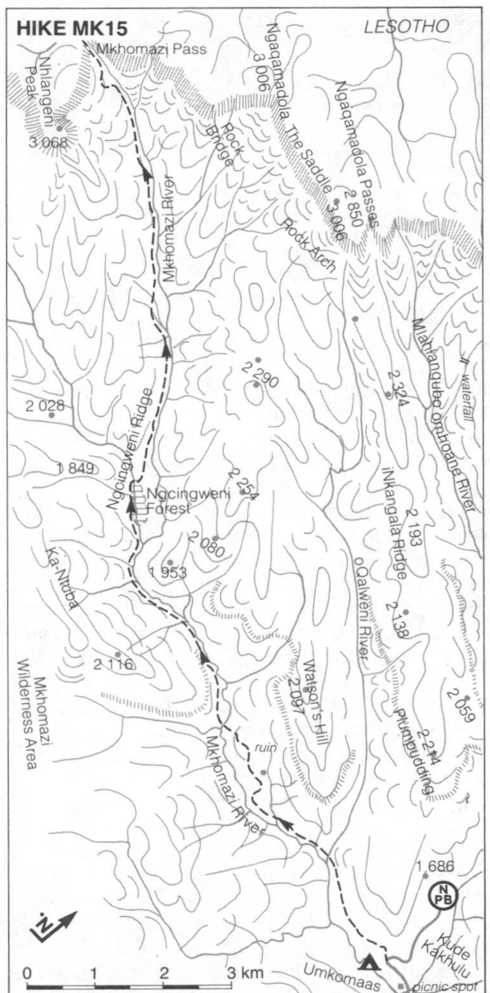

A Cave Sandstone formation in the Mkhomazi Wilderness Area. The sandstone layer is soft and highly erodable, forming the characteristic large caves and overhangs beneath the basalt walls of the Escarpment.

second one and you will come to another fork. The right-hand branch crosses the Mkhomazi River, but take the left-hand path along the left-hand bank of the river for another 2 km to the Contour Path. Carry on along the left-hand river bank up the pass; after about 1,5 km the path veers away from the river and then back again before reaching the top. On reaching the watershed (the border) you will be looking down into the valley of the Boja-bo-tsotse River. A vague path continues straight on and crosses the river in a potentially boggy section of the valley, contouring around its western slope.

FOOD

The principle here is 'light but tasty', although essentials like coffee, tea, milk powder, rice and chocolate should not be forgotten (potatoes are not recommended). Hearty, tasty meals can be made in the mountains by using mainly dehydrated vegetables, rice and meat substitutes and by adding small amounts of strong-flavoured herbs and spices. Garlic goes a long way to improving any meal. Mushrooms, onions, bean sprouts and green peppers are also light and tasty.

For breakfast, muesli and powdered milk satisfy most hikers, although you can safely take eggs along, by wrapping them in cloth and placing them in a pot. Salami and cheese with biscuits can be supplemented with fruit for lunch. Don't forget sundowners, as this is where the principle of light but tasty really pays off – pâté and oysters with wine or liqueurs enhance the sunsets and disguise the taste of soya mince! Learn how to make bread with self-raising flour (this is actually quite simple) and your status as a mountaineering gourmet will soar. Chocolate and whiskey are essential emergency rations, so don't skimp.

Nhlangeni Pass and Cave

Hike MK16

Route: *Vergelegen Nature Reserve to Nhlangeni Cave*
Distance: *21 kilometres*
Duration: *8 to 9 hours*
Grade: *Extreme*
General: *This hike follows the Mkhomazi and Nhlangeni rivers, into a deep cutback. The area is rugged and cut by myriad streams, with numerous caves to explore. The gradient is not extreme, but it just seems never to stop. You will need two days to reach the summit if the trip is to be enjoyed. Carefully consult the map for interesting variations of this route description which, as usual, takes the easiest way between departure point and destination.*

▶ Begin at the right-angle bend in the road near the Vergelegen picnic spot (Hike MK15) and follow the same route for 9 km. Just past the second main fork in the river (where there is a fork in the path and the Mkhomazi route follows the left bank of a tributary), our route takes the left-hand prong and climbs above the stream, looking down to the Ngcingweni Forest. The Mkhomazi path then crosses the stream and heads past the forest over a low ridge; but the Nhlangeni path crosses a few streams and then curves around to the left, gradually approaching the same tributary that has also curved around to the left.

▶ The path reaches the left-hand bank of the stream, the Nhlangeni, and follows it for about 1 km to yet another fork. At this point a decision must be made: whether to be adventurous and take the longer left-hand loop uphill to a sulphur spring, or rather cling to the river course for the 2-km shorter trip. The first path goes up a tributary 2 km to the spring near the Contour Path where you can soothe your weary spirit. To regain the Nhlangeni path, keep right for another 2 km, which is in effect the Contour Path. On reaching the Nhlangeni River the path

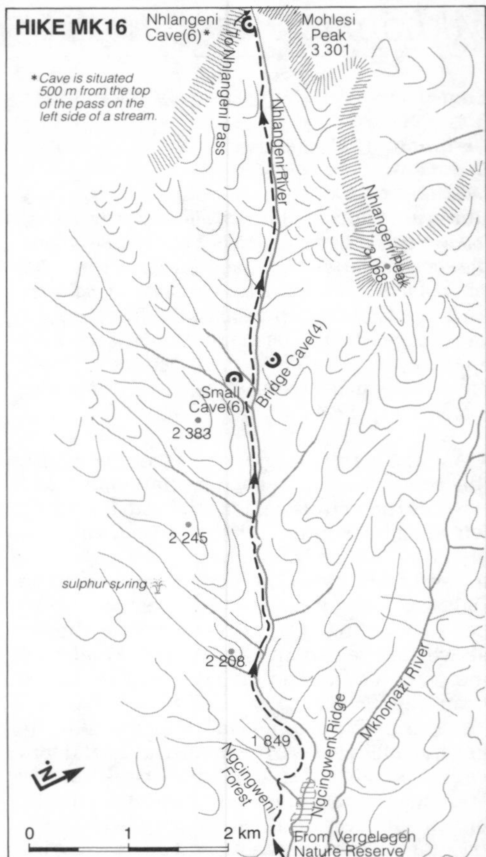

lies at a relatively low altitude (2 050 m) and the pass is a 5-km climb, gaining 1 150 m to reach an altitude of 3 200 m.

▶ A tributary is reached on the left after 1 km and Small Cave can be found some way up to your left. Another 400 m up the pass, another tributary can be found on the same side of the river, pass this tributary, then the first on the other side after another 400 m. The slightly larger Bridge Cave can be found up this gully.

▶ Both Small Cave and Bridge Cave are off the main route and finding them requires some searching – so don't depend on using them. Another 1,5 km upstream brings you to another fork: be sure to take the left-hand branch as the right-hand one will lead you into trouble. Now you are still 3 km from the summit and 2,5 km from the Nhlangeni Cave, which is easily found to the left of the path. Once on the Escarpment you can see ka-Ntuba peak a few kilometres to the south.

Sani Pass *Hike MK17*

Route: *NHW car park to Sani Pass*
Distance: *14 kilometres*
Duration: *6 to 7 hours*
Grade: *Extreme*
General: *Because there is a gravel road all the way up Sani Pass it is not often thought of as a hike, but it should be, as the trip is quite spectacular and rewarding – especially the destination, where hikers can enjoy the comfort of the Mountaineers' Chalet. Something beyond the scope of this book, but worth mentioning, this pass is the gateway to one of the world's most underrated and unexplored hiking wildernesses. Lesotho offers nearly all that places like Tibet and India can, except the grand vistas of the Himalayas. But, as I have written elsewhere, this is an African adventure among the mountains that are old and wise, harbouring secrets more complex than 'youngsters' such as the Alps, the Rockies or the Himalayas. Sani Pass is also the conclusion of the ultimate 'Berg traverse along the summit from Mont-aux-Sources. Distance given for this hike is from the NHW car park about 5,5 km past the Sani Pass Hotel.*

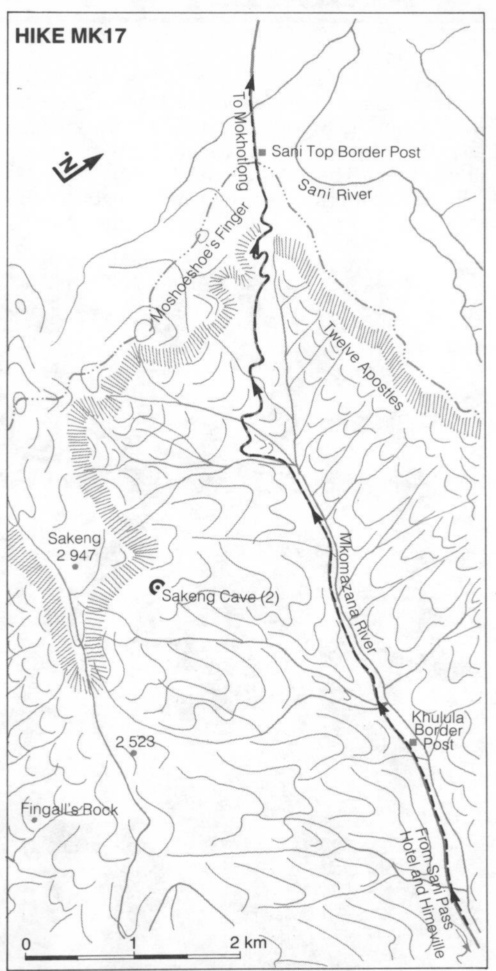

A mountain reedbuck ewe.

▶ No description is needed for the hike that follows the road along the Mkhomazana River, between the Twelve Apostles and the Giant's Cup, finishing above the engineered hairpin zigzags near the prominence called Moshoeshoe's Finger. It was he who galvanized the riff-raff of the Difaqane wars into the mountain-dwelling nation that neither Shaka nor Mtsilikatsi, Briton nor Boer could dislodge or subjugate.

While liquor is available at the summit lodge, visitors must arrange to get their own food up there; you can arrange this through Mokhotlong Mountain Transport Company and save your energy for enjoying the magnificent surroundings. The top of the pass opens out onto the Tsani Flats, with the higher Maluti peaks in the near distance. Skiing is possible nearly every year. It is also possible to continue into the interior and all the way to Maseru, some 200 km away.

MZIMKHULU

The last section of the Natal Drakensberg is another vast, predominantly Wilderness Area. With the exception of a few peaks at the northern end, around the Rhino and at the southernmost tip, the Escarpment here is far less spectacular and inviting than it is to the north. There are no forests in this area whatsoever and the only bush to be found is along river courses where mountain sage, ouhout and *Rhus* species predominate. Occasionally one encounters proteas on open slopes and the Cape holly, yellowwood or cabbage tree. The low, rust-coloured *Protea dracomontana* is sometimes found in dense communities on the grassy knolls of the Little Berg. In seepage areas and along stream banks there is an abundance of large tree ferns (*Alsophila dregei*). These trees, as well as cycads, are protected in South Africa.

The overwhelming impression of the area is of vast expanses of golden grassland (*Themeda* sp. and *Festuca* sp.) of the Little Berg and relatively low grey basalt ramparts beyond. In the extreme north, the most impressive physical feature of the range, the Giant's Cup or Hodgson's Peaks, can be found. The main holiday area of the region is Garden Castle, where one finds one of the finest, traditional 'Berg hotels with more than the usual facilities, including a heated swimming pool and watersports on the nearby Todd's Farm.

While the area is named after a Cave Sandstone formation standing way out from the Escarpment, the predominant feature of this area is the Rhino, which juts out from the Escarpment and resembles a rhino's horn. (It is an old tradition that every Thursday the hotel arranges an ascent of the peak.) For those preferring their trekking to be of the equestrian variety, this is the ideal area. Horses may be hired from the two forest stations in the area for as little as R2,00 a day, as well as from the hotels and Sehlaba-Thebe Lodge in Lesotho.

In the Mzimkhulu area and at Sehlaba-Thebe there are more tarns than in any other part of the Drakensberg, with an area near Cobham being called the 'Lake District'. Waterfowl congregate on these lakes, while buck and other wildlife make ample use of the water. The many rivers in this section are a haven for otters, as the lack of human interference allows these shy creatures to live unmolested. The only evidence

of their presence is their pure white droppings, rich in calcified crab shell.

The main forest station is at Cobham, where fishermen and hikers alike enjoy camping beside the Pholela River. From here the distant Giant's Cup is most impressive. Although the facilities of the smaller camp site at the Garden Castle Forest Station are basic, one is enveloped here by the high peaks. For those interested in rock art, only the magnificent Ndedema Gorge rivals the Bushman's Nek area, but most of the really spectacular caves are not marked on any map. Between Cobham and Mzimkhulwana there is the Siphongweni Cave, which has been declared a national monument to protect the rock paintings; nevertheless, vandals persist in desecrating them. At Bushman's Nek there is a small and informal hotel but no forestry facilities, although there is a forester on duty at the car park where you can obtain wilderness permits.

Sehlaba-Thebe, meaning 'the shield', marks the end of our journey through the Drakensberg. Being too high to be considered Little Berg and yet below the Drakensberg summit, this extraordinary, wide plateau harbours a number of endemic species and is an environmentalist's delight. The cluster of peaks above the shield is known as Thaba-Ntsu, 'the mountain of the lammergeier', or less originally as the Devil's Knuckles. It is possible to hire the lodge at Sehlaba-Thebe, Lesotho's only national park, or to camp out on the plateau or in the numerous caves there. Once again, if you prefer the hoof to the boot, it is possible to arrange horses to meet you at the Bushman's Nek Police Post for the journey up to the Park.

A peaceful scene at a large tarn in the 'Lake District' above Cobham Forest Station.

Giant's Cup Trail — Hike MZ1

Route: *Sani Pass to Bushman's Nek*
Distance: *60,3 kilometres*
Duration: *5 days*
Grade: *Moderate to Severe*
General: *This NHW trail keeps to the plateaux and valleys of the Little Berg and is an excellent introduction to Drakensberg hiking. Bookings must be made through the NHW Board offices in Pietermaritzburg, from where maps, permits and other literature are available. The trail is designed to give the hiker as much diversity as possible within the restrictions of the allotted land. While organized trails are not everyone's idea of a good time, this hike can be considered as the most southerly extension of the Contour Path route which I have charted from Mnweni (see page 46). Perhaps one day this challenging proposition will be met. I certainly have done long sections of it, but never continuously. Accommodation on the hike is generally far more luxurious than other NHW trails, with soft beds, fireplaces and even wood stoves and hot showers at some huts. The path follows the general line of the Escarpment and between 10 to 15 km east of it. My experience along this path was marred by a line of sweet papers from one end to the other – I collected them all with the intention of catching up with the offender but was not lucky enough to accomplish this. Transport arrangements must be made for the end of the hike.*

▶ **Day 1** (13,3 km): Park at the guarded NHW site, about 5 km above the Sani Pass Hotel. The hike begins two hairpin bends above the car park. Few parties seem to complete the proposed distance of the first day's hike, which I consider to be the best of the entire trail. After an easy 2,5 km stroll along a platform formation, the path climbs for about 600 m, contours for another kilometre and then descends to the Gxalingenwa River. The slope down to the magnificent iNgenwa Pool is scattered with small protea trees. If the main pool is occupied, just venture upstream and you will find many cascades and secluded pools from which to choose. This area makes a fine lunch spot, but if the weather is bad continue up the opposite slope to a cave.

▶ From the cave the path undulates around Ndlovini Hill and then down to the Trout Beck.

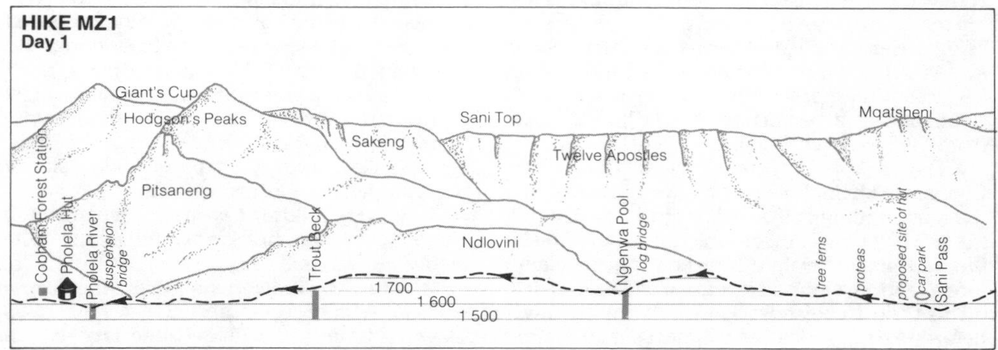

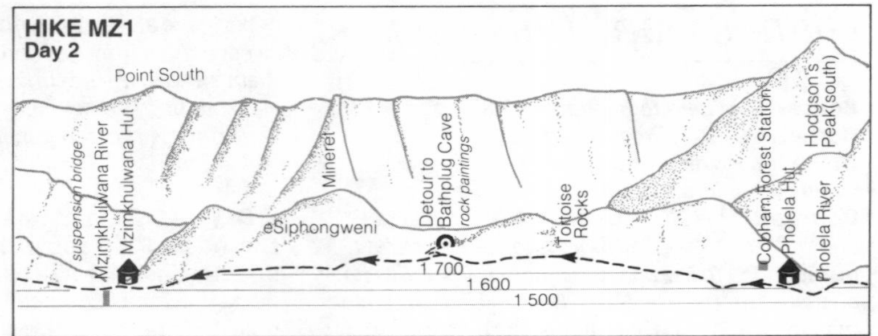

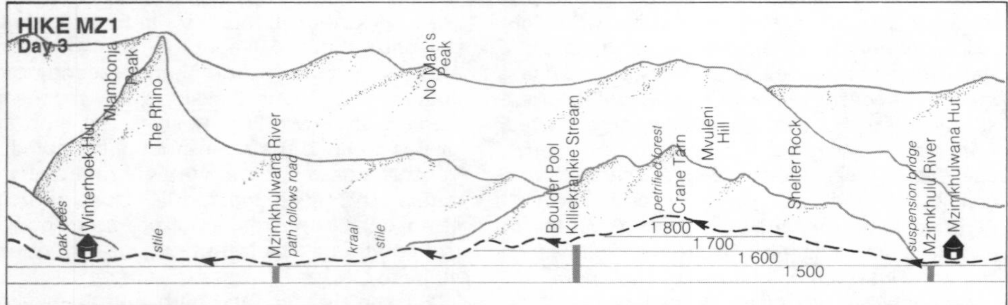

Follow the river to Cobham Forest Station, passing through a game fence and over a suspension bridge. Here Pholela Hut, once a farmhouse, awaits you with hot showers and other luxuries. There are trout in the rivers around Cobham, but a permit must first be obtained from the Himeville Hotel.

▶ **Day 2** (9 km): This short section, from Cobham to Mzimkhulwana, allows you to explore the surrounding countryside or to laze around the pool, downriver from the hut. From Pholela the path skirts around between the river and forest station, climbs a steep hill and then eases off to pass Tortoise Rocks and Bathplug Cave before taking a long, gentle descent to Mzimkhulwana Hut. It is possible to follow the river upstream from the hut for a few kilometres and then ascend a steep grass slope to Siphongweni Cave and Shelter. This detour affords great views of the area and leads to some of the most recently discovered rock art. Before undertaking this trip read the route description for Hikes MZ4 and MZ5, because the paths on this side of the eSiphongweni Hill are vague to nonexistent.

▶ **Day 3** (12,2 km): Cross the suspension bridge below the hut and then climb quite steeply up to the Little Bamboo Mountain, named after the indigenous grass, *Arundinaria tessellata*, which grows here. On a high plain below the little mountain is Crane Tarn, which is frequented by blue cranes and sometimes the rare wattled crane. Petrified wood can be found in the vicinity, but don't remove souvenirs, as by the fifth day you will be sore and tired, and then you will just throw it away where no-one can see it, or where it may confound geologists.

▶ From Crane Tarn the path begins its descent to Killicrankie Stream and an irresistible pool beneath a large boulder. Along this section the path passes a community of *Protea subvestita*, with *Helichrysum* sp. and other flowers, which attracts a confetti-fall of butterflies and ladybirds. This is the place to linger, and to have lunch at the pool, for after this section the path becomes domesticated; it crosses private land past houses and kraals, and then follows the Garden Castle road for 1 km to the Mzimkhulu River. Just past the river the path turns off to the left and for some seemingly sadistic purpose goes directly over a hill and down the other side instead of around it, crosses a stream at a shallow dam and arrives at the Winterhoek thatched bungalows shaded by large oak trees.

▶ **Day 4** (12,8 km): This section, from Winterhoek to Swiman at the Garden Castle Forest Station, typifies the southern Drakensberg; thick grassland in all directions is broken only by the occasional protea tree. In spring and summer, however, the veld comes alive with flowers, including orange and crimson watsonias, yellow and mauve asters and everlastings. By 'Berg standards the first part of this section, up Black Eagle Pass on the lower slopes of Garden Castle itself, is easy, but in terms of this trail it is the hardest section. Once up the pass, however, it is easy going through the grassland, with sweeping views of the Escarpment on either side of Rhino Peak. Below you stretch the valleys of the Mzimkhulu and Mlambonja rivers to the right, and the Mzimude River with its tight meanders and oxbow lakes on the left.

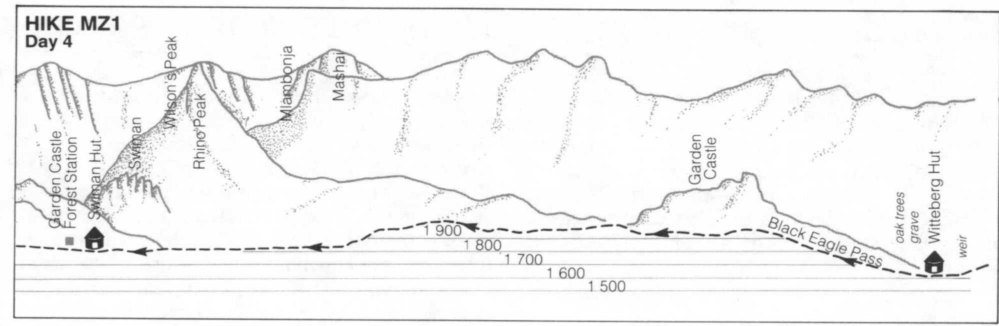

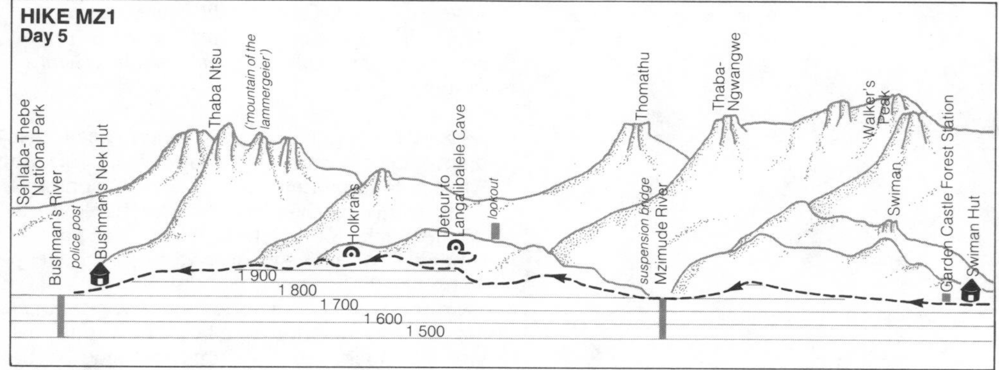

Thaba-Ntsu (or the Devil's Knuckles) is a prominent feature at the end of the Giant's Cup Trail.

There is precious little water to be found on this exposed section of the trail, so be sure to carry your fill; this minor shortcoming is compensated by the frequent sightings of black eagles and lammergeiers. Swiman Hut is set among the pine and blue gum trees at Garden Castle, with the sandstone masses of The Monk and Swiman directly above and the Rhino nudging the sky to the north. Despite the unexpected luxury, I was disappointed with this hut, which looks like a low-cost, government-issue house, complete with security wall, and not like a mountaineer's hut at all.

▶ **Day 5** (13 km): This final stretch to Bushman's Nek begins gently over Bucquay Nek and down to the Mzimude River and pool, 5 km from Swiman. The main peaks that you pass on the right are (with the Rhino behind) Mlambonja (3 309 m), Wilson's Peak (3 276 m), Mashai (3 313 m), Mzimude (3 210 m) and Walker's Peak (3 306 m) opposite Langalibalele Cave. After crossing a suspension bridge, the path rises in terraces to the cave, which faces back towards the Rhino, from just above a stream below the hill called Langalibalele (see page 126) (the stream is a good lunch spot). Two easy sections lead uphill to the final 3-km descent to the Bushman's Nek Hut. The hut stands on a spur some way off the path, but by this stage most people seem to rush on to the car park at the forest station and head immediately for home, no doubt having had enough of being 'away from it all'.

iNgenwa River and Emerald Stream *Hike MZ2*

Route: *Cobham Forest Station to Emerald Stream*
Distance: *24 kilometres*
Duration: *9 hours or 2 days*
Grade: *Severe*
General: *This hike takes one through fertile country with a magnificent view of Giant's Cup. It is an easy two-day outing, including camping beside the Gxalingenwa River with ample time to fish and explore. Cobham itself is a pleasant camp site on the Pholela River, surrounded by large trees.*

▸ Starting at Cobham, cross the suspension bridge over the Pholela River and then backtrack along the Giant's Cup Trail (marked by painted footprints) for 8 km, following the Trout Beck. About 2,5 km from the bridge the path circles the Ndlovini Hill and then descends past a cave to the enticing iNgenwa Pool. This stretch of river has many gloriously secluded pools where you can strip down and bathe at leisure. It is also the best lunch spot along the hike.

▸ After a rest and sunbathe here, do not cross the log bridge but continue up the left-hand bank. A pleasant 4-km walk up the river brings you to the branching off of two paths to the left; continue straight on and pass below Baboon Rock to two river crossings within 100 m of each other. This path carries on all the way up the Giant's Cup, but between the two river crossings is a tributary coming in from the left (south). Follow the path along this stream up to the Gxalingenwa Cave, which sleeps 12 people, or carry on up the river as far as your curiosity takes you.

▸ Return from the cave along the river for 1,5 km past Baboon Rock and turn right at right-angles away from the river. An undulating, curving traverse below Pinnacle Rock and then along an intermittent stream brings you to the Emerald Stream. Cross the stream twice. The path then veers away from the stream, past its confluence with the Pholela River, which you cross 9 km from the previous turn-off. From here the tall trees and English country-style buildings of Cobham can be seen 1,5 km downstream.

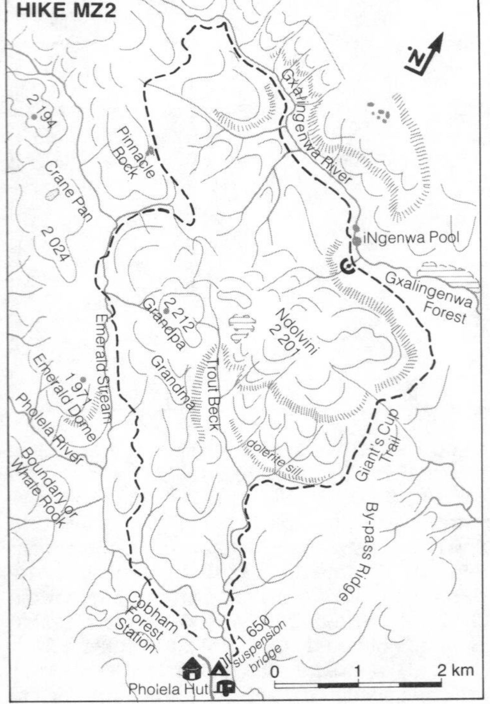

Hodgson's Peaks *Hike MZ3*

Route: *Cobham Forest Station to Hodgson's Peaks*
Distance: *19 kilometres*
Duration: *8 to 9 hours or 2 to 3 days*
Grade: *Severe to Extreme*
General: *Depending on whether you choose to overnight within the bowl of Giant's Cup or below the Escarpment, this will be a two- or three-day hike. It is also possible to make the caves at the base of the pass your objective, in which case it becomes an easy two-day hike. In my opinion, the Pholela River flows through the most attractive valley in the southern Drakensberg, and the twin Hodgson's Peaks which make up the rim of Giant's Cup are the most aesthetically pleasing peaks south of Giant's Castle.*

▸ From the camp site at Cobham, head east upstream along the left-hand bank of the Pholela River. After 2 km the path contours away from the river and rejoins it below the Whale Rock; for the next 1,5 km the path is sandwiched between the river and the steep slope of eSiphongweni on the left. (The cave near the top of this mountain is a national monument – but more of it later.) Continue past Monster Rocks on the right-hand side of the river.

In this area you are likely to see a number of small raptors, including gliding rock kestrels and darting lanner falcons. The abundance of shell-encrusted droppings should reveal just how many of otters lie up during the day along the rivers. Consider yourself extremely privileged if you chance upon one of these shy creatures at its resting holt, either sunning itself on a rock or snoozing on its back under an overhanging bank. The Cape clawless otter spends much of its active life in water but may forage some distance inland in search of crabs, frogs, insects and other small prey. They are equally at home in fresh or salt water – this is the same species found along the Tsitsikama coast.

▶ About 1,5 km further on from the Monster Rocks you will pass a shelter and then reach a fork in the path and in the river. Cross the iNhlabeni River (coming in from the left) and bear right, continuing up the left-hand bank of the Pholela River. Shortly hereafter the valley closes in on both sides and the river reverts to its youthful stage; the wall on the left is straight while on the right it comprises a series of steep stream-cut folds. About 4 km past a rare patch of bush, there is a four-way crossing of river and paths on the left-hand river bank. You can detour to Spectacle Cave by veering left, below a waterfall, for 100 m; alternatively, you can reach Gorge Cave by turning right up another side stream and gully for the same distance or carry straight on for 1 km to Pholela Cave. These caves each sleep 12 people, so choose the best shelter to suit the weather, taking into account wind direction and where the sun will set and rise. There is something magical in seeing a sunrise from a Drakensberg cave.

These caves are situated perfectly for a day's hike, 14 km from the start. For those going on up the pass eat heartily for, to paraphrase an old story, the path is steep and getting steeper (see page 6). Decide whether you intend to be up and back down the pass by nightfall or whether you will sleep in the embrace of Hodgson's Peaks. (It is interesting to think that only 60 years ago it was believed that no-one could survive a night on top of these mountains, but then they didn't have lightweight tents and sleeping bags and thermal clothing.)

The profile of the day's walking is parabolic, up the spectacular Masubasuba Pass to the bowl of the Giant's Cup. This feature was named by an early explorer looking for a safe passage from Natal, through the land of the then hostile Xhosa, and on to the Cape Colony. The twin peaks which form the cup's rim were named after Thomas Hodgson who was accidentally shot dead in 1862 while out on commando in the area, chasing Bushman cattle raiders.

▶ At the four-way junction in the vicinity of the caves, the path leading up Masubasuba Pass turns right, passes Gorge Cave and then veers left; do not take the right-hand fork after the cave, but stick to the left-hand bank of the Pholela River along the now ill-defined path. From here onwards it is 'simply' a matter of ascending to the top of this formidable amphitheatre, with towering walls on three sides. The path tops the Masubasuba Pass at an altitude of 3 050 m, some 200 m below the two peaks.

▶ Both peaks are easy to climb from the saddle at the top of the pass and anyone who has made it this far would surely take the hike to its natural conclusion. It is rumoured that on a fine day you can see clear from the summit to both poles! The distance from Gorge Cave to the top of the pass should take about three to three and a half hours (4 km), and another 20 to 30 minutes to ascend either of the two peaks – the southern one being some 12 m higher than the northern (3 256 and 3 244 m respectively). Like an analogy of life, after this it is all downhill.

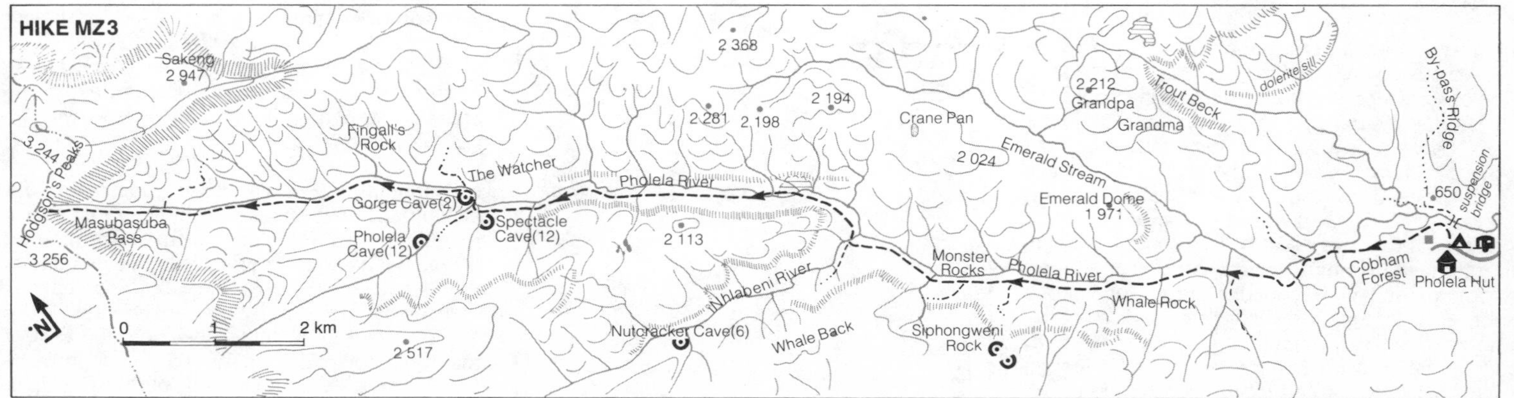

Siphongweni Shelter and Rock *Hike MZ4*

Route: *Cobham Forest Station to Siphongweni Rock*
Distance: *11 kilometres*
Duration: *4 hours 30 minutes*
Grade: *Moderate to Severe*
General: *This interesting hike takes you up a mountain which affords 360-degree views. The shelter cave has been declared a national monument as it houses some unusual Bushman paintings of remarkable quality. They depict Boers on horseback and other scenes dating from the 1860s, marking the coming of white men to this area and the subsequent demise of the Bushmen. In spite of the fact that the shelter is a national monument, vandals still persist in defacing the paintings with the same barbarism that killed the people who painted them. If time and one's feet are limiting factors it is possible to cut 3 km from the trip by taking a steep short-cut up the mountain from the Pholela River to the caves.*

▶ Starting from Cobham follow the Pholela River upstream for 6 km (Hike MZ3) to the area below the Monster Rocks, where the short-cut goes steeply up eSiphongweni mountain on the left. Carry on up the river for another 1 km to the third side-junction to the left. Turn left here and proceed up to the top of Whale Back and then turn left to descend towards the wide plateau to the south, looking towards Siphongweni and the tarns scattered on the elevated plain. Follow the edge of the ridge above the Pholela River towards the peak, looking down to where you came up the river, the path along the Escarpment edge is vague to nonexistent, but it is marked by the occasional cairn.

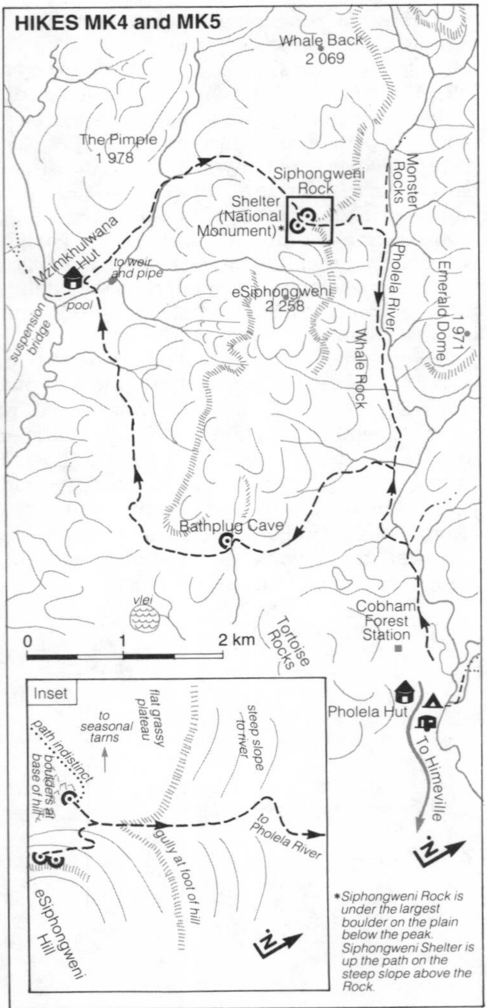

You will eventually come to a gully at the top of the short-cut path, where eSiphongweni Peak rises up from the plateau. Turn right here and ascend the slope to the Shelter which houses the famous Bushman paintings. Siphongweni Rock is found under the largest of the massed boulders on the slope below the cave, where a gap exists between the ground and the boulder thereby forming a large, dark, cave-like overhang.

Siphongweni *Hike MZ5*

Route: *Round trip from Cobham Forest Station via Siphongweni Rock*
Distance: *22 kilometres*
Duration: *8 hours*
Grade: *Moderate to Severe*
General: *This hike goes up the Pholela River to the Siphongweni Rock and then down into the river valley of the same name, before backtracking up the Giant's Cup NHW Trail from the Mzimkhulwana Hut. The middle third of the hike requires some skilled map reading and orienteering, not to mention sure footwork where old paths cease to exist. After a rescue mission here, I had to descend this way alone in the dark and it now amazes me that I didn't break a leg or an ankle on the rough terrain with its brambles and dongas, all of which can be avoided by sensible pathfinding.*

▶ Follow the Pholela River upstream out ofCobham and then take either the short-cut up to eSiphongweni or up to the beginning of Whale Back and back along the plateau edge to the Siphongweni Cave (Hike MZ4). The cave is 11 km from Cobham by the longer route. From Siphongweni Rock take a bearing due east of magnetic north (line up the right-most pinnacle of Whale Back with the middle of Giant's Cup to get a north-east bearing from the rock) and walk along the plain to its narrowest point, above a forked gully. Skirt around to the right of the main gully and make for a spur (the right-hand edge of the gully with its intermittent stream). This is shown on Slingsby's map as a well-defined path, but it no longer exists.

▶ Half-way down the spur veer to the left in a gentle arc down to the Siphongweni River, finding the easiest route. Cross the river and proceed down the right-hand bank where you should pick up an indistinct path (shown clearly on the map). About 1,8 km downstream you will reach Mzimkhulwana Hut, where you can enjoy the pleasures of the deep pool there. After you have dried off, cross the river (there is a bridge just downstream from the pool), and retrace the NHW path – just follow the little white footprints for 8 km back to Cobham. This last section is easy, going gently up to Bathplug Cave and then gently down, past Tortoise Rocks to the Pholela River.

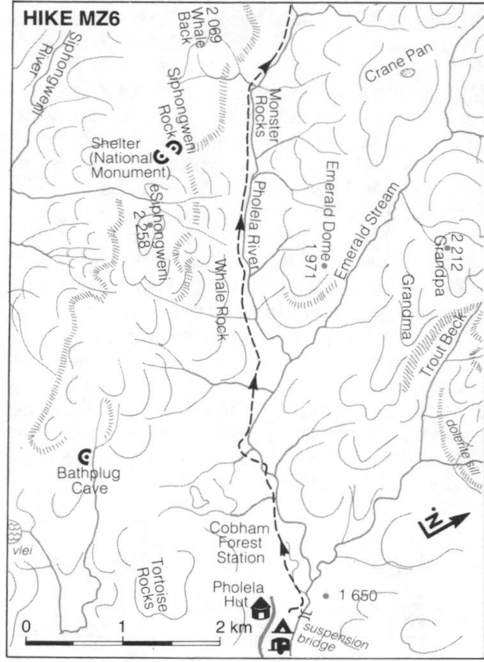

(Above, top.) Petrified wood can be seen scattered along the trail below the Little Bamboo Mountain. (Above.) This pool on the Giant's Cup Trail is a welcome respite between the Mzimkhulwana and Winterhoek huts.

The Pholela River Walk

Hike MZ6

Route: *Cobham Forest Station to the Pholela River*
Distance: *9 kilometres*
Duration: *3 hours 30 minutes*
Grade: *Fair*
General: *It is possible to amble from Cobham up one or all of the three rivers which cut the valley to the north: the Pholela River, Emerald Stream and Trout Beck. These hikes form parts of longer hikes that have already been described in this chapter. As the outbound and return journeys follow the same routes, it is up to the hiker to decide where the turnabout point will be: the descriptions which follow are really just of my own making but are nevertheless convenient distances. If the idea of braaied trout is appealing, be sure to carry a rod and flies, and a licence, which must be obtained from the Himeville Hotel before you arrive at Cobham, otherwise you will be poaching.*

▶ Starting from the Cobham camp site take the path up the left-hand bank of the Pholela River; in other words, do not cross the suspension bridge. Follow the river bank for 2,5 km past the fork in the path which leads off to the right and crosses the river and past the right-angle turn-off to the right. Carry straight on here and you will meet up with the river after another 2 km, passing a side junction to the left. For the next 4 km, the path hugs the left-hand bank of the river, passing Whale Rock, eSiphongweni, Monster Rocks and finally the tail end of Whale Back before coming to the Shelter on the banks of the Pholela River (not to be confused with Siphongweni Shelter at the top of that hill). All these landmarks are on your left. The fork in the river here marks the end of the walk, but it is possible to carry on either up the Pholela River on the right or the iNhlabeni Stream to the left.

Emerald Stream Hike

Hike MZ7

Route: *Cobham Forest Station to Emerald Stream*
Distance: *8,5 kilometres*
Duration: *3 hours*
Grade: *Fair*
General: *The same comments apply here as for the previous hike. This river is a 9 km-long tributary of the Pholela River.*

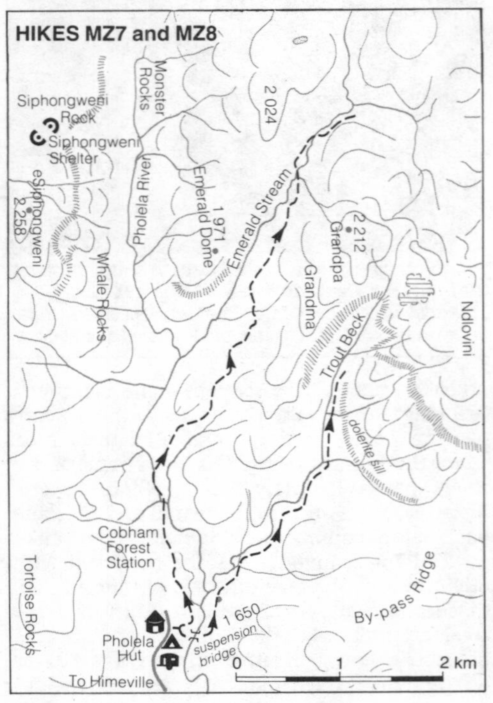

▶ Follow the left-hand bank of the Pholela River upstream for 2 km (Hike MZ6), but then turn right to cross the Pholela River and climb up a spur between two stream gullies for 1 km, rising 100 m in altitude. From here you can look down on to the confluence of the Pholela River and Emerald Stream on your left. Carry on parallel to and above the right-hand bank of the Emerald Stream, alternatively contouring and climbing above the river for 3 km, passing Emerald Dome on the opposite side of the river, until the river is met and crossed. The path recrosses the river after 800 m and follows it for nearly 1 km. A short tributary branches off to the right on its way to the Gxalingenwa River and the path veers off to follow it, thus marking the end of this hike. On the top of the hill on the opposite side of the river is Crane Pan where blue and sometimes even wattled cranes congregate, so it may be worth a detour.

Trout Beck River Walk

Hike MZ8

Route: *Cobham Forest Station to Trout Beck*
Distance: *Approximately 3 kilometres*
Duration: *1 hour*
Grade: *Easy*
General: *This is probably the easiest hike in the vicinity of Cobham, backtracking up the Giant's Cup Trail for 3 km. This path is well trodden by men with fishing rods in hand and feathered hooks in their hats.*

▶ Cross the suspension bridge over the Pholela River and then proceed along and through the game fence. Follow the little white footprints and you can't go wrong. Keep following the right-hand bank of the river, as the Trout Beck branches off to the right where paths also branch off from the NHW trail, which can usually be identified by the litter left along the way. The Trout Beck is a gentle meandering stream marked by many small pools and lush tree ferns.

The Lake District Hike MZ9

Route: *Round trip from Siphongweni Shelter via the Lake District*
Distance: *14,5 kilometres*
Duration: *6 hours*
Grade: *Moderate*
General: *A hike of the Lake District should definitely be considered as a multi-day outing, using the many caves in the vicinity, including the two Venice Caves and Chameleon Cave at the eastern extremity of the 'district', Nutcracker Cave near Lakes Cave and the Siphongweni Rock overhang at the western end of the area, and there are still more for you to find. A network of paths connects the caves and places of interest and allows hikers to amble around this section of the Little Berg. The following description outlines a circular hike of the area from Siphongweni Shelter to Chameleon Cave (37,5 km from Cobham), while the distance given is the shortest route from Cobham to a favourite resting place in the Lake District, Lakes Cave.*

▶ Follow the left-hand bank of the Pholela River from Cobham, past Whale Rock and eSiphongweni, up to Whale Back (Hikes MZ4 and MZ5). Here you can turn left to make for the Siphongweni Shelter and Rock as a lunch spot or even for the first night's stopover. Retrace the cliff line back to the tail end of Whale Back and then take the path around the far side of Whale

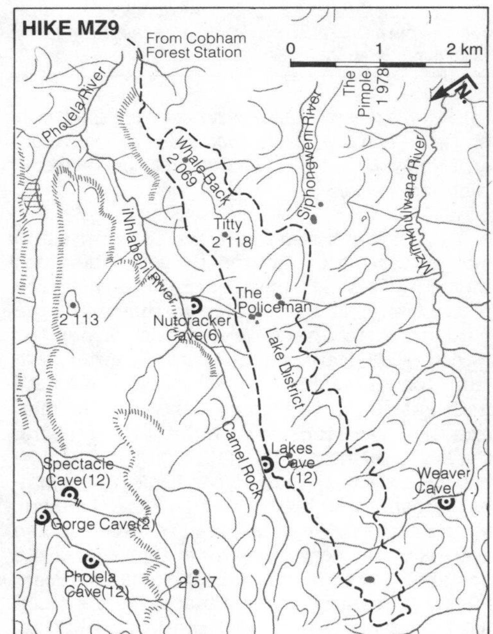

Back; the first path you reach follows the near (southern) flank of Whale Back to reach Venice Caves after 11 km. Traverse along the northern flank of Whale Back for 3 km to The Policeman outcrop on the left, and then a further 3 km to a junction near a group of three tarns. Most of the tarns of the Lake District are to be found between here and The Policeman, above the level of the path on Whale Back.

▶ Lakes Cave is reached by turning sharp right at the junction. It faces out over a stream about 500 m back from the junction below Camel Rock. This cave is 13 km from Cobham by the shortest route and so could be the first or second night's stopover. In fact, you could even proceed on to Venice or Chameleon caves on the first day as this would increase the distance by only 4 km. Retrace your steps back to the junction near the tarns and cross straight over. Go in and out of numerous gullies, generally losing height until the path curves at right-angles to the left after 1,6 km and then descends a spur to a T-junction. This point marks the end of the Lakes District.

▶ To get to Venice Caves, turn right here to descend into a gully and then climb up the other side, curve around one bulge into another gully, ascend around a second bulge and descend to cross the Mzimkhulwana River. Turn right here and the two Venice Caves are found about 700 m upstream, one on either side of the river.

▶ To reach Chameleon Cave, continue on the path away from the river for another 300 m. Retrace your steps for 2 km to the beginning of the Lake District and bear right for 9 km, following an undulating contour to the south-eastern corner of Whale Back. The path goes continually up and down, in and out of the stream gullies along this stretch. Only one permanent stream is encountered, about 3 km from the previous junction. The mere 30-m difference in altitude between the beginning and end of this 9-km section is hard won. You will now be standing on an escarpment lip overlooking the Pholela River, with the Siphongweni Shelter on the slope at the far end of the wide plateau. Bear left here and then right after about 500 m and descend to meet the path on the bank of the Pholela River. Follow the river back to Cobham, 9 km away.

At one of the most southerly points explored in this guide, hikers watch waterfowl while skirting around a large tarn near Sehlaba-Thebe.

There is something magical about watching a sunrise or sunset from a Drakensberg cave, in this case from Tarn Cave at Sehlaba-Thebe.

The Monk and Sleeping Beauty Cave *Hike MZ10*

Route: *Garden Castle Forest Station to Sleeping Beauty Cave*
Distance: *4 kilometres*
Duration: *1 hour 30 minutes*
Grade: *Fair*
General: *This is one of the more popular short walks in this area and deservedly so. There are grand views, river and mountain scenery, and caves for those wishing to spend the night out. I would recommend this as a night's outing for young hikers on their first 'Berg trip, as it offers safety with the possibility, as far as the spirit takes one – while the older folk can 'armchair climb' in the excellent hotel below, or from their folding chairs in the camp site.*

For R2,00 a day you can hire horses from the Forestry Office and explore the mountain wilderness in style, but you should be a competent rider as there is no supervision.

▶ If you are not staying in the Forestry camp site you can park your car at the gate, where you must buy a wilderness permit and sign the mountain register. From here you just follow the path up the right-hand bank of the river, past the foresters' quarters and the camp site. After 1 km from the camp site, the valley narrows as the path enters the sandstone portals of Swiman and then The Monk, with Rhino Peak nudging the sky to the north. The path along this section can become rank with *Hyparrhenia* and *Danthonia* grasses and bracken (*Pteridium aquilinum*), which is the most widespread of all ferns. The path is never very steep as it approaches the castle towers of Mlambonja and Wilson's Peak. Sleeping Beauty Cave is situated on the steep slope above the river and can be reached by crossing the river 1 km past the head of The Monk. Engagement Cave is in a side gully on the right, 700 m upstream.

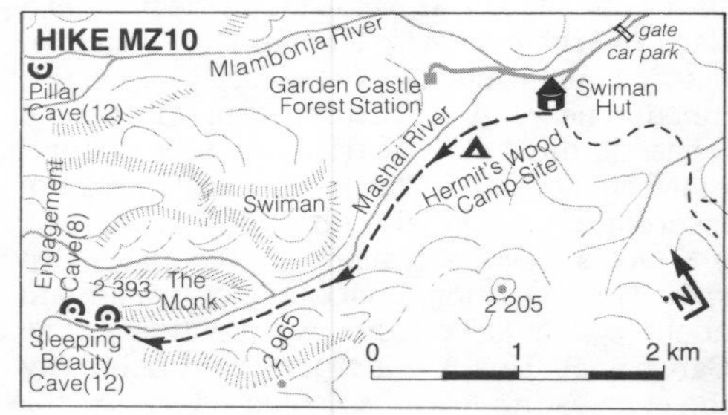

Hidden Valley Hike MZ11

Route: *Garden Castle Forest Station to Hidden Valley*
Distance: *9 kilometres*
Duration: *3 hours*
Grade: *Moderate*
General: *For those with an interest in geology, this hike up the Mzimude Valley offers interesting formations as well as some unusual erosion features. The return trip is an all-day outing, going for part of the way along the NHW trail.*

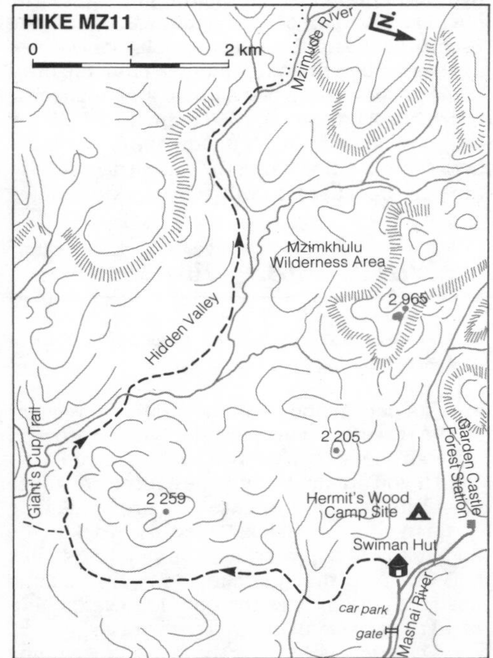

▸ The path begins behind Swiman NHW hut (follow the signs from the Forestry gate – after 1,8 km take the right-hand fork to Bushman's Nek). The path goes gently up past Sunken Valley and up to Bucquay Nek. One kilometre above the river the Hidden Valley path branches off to the right from the NHW path: this is a pleasant detour down to the suspension bridge across the river. The path to Hidden Valley goes gently uphill and then levels off before descending to the river after 2 km.

▸ Cross the river where the path goes uphill and away from the river for about 1 km before entering the valley that is enclosed in the embrace of sandstone arms stretching out from the main body of the mountains. The path actually carries on for another 7 km up the Mzimude Pass, but that is another hike. There are trout in the river for the catching and a peaceful seclusion to be savoured – unless, like me, you choose a day when a school outing decides to 'discover' this hidden world; not that I dislike school children . . . It is up to you to decide when to turn back, but I have fixed the spot where the valley narrows considerably and the path becomes steep.

Three Pools and Bushman's Rock Hike MZ12

Route: *Garden Castle Forest Station to Bushman's Rock*
Distance: *4,5 kilometres*
Duration: *1 hour 30 minutes to 2 hours*
Grade: *Fair*
General: *This pleasant, occasionally steep, short walk has two variations; both lead to pools and the extra distance is more than worth the small effort.*

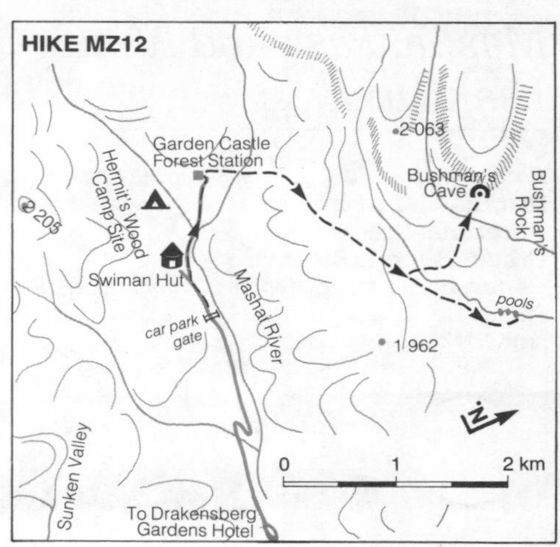

As Bushman's Cave is in the Mzimkhulu Wilderness Area, a permit will be necessary.

▸ Start at the Forestry gate and follow the road to the offices. From here the path goes off in a NNE direction, across the Mlambonja River and up the steep hill on the other side. After about 1 km there is a short respite and then it's up again for another kilometre to the top of a ridge. Descend the slope in front of you and cross a stream after 1 km before coming to a fork. Take the right-hand cul-de-sac to Three Pools and to Champagne Pool, 400 m further on. Return to the fork after your swim and turn right to take the other path for 1,5 km to Bushman's Rock and then for another 500 m to Bushman's Cave. Hikers may not sleep in any of the rock shelters in this area, but you can camp out. On the path to the cave there is a short 'loop' detour that leads you to Queen's Pool should you wish to swim once more (this path is not on Slingsby's map).

Mashai Pass and Rhino Peak *Hike MZ13*

Route: *Garden Castle Forest Station to Rhino Peak*
Distance: *11 kilometres*
Duration: *5 hours*
Grade: *Severe to Extreme*
General: *As a result of some inherent aesthetic magnetism, some peaks in the Drakensberg demand to be tackled. Rhino Peak is such a climb and guests at the Drakensberg Gardens Hotel will discover that on Thursdays they are expected to be out and up the peak by lunchtime. I met an elderly man who was there for his fourth attempt to reach the summit. Three times he had been driven back by violent thunderstorms and blizzards and on the day I met him it had started to snow lightly. I never did find out if he made it or not, but this anecdote is a reminder to anyone attempting such a route: always be prepared for the worst, but enjoy yourself all the same.*

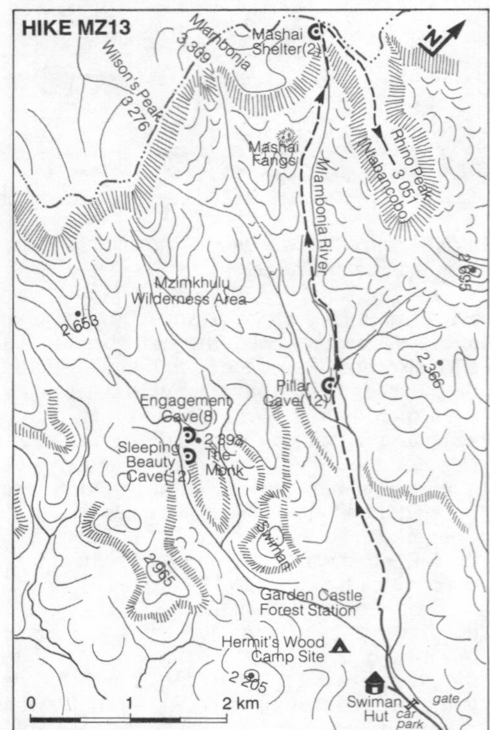

▶ Get your permit from the forester at the gate and follow the Forestry road to the offices. Continue in a north-westerly direction, parallel to the Mlambonja River (for some cartographical or historical reason the Mashai Pass does not follow the river of that name, perhaps so as not to confuse this pass with the Mlambonja Pass in the Cathedral area). From the Forestry office you can see the river on the right and the path veers towards it for about 1,5 km and then follows the left-hand bank for another 1,5 km past Pillar Cave. Shortly thereafter it crosses the river. Another path, not shown on the map, branches off just below Pillar Cave and goes up to the three Little Caves before rejoining the Mashai Pass path.

▶ From the river crossing above Pillar Cave the 4-km slog up the pass begins. There are several river crossings midway up the pass, then you will pass the Mashai Fangs on the left, and the Mashai Shelter – for it is no more than that – marks the top of the pass. The path takes the obvious line across the saddle between the Escarpment and the peak, which juts out like the head after which it is named. From the head of the pass to the tip of the Rhino's (Ntabancobo) horn, it is 2 km, gaining 150 m in altitude. If the weather is anything but fair, think carefully before proceeding along the knife-edge ridge to the horn because you will be very exposed.

Bushman's Cave and Ngwangwane Pass *Hike MZ14*

Route: *Bushman's Nek Police Post to Ngwangwane Pass*
Distance: *11 kilometres*
Duration: *5 hours*
Grade: *Severe to Extreme*
General: *This hike leads past one of the many caves that were used by Bushmen in what was once a stronghold of these legendary hunters and spirits of the wilderness. Some of the most famous caves containing Bushman rock art in the Drakensberg are to be found in this area, but they are not marked on the map, so it is up to you to find them if you're interested. The hotel has a display on the rock art in the area and directions to some of the better-known caves – just remember to 'take only photographs and leave only footprints'.*

▶ Buy a permit and fill in the mountain register at the Forestry car park and then proceed through the security fence to the Police Post – even if you are not leaving the country, all hikes pass through here in case you are smuggling cattle in your backpack. Follow the track to the Bushman's River, cross over the stepping stones and take the first path to the right, heading upstream. From here the path follows the left-hand river bank all the way to the cave.

▶ The going is easy for the first 4 km, gaining

only 100 m in altitude over this distance. Three kilometres after entering the Bushman's River valley, the path crosses a tributary and passes to the right of a ridge. The valley then becomes a gorge. The path crosses another tributary after 1,5 km and the gorge steepens and narrows again. You are now half-way to the cave.

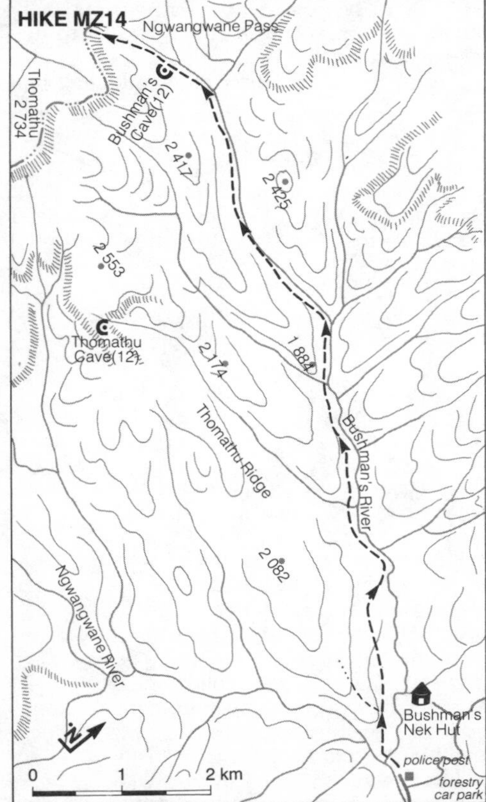

Although the path does become less distinct the further you go, just stick to the left-hand bank of the river, bearing left where a gorge branches off to the right (north) parallel to the Escarpment, and you will reach the cave 1 km below the summit. (The gorge that branches off to the right will be recognized by the observant as being the main river course, but even then just keep to the left).

The average height of the Escarpment and peaks in this area is some 300 to 400 m lower than to the north and the landscape is less rugged. The caves are found mostly on the southern, north-facing slopes near the head of river valleys, facing to the north-east. The obvious place to look for them is at the base of sandstone crags that cap the characteristic parallel ridges jutting out at right-angles from the Escarpment.

Thomathu Cave and Pass

Hike MZ15

Route: *Bushman's Nek Police Post to Thomathu Cave*
Distance: *10 kilometres*
Duration: *4 hours 30 minutes*
Grade: *Severe to Extreme*
General: *This hike goes up a well-defined path on the northern flank of the Thomathu Ridge. Like all the large caves in the area, this one faces north-east and could sleep an army.*

▶ From the Police Post follow the dirt track across the Bushman's River just above its confluence with the Ngwangwane, which is the main river that drains this area, and then turn first right along the first section of the Bushman's River path. After walking parallel to the river for several hundred metres, you will see a path that turns off to the left to ascend the dominant ridge – take heart, for this is the route you must follow. By Drakensberg standards this is nothing like an epic hike and you should consider taking all the luxuries that make camping so enjoyable – smoked oysters, pâté, wine, 15 kg of camera gear or whatever else takes your fancy.

The peak of the Rhino (3 051 metres) juts from the rest of the range in the Garden Castle Area.

▸ A small consolation is that the worst of the climbing is done in the first two-thirds of the hike and the 3-km section from the cave to the summit ascends only 200 m. The unbroken grasslands stretching away in all directions comprise mainly *Themeda triandra* and *Festuca costata* species, with a few other types of grasses found particularly in moist places. Thomathu Cave is presumably named after the ridge on which it is situated.

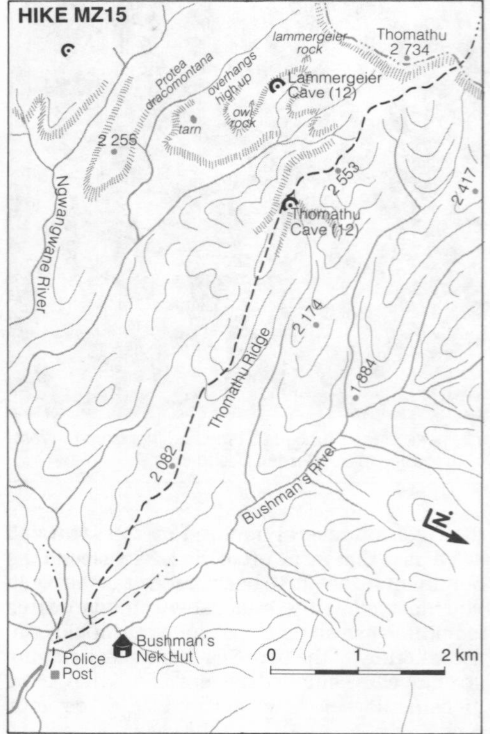

Lammergeier Cave   Hike MZ16

Route: *Bushman's Nek Police Post to Lammergeier Cave*
Distance: *10,5 kilometres*
Duration: *5 hours*
Grade: *Severe*
General: *The extra time allowed here is due to the fickleness of the path – anyone who manages to stay on one continuous path should be awarded a mountaineer's merit badge. In the Ngwangwane Valley there are too many paths, which cause to some confusion, while higher up the ridges they are less obvious than the map would imply, which is even more confusing. For the first half of the way, I hiked close to the river which runs below the ridge leading up to the cave, and thereafter I bundu bashed my way up the stepped ridges leading to a gully below the high sandstone crags. I had to search the area around the nose of the ridge before I discovered the cave at the head of the gully on the northern side of the ridge (a closer look at the map makes this obvious in the clear light of hindsight). The cave is the largest but the least comfortable in the area; in fine weather, however, you can camp on the grass below. Below the 'nose' of the ridge there is a small plateau with a tarn and, down a side gully, you will find a remarkable cave with hundreds of Bushman paintings, covering a long period of occupation.*

▸ Starting at the police post, cross the Bushman's River, bear left along a multi-lane footpath and cross the Ngwangwane River shortly afterwards. The path then follows the left-hand bank of the river for 5 km, past a fork (keep to the river bank) and a prominent hill on the right, to a four-way intersection where one path goes uphill to the left, another continues up the left-hand river bank and a third path goes across the river to the right. Take the third alternative to the right over the river and then proceed up and over a saddle behind the prominent hill which you passed some way back. From the saddle the path turns left up a ridge for 80 m, traverses to the right to cross a stream and then carries on straight up a ridge parallel to the stream on the right.

The cave is situated in a picturesque corner at

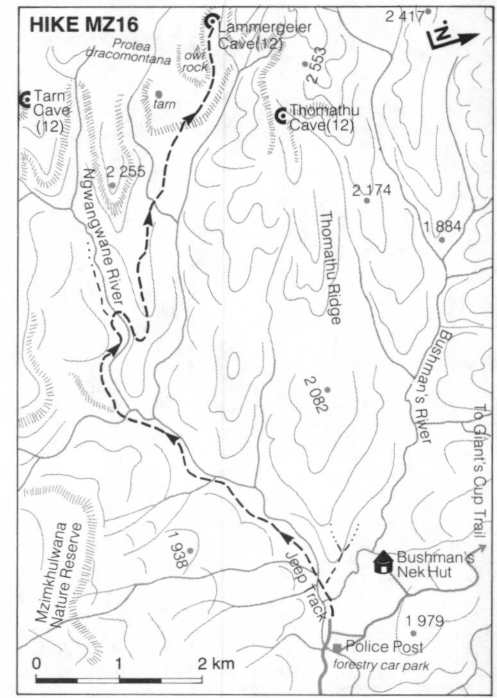

During the early part of the nineteenth century Thaba-Ntsu was the site of bitter fighting between the Amahlubi and Amangwane tribes. A member of the former is reported to have said that there was a 'white mark from the Tugela to Thaba-Ntsu and that mark was (their) bones'.

the head of a stream gully, surrounded on three sides by high sandstone battlements. The cave gets its name from a rock formation above the cave which resembles a monumental bearded vulture, while another rock further along the ridge looks like a giant owl. This is indeed a place of birds: hundreds of rock pigeons roost in the sandstone crags and martins sometimes fill the air above the valley like locusts. I watched a lanner falcon swooping after a rock martin in prolonged aerial combat. Although one of the fastest and most aerobatic raptors, the lanner falcon should have known better than to take on a martin in mid-air. It then went after siskins, but they took to the grass whenever the lanner swooped on them and after about half an hour the lanner glided off over the ridge.

MOUNTAIN PHOTOGRAPHY

I have spent a lot of time and money over the years improving my photographic equipment for hiking in order to reduce weight but maintain quality. Nothing beats a good eye and being in the right place, but practice does seem to increase one's luck.

A 35 mm, single reflex camera is the most popular body format, but some people use smaller or larger format bodies as a compromise between weight and picture clarity. While 50 mm is the standard lens size (focal distance of the lens), modern zoom lenses lose less in clarity than the eye can detect, so I use a 28 – 80 mm zoom lens as my standard. For very close-up work and less distortion I carry a 50 mm lens with a macro-facility. A flash is very useful for close-up work and for photographing flowers, as it highlights the focal object and fills in shadows. Bird enthusiasts cannot get away with carrying anything smaller than a 300 mm lens. In fact I use an 80 – 300 mm zoom which can be hand-held at fast speeds, while my hiking stick doubles as a tripod for slower speeds, as well as for close-up work. Using only slide film, I keep a polarizing filter on the lenses for most of the time; this filter eliminates glare, enriches natural colours and deepens the blue of the sky while emphasizing clouds (it also doubles as a neutral density filter for flowers). When there is no direct sunlight, I merely swap this for a skylight filter to protect the lens.
Like trout fishing, successful photography is a matter of practice and patience.

Bushman's Nek to Sehlaba-Thebe Hike MZ17

Route: *Bushman's Nek Police Post to Sehlaba-Thebe*
Distance: *14 kilometres*
Duration: *5 hours 30 minutes to 6 hours*
Grade: *Severe*
General: *The distance given is from the police post to the lodge in Sehlaba-Thebe, Lesotho's only national park, which was proclaimed to protect the unique habitat and endemic species. The shield-like plateau lies higher than the rest of the Little Berg yet lower than the Escarpment and is a naturalist's haven where many large tarns attract a host of animals and birds. There are extraordinary natural rock formations as well as many ruins of large kraals and shelters. The lodge, which looks somewhat like a displaced suburban house, sleeps 12 people and can be booked. The three-peaked Thaba-Ntsu dominates the Park from the north-western corner and dares one up its jagged basalt slopes.*

▶ After getting your passport stamped at the Police Post, follow the previous hike's (Hike MZ16) route over the Bushman's River and then up the left-hand bank of the Ngwangwane River for 4 km. Stop along the way for a swim if the weather permits, for there is a long haul after this, with no chance of swimming until you reach the tarns on the high plateaux. Turn left at the first path that leads that way, but keep to the main track as this area has become badly eroded. The path leads up a series of spurs which are not particularly steep, although a heavy pack will take its toll.

▶ After 1 km from the river, bear to the left for a short way before going through a section of sharp boulders; this is where the pass was blasted many years ago in an attempt to stop Bushmen and later Basutho tribesmen from using the pass for cattle rustling, which still plagues the area. This is also a good spot to be on the lookout for eagles and lammergeiers.

▶ On reaching Bushman's Nek itself, there is a series of large tarns on the plateau stretching off to the left. After this there is only one more long spur that must be climbed. Do not bother taking the path off across the plateau to the left to a group of small white buildings marked as Jonathan's Gate, firstly because you are unlikely to find anyone at the border post, and secondly because the gate has fallen into disuse.

▶ At the top of the spur you will come to the border fence, and trip over it if you arrive in the dark as I did. There are some old stone ruins here and grey rhebuck are common on the grass slopes. You will cross a stream 1,5 km past the fence and then the lodge will be seen straight ahead up the main valley. There is a profusion of tracks and paths here, so choose the path of least resistance and don't rely on the map to guide you – the most direct route is the best one. A day spent exploring the hills and tarns around the lodge will be a day well spent, especially if you are there in mid-summer when the brilliant white water lilies, called 'the crown jewels of Sehlaba-Thebe', bloom. This buttercup-like flower (*Aponogeton ranunculiflorus*) which is inset with tiny yellow stamens, was discovered in 1970 and is not known to exist anywhere else.

Yellowbilled and black ducks glide on the tarns, while wagtails bob around the shores; secretary birds strut the thick grasslands and sparrow-like Drakensberg siskins grow fat on the dense seed heads; black and martial eagles, as well as lammergeiers, may be seen soaring across the plains in search of food. Even the striking but rare bald ibis may be seen foraging

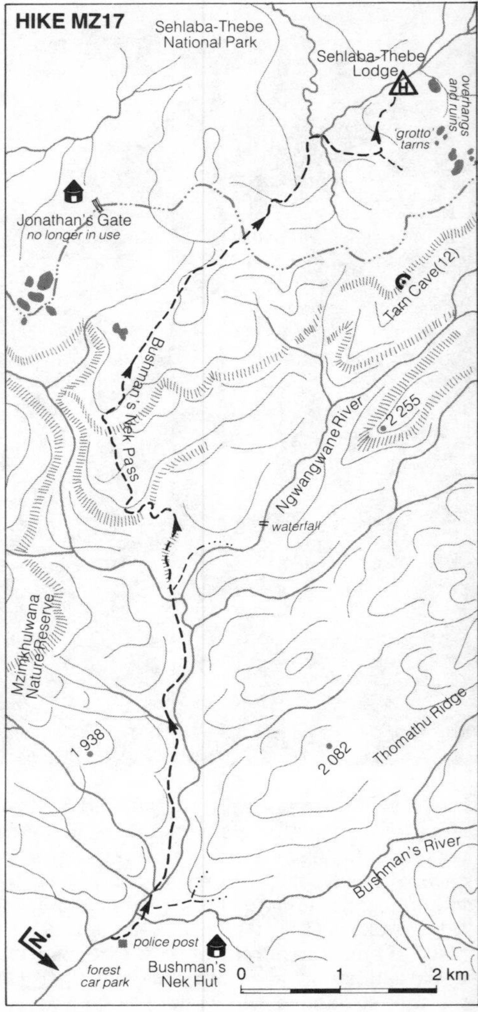

in the grass here. Small animals like water mongooses and wild cats are seldom seen, but their spoor is evident in the mud around the tarns.

Caves Traverse *Hike MZ18*

Route: *Bushman's Nek Police Post to Lammergeier, Thomathu and Bushman's caves*
Distance: *35 kilometres*
Duration: *4 days*
Grade: *Severe*
General: *This hike is really only for experienced hikers who like to explore off the beaten track. You will need to be fit and have good mountain sense and map-reading abilities and even then you are sure to get lost once or twice. One of the main objectives of this hike, which to me remains one of the highlights of many years of hiking in the Drakensberg, is to locate caves with Bushman paintings. There is no finer challenge and no better reward than finding them, lost, forgotten or just guarded by secrecy, and to share the spirit of the mountains as distilled by the Bushmen and captured in their art. The terrain for this hike is rugged and this description is meant only as a guideline – the route which each party takes is up to its own creative map reading.*

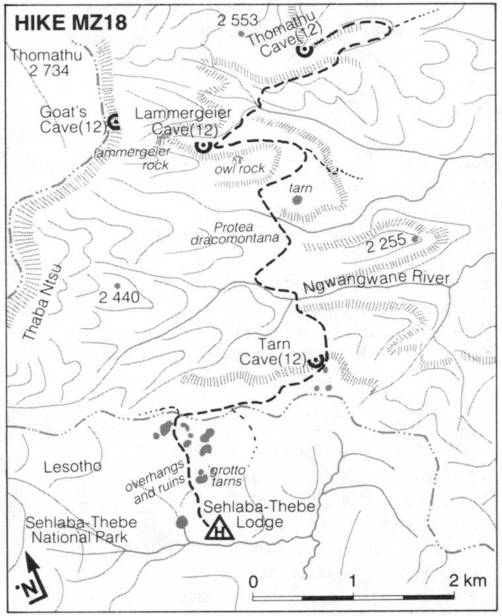

▶ The general objective is to ascend to Sehlaba-Thebe (Hike MZ17), then find your way to Tarn Cave on the lip of the Park's boundary crags and then over the grassy knolls and across the intervening, converging river valleys to Lammergeier, Thomathu and Bushman's caves (look out for cairns to guide you to the cave). There will be time each day to laze around the rivers, ambushing otters and water fairies that are known to live here but are so elusive. Tarn Cave is easy to find, being just over the lip of the plateau north-east of the lodge. From the lodge, hike to the large tarns starting about 1 km to the north and then veer to the right making for the plateau edge, 1,5 km from these lakes. As can be expected, there are small tarns on the plateau just above the cave. The paths up to the cave are obvious.

From here on, however, it is up to you to find the way. The trip relies on accurate map reading, so carefully count contour lines, ridges and valleys and line them up with major peaks. The next three caves in the sequence are described in previous entries in this chapter, so you will have more clues than I did when I started out. Any cave not shown on Slingsby's map is out of bounds for camping or anything other than appreciating – if you find one you will see why.

The three high peaks on the Escarpment to the south of the hut are known as Thaba-Ntsu, 'the mountain of the lammergeier', the Devil's Knuckles or the Three Bushmen. This is generally considered to be the tip of the dragon's tail, although the Drakensberg basalt formation continues into the north-eastern Cape to Ben Macdui near the village of Rhodes. This most southerly part of the Drakensberg is not included in this guide, as it is quite limited in terms of hiking but is used as a skiing base. Its charms should not be neglected; it certainly has more than its fair share of Bushman paintings in very much more accessible caves than those in the area that I have described.

And so our journey ends, but remember that this is really only the beginning, for the Dragon mountains and the land beyond are vast – I have described only the better-known parts, leaving the rest for wilderness lovers to discover for themselves. Perhaps one day we'll meet there.

APPENDIX 1
Common and scientific names referred to in the text

BIRDS

Batis *Batis* spp.
Bokmakirie *Telophorus zeylonus*
Buzzard, jackal *Buteo rufofuscus*
Chat, mountain *Oenanthe monticola*
Cisticola, cloud *Cisticola textrix textrix*
Coot, redknobbed *Fulia cristata*
Cormorant *Phalacrocorax* spp.
Darter *Anhinga rufa*
Dove, laughing *Streptopilia capicola*
Dove, turtle *Stigmatoplia senegalensis*
Duck, black *Anas sparsa*
Duck, yellowbilled *Anas undulata*
Eagle, black *Aquila verreauxii*
Eagle, martial *Polmaetus bellicosus*
Falcon, lanner *Falco biarmicus*
Fiscal *Lanius collaris collaris*
Flycatcher, fiscal *Sigelus silens*
Francolin, redwing *Francollinus levaillanthii levaillanthii*
Hadeda *Bostrychia hagedash*
Hamerkop *Scopus umbretta*
Harrier, black *Circus maurus*
Ibis, bald *Geronticus calvus*
Kestrel, rock *Falco tinninculus rupicola*
Kite, black-shouldered *Elanus caeruleus*
Lammergeier *Gypaetus barbatus*
Martin, rock *Hirundo fuligula*
Neddicky *Cisticola fulvicapilla fulvicapilla*
Pigeon, rock *Columba guinea*
Quail, African *Cortunix cortunix*
Robin, Cape *Cossypha caffra*
Secretary bird *Sagittarius serpentarius*
Siskin, Cape *Serinus totta*
Starling, redwinged *Onycho gnathus morio*
Sugarbird, Guerney's *Promerops gurneyi gurneyi*
Sunbird, black *Chalcomitra amethystina*
Sunbird, collared *Anthreptes collaris*
Sunbird, malachite *Nectarinia famosa*
Swallow, black saw-wing *Psalidoprocne holomelaena*
Swallow, European *Hirundo rustica*
Swallow, greater striped *Cecropis cucullata*
Swift, Alpine *Apus melba*
Swift, white-rumped *Apus caffer*
Thrush, groundscraper *Turdus litsipsirupa*
Vulture, bearded *Gypaetus barbatus*
Vulture, Cape *Gyps coprotheres*
Warbler, Victorin's scrub *Bradypterus victorini*
White-eye, Cape *Zosterops pallidus*
Woodpecker, olive *Mesopicos griseoccephalus*

MAMMALS

Aardwolf *Proteles cristatus*
Baboon *Papio* spp.
Blesbok *Dalmaliscus dorcas phillipsi*
Bushbuck *Trageliscus scriptus*
Dassie, rock (hyrax) *Procavia capensis*
Dassie, tree *Dendrohyrax arboreus*
Duiker, grey *Sylvicapra grimmia*
Eland *Taurotragus oryx*
Gemsbok *Oryx gazella*
Hare, Natal red *Pronolagus crasscaudatus*
Hare, southern bush (scrub) *Lepus saxatils*
Hartebeest, red *Alcelaphus buselaphus caama*
Jackal, black-backed *Canis mesomalis*
Klipspringer *Oreotragus oreotragus*
Leopard *Panthera pardus*
Lynx *Felis caracal*
Mongoose, Cape grey *Herpestes pulverulentus*
Mongoose, Egyptian (large grey) *Herpestes ichneumon*
Mongoose, water *Atilax paludinosus*
Mongoose, white-tailed *Ichneumia albucauda*
Oribi *Ourebia ourebi*
Otter, Cape clawless *Aonyx capensis*
Porcupine *Hystrix africae-australis*
Reedbuck, mountain *Redunca fulvorufula*
Rhebuck, grey *Pelea capreolus*
Serval *Felis lybrica*
Springbok *Antidorcas marsupialis*
Wild cat *Felis lybica*
Wildebeest, black *Connochaetes gnou*
Zebra, mountain *Equus (Hippotigris) zebra zebra*

REPTILES

Adder, berg *Bitis atropos atropos*
Adder, puff *Bitis arietans*
Agamas (koggelmannetjies) Agamidae (family)
Cobra, spitting (rinkhals) *Hemachatus haemachatus*
Gecko Gekkonidae (family)
Lizards, legless Amphisbaenadae (family)
Lizards, true Lacertidae (family)
Skink Scincidae (family)

PLANTS

Ash, Cape *Ekebergia capensis*
Assegai *Curtesia dentana*
Asters Asters (family)
Beech, Cape *Rapanea melanophloeos*
Bottlebrush, Natal *Greyia sutherlandii*
Bracken *Pteridium aquilinium*
Cabbage tree, highveld *Cussonia paniculata*
Cedar, mountain *Wilddringtonia nodiflora*
Cycad *Encephalartos ghellinckii*
Crown jewels of Sehlaba-Thebe *Apongeton renunculiflorus*
Dagga, wild *Leonotis leonurus* var. *leonurus*
Erica Ericaceae (family)
Everlasting *Helichrysum* spp.
Fern, tree *Alsophila dregei*
Holly, African *Ilex mitis*
Iris, wild *Dietes grandiflora*
Ironwood *Olea capensis*
Lily, Guernsey *Nerine sarniensis*

Lily, river *Schizostylis coccinea*
Monkey's rope *Secamone* spp.
Moraea *Moraea* spp.
Nana-berry *Rhus dentata*
Old man's beard *Usnea* spp.
Olinia, mountain *Olinia emarginata*
Olive, wild *Olea europea* subsp. 'africana'
Ouhout *Leucosidea sericea*
Peach, wild *Kiggelaria africana*
Protea, Drakensberg *Protea dracomontana*
Protea, highveld *Protea caffra*
Protea, lipped *Protea subvestita*
Protea, Natal *Protea multibracteata*
Protea, nubigena *Protea nubigena*
Protea, silver *Protea roupelliae*
Red grass *Themeda triandra*
Red-hot poker *Kniphofia* spp.
Sage, mountain *Buddleja corrugata*
Sage, wild *Tarchonanthus camphoratus*
Sagewood *Buddleja salviifolia*
Spike thorn *Maytenus heterophylla*
Stinkwood *Ocatea bullata*
Stinkwood, white *Celtis africana*
Taaibos, mountain *Rhus dentata*
Tussock grass *Festuca costata*
Waboom *Protea nitida*
Watsonia *Watsonia densiforma*
Wattle, black *Acacia mearnsii*
Yellowwood, Outeniqua *Podocarpus falcatus*
Yellowwood, real *Podocarpus latifolius*

APPENDIX 2
Useful addresses and telephone numbers

Berhaven Cottages, P.O. Box 192, Winterton 3340; tel. (03682), ask for 3712.
Bushman's Nek Hotel, Private Bag 137, Underberg 4590; tel (03372) 103.
Cathedral Peak Forest Station, Gewaagd, P.O. Winterton 3340; tel. (03682) 3621.
Cathedral Peak Hotel, P.O. Winterton 3340; tel. (03682), ask for Cathedral Peak Hotel.
Cathkin Park Hotel, Private Bag 12, Winterton 3340; tel. (03642), ask for Mont-aux-Sources 1.
Cavern, The, P.O. Box 3340; tel. (03642), ask for Dragon Peaks 1.
Champagne Castle Hotel, Private Bag 8, Winterton 3340; tel. (03642), ask for Champagne Castle 2.
Cobham Forest Station, P.O. Himeville, 4585; tel. (033722) 1331.
Dragons Peaks Park, P.O. Winterton 3340; tel. (03642), ask for Dragon Peaks 1.
El Mirador, P.O. Winterton 3340; tel. (03642), ask for Dragon Peaks 1.
Garden Castle State Forest, P.O. Box 90, Underberg 4590; tel. (033712) 1722.
Giant's Castle Game Reserve, Private Bag 7055, Estcourt 3310; tel. (03631) 2418.
Golden Gate Highlands National Park, (for accommodation) The Chief Director, National Parks Board, P.O. 787, Pretoria 0001; tel. (012) 44–1191/98.
Highmoor State Forest, P.O. Box 51, Rosetta 3301; tel. (033332) 1322.
Hillside Camp Site, P.O. Box 288, Estcourt 3310; tel. (03631) 24435.
Hlalanathi Resort, Private Bag 621, Bergville 3350; tel. (03642) 182/172.
Injasuti Camp, Private Bag 7010, Estcourt 3310; tel. (Loskop) 1311.
Inkosana Lodge, P.O. Box 60, Winterton 3340; tel. (03682), ask for 3520, evenings only.
Kamberg Nature Reserve, P.O. Rosetta 3301; tel. (033332) 1431.
Little Switzerland Hotel, Private Bag 661, Bergville 3350; tel. (03642) Robber's Roost 2.
Loteni Nature Reserve, P.O. Box 14, Himeville 4585; tel. (033772) 1540.
Mdedelelo Wilderness Area (Monk's Cowl Forest Station), P.O. Box Winterton 3340; tel. (03682) 2204.
Mkhomazi Wilderness Area, P.O. Box 105, Nottingham Road 3280; tel. (033312) 1902.
Monk's Cowl Forest Station, P.O. Winterton 3340; tel. (03682) 2204.
Mont-aux-Sources Hotel, Private Bag 1, Mont-aux-Sources 3353; tel. (03642), ask for Mont-aux-Sources 7.
Mountain Club of South Africa, (head office) 97 Hatfield Street, Cape Town 8001; tel. (021) 45–3412.
Mountain Splendour Caravan Park, Private Bag 23, Winterton 3340; tel. (03682) 3503.
Mountaineer's Chalet, P.O. Box 12, Himeville 4585; tel. (0020), ask for Himeville 1302.
Mzimkulu Wilderness Area, The Regional Director, Natal Forest Region, Private Bag 9029, Pietermaritzburg 3200; tel. (0331) 28101.
Natal Parks Board, P.O. Box 662, Pietermaritzburg 3200; tel. (0331) 51221 (8 lines).
National Hiking Way Board, Private Bag 9029, Pietermaritzburg 3200; tel. (0331) 28101.
National Parks Board, P.O. Box 787, Pretoria 0001; tel. (021) 441191–8.
Nest, The, Private Bag 14, Winterton 3340; tel. (03642), ask for The Nest 2.
Royal Natal National Park, P.O. Mont-aux-Sources 3353; tel. Bergville, ask for Mont-aux-Sources 3.
Royal Natal National Park Hotel, Private Bag 4, Mont-aux-Sources 3353; tel. (03642), ask for Mont-aux-Sources 1.
Rugged Glen Nature Reserve, The Officer-in-Charge, Rugged Glen Nature Reserve, P.O. Mont-aux-Sources 3353; tel. (03642) 7104.
Sani Pass Hotel, P.O. Himeville 4585; tel. (033722), ask for 29.
Sehlaba-Thebe Lodge, Lesotho National Parks, P.O. Box Maseru 60, Ficksburg 9730; tel. (0563) 3434/3131.
Vergelegen Nature Reserve, P.O. Box Himeville 4585; tel. (03392) 1712.
Witzieshoek Mountain Resort, P.O. Box 5581, Phuthaditjhaba 9866; tel. (01432) 9302.

APPENDIX 3

Further reading

Bannister, A., 1984. *The National Parks of Southern Africa*. C. Struik, Cape Town.

Bristow, D. and Ward, C. 1985. *The Mountains of Southern Africa*. C. Struik, Cape Town.

Burman, J., 1966. *A Peak to Climb*. C. Struik, Cape Town.

Clarke, J. and Coulson, P., 1984. *Mountain Odyssey*. Macmillan, Johannesburg.

Dodds, D.A., 1975. *Cradle of Rivers: The Natal Drakensberg*. Centaur, Cape Town.

Irwin, P., Ackhurst, J. and Irwin, D., 1980. *A Field Guide to the Natal Drakensberg*. Wildlife Society of Southern Africa, Durban.

Journals of the Mountain Club of South Africa, 1897 – 1986.

Killik, D.J.B., 1963. *An Account of the Plant Ecology of the Cathedral Peak Area of the Natal Drakensberg*. Botanical Survey of South Africa, Memoir No. 34.

Levy, J., 1982. *Everyone's Guide to Trailing and Mountaineering in Southern Africa*. C. Struik, Cape Town.

Levy. J., 1987. *The Complete Guide of Walks and Trails in Southern Africa*. C. Struik, Cape Town.

Liebenberg, D., 1972. *The Drakensberg of Natal*. Bulpin, Cape Town.

McLachlan, G.R. and Liversidge, R., 1984. *Robert's Birds of Southern Africa*. The Trustees of the John Voelcker Bird Book Fund, Cape Town.

Moll, E.J., 1981. *Trees of Natal*. University of Cape Town Eco-Lab Trust, Cape Town.

Pager, H., 1971. *Ndedema*. Akademische Druck Verlag Anstalt, Graz.

Palgrave, K.C., 1977. *Trees of Southern Africa*. C. Struik, Cape Town.

Pearse, M., 1980. *A Camera in Quathlamba*. Howard Timmins, Cape Town.

Pearse, R., 1973. *Barrier of Spears: Drama of the Drakensberg*. Howard Timmins, Cape Town.

Pearse, R., 1978. *Mountain Splendour: The Wild Flowers of the Drakensberg*. Howard Timmins, Cape Town.

Pearse, R., 1986. *The Dragon's Wrath*. Macmillan, Johannesburg.

Trauseld, W., 1977. *Wild Flowers of the Natal Drakensberg*. Purnell, Cape Town.

Truswell, J., 1977. *The Geological Evolution of Southern Africa*. Purnell, Cape Town.

Walker, C., 1986. *Signs of the Wild*. C. Struik, Cape Town.

Willcox, A., 1973. *Rock Paintings of the Drakensberg, Natal and Griqualand East*. C. Struik, Cape Town.

INDEX

Individual birds, mammals, reptiles and plants are not included in the index. Page numbers in *italics* indicate that the subject is illustrated. Entries and page numbers in **bold** refer to individual hikes.